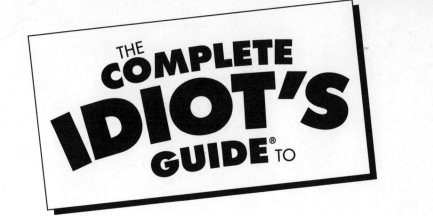

THE COMPLETE IDIOT'S GUIDE® TO

Social Security and Medicare

Second Edition

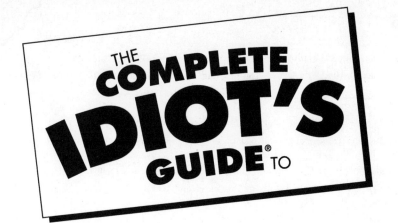

THE COMPLETE IDIOT'S GUIDE® TO

Social Security and Medicare

Second Edition

by Lita Epstein

ALPHA

A member of Penguin Group (USA) Inc.

For my parents, whose love and support gave me the foundation to follow my dreams.

ALPHA BOOKS

Published by the Penguin Group

Penguin Group (USA) Inc., 375 Hudson Street, New York, New York 10014, U.S.A.

Penguin Group (Canada), 10 Alcorn Avenue, Toronto, Ontario, Canada M4V 3B2 (a division of Pearson Penguin Canada Inc.)

Penguin Books Ltd, 80 Strand, London WC2R 0RL, England

Penguin Ireland, 25 St Stephen's Green, Dublin 2, Ireland (a division of Penguin Books Ltd)

Penguin Group (Australia), 250 Camberwell Road, Camberwell, Victoria 3124, Australia (a division of Pearson Australia Group Pty Ltd)

Penguin Books India Pvt Ltd, 11 Community Centre, Panchsheel Park, New Delhi—110 017, India

Penguin Group (NZ), cnr Airborne and Rosedale Roads, Albany, Auckland 1310, New Zealand (a division of Pearson New Zealand Ltd)

Penguin Books (South Africa) (Pty) Ltd, 24 Sturdee Avenue, Rosebank, Johannesburg 2196, South Africa

Penguin Books Ltd, Registered Offices: 80 Strand, London WC2R 0RL, England

International Standard Book Number: 1-59257-519-6
Library of Congress Catalog Card Number: 2006924597

08 07 06   8 7 6 5 4 3 2

Interpretation of the printing code: The rightmost number of the first series of numbers is the year of the book's printing; the rightmost number of the second series of numbers is the number of the book's printing. For example, a printing code of 06-1 shows that the first printing occurred in 2006.

Printed in the United States of America

Note: This publication contains the opinions and ideas of its author. It is intended to provide helpful and informative material on the subject matter covered. It is sold with the understanding that the author and publisher are not engaged in rendering professional services in the book. If the reader requires personal assistance or advice, a competent professional should be consulted.

The author and publisher specifically disclaim any responsibility for any liability, loss, or risk, personal or otherwise, which is incurred as a consequence, directly or indirectly, of the use and application of any of the contents of this book.

Most Alpha books are available at special quantity discounts for bulk purchases for sales promotions, premiums, fund-raising, or educational use. Special books, or book excerpts, can also be created to fit specific needs.

For details, write: Special Markets, Alpha Books, 375 Hudson Street, New York, NY 10014.

Publisher: *Marie Butler-Knight*
Editorial Director: *Mike Sanders*
Managing Editor: *Billy Fields*
Senior Acquisitions Editor: *Paul Dinas*
Development Editor: *Jennifer Moore*
Production Editor: *Megan Douglass*
Copy Editor: *Emily Garner*

Cartoonist: *Shannon Wheeler*
Book Designers: *Trina Wurst/Kurt Owens*
Cover Designer: *Kurt Owens*
Indexer: *Brad Herriman*
Layout: *Brian Massey*
Proofreader: *Mary Hunt*

Contents at a Glance

Contents

Foreword

Social Security and Medicare together have an average value for each working American in excess of $500,000—more than most of us will ever be able to save ourselves. This value has made them the most important government entitlement programs we will receive. However, with the changes and proposed changes in these benefits, we have a difficult time keeping track of what the actual benefits are, particularly as pertains to Medicare. In fact, over the past 15 years, the annual Retirement Confidence Survey has found that the public doesn't have a good grasp of either Social Security or Medicare. Too often when we go looking for answers we run into complicated bureaucratic gobbledygook that was been written by a team of lawyers. We need to know as much as we can to protect ourselves.

Lita Epstein has provided just what the public ordered with her completely updated revision of *The Complete Idiot's Guide to Social Security and Medicare*. It is complete, clear, and easy to understand. Give it a prominent place on your bookshelf. Make it required reading for your children. It could make a big difference in your future.

Between these covers, you'll find the answers to such critical questions as:

What benefits can you get from Social Security? How long do you need to work to get a benefit? What do you lose if you begin Social Security at age 62 instead of waiting until age 66 or later? What benefits are your spouse and kids going to get if you die before either age? What happens to benefits in the event of a divorce? If you get a Social Security benefit does it mean you will always get Medicare?

What is the difference between Medicare Parts A, B, and D? What do the new drug plans really offer and how can you get the best plan for your needs? What can you expect to pay? How does long-term care insurance compare to Medicare coverage for nursing home care? Once you have Medicare can you lose it? For example, if you get a divorce?

The Complete Idiot's Guide to Social Security and Medicare gives full, current answers to these and hundreds of other questions that pertain directly to you and your family—and in language that everyone will be able to understand. It even includes a complete resource section for more information if you need it.

Simply put: buy this book. Give it to those you love. It's the best investment you'll make to ensure a lifetime of security and protection.

Dallas L. Salisbury

Dallas L. Salisbury is President and CEO of the Employee Benefit Research Institute (www.ebri.org) in Washington, D.C. He has been running EBRI since 1978, and is one of the nation's most frequently cited experts on Social Security, Medicare, health insurance, retirement, and savings.

Introduction

Imagine your life without a Social Security number. Without that nine-digit number, you wouldn't be able to work or to open any type of bank or other financial account. You probably would have difficulty applying for a driver's license, getting a loan, or even obtaining a credit card.

A Social Security identification number becomes part of your life when you are born and can stay around long after your death. Today, parents must get a Social Security number for their baby before they can claim a newborn as a tax deduction. After your death, your spouse, children, and even your parents may be eligible to collect benefits on your work record.

When President Franklin D. Roosevelt pushed and prodded to create Social Security, he ran into major opposition because many politicians and the general public worried that it was a communist plot. Medicare was opposed for years because people feared it was the start of socialized medicine.

Today, Social Security and Medicare are two of the most popular government programs. While people may fear that the programs won't be around when it comes time for them to collect, few folks would advocate that either program should be disbanded.

In this book, we'll take a journey to find out why these programs have become such a huge part of our lives and to find out the answer to the proverbial question, "What's in it for me?"

For the second edition, an entirely new chapter about the Medicare prescription drug benefit, which started in January 2006, was added to the book. In addition, income, tax, and other key financial statistics were updated throughout the book. The politics of Social Security and Medicare are in a constant state of flux, and information that impacts the politics of these programs was updated as well.

How I've Organized the Book

We'll start our journey by reviewing how all this got started. Then we'll visit the question of how the laws developed into what they are today. After that, we'll head off into the world of current benefits. Finally, we'll look at what's next for the country's most popular programs.

I've organized the book into six parts:

Part 1, "Hatching the Nest Egg," talks about how Social Security got started and how more than a hundred pieces of legislation hatched the nest egg that is now part of almost everyone's retirement program.

Part 2, "Getting Your Share," focuses on the benefits you can expect and how to collect those benefits.

Part 3, "Cracking Open Your Nest Egg," discusses the major life changes that can affect your Social Security benefits and what parts of the nest egg you can still count on even after divorce, the death of a spouse, or disability.

Part 4, "Living Right," gives you some ideas for how to live on your Social Security benefits and reviews some things you should consider regarding your other retirement assets.

Part 5, "Staying Healthy," reviews the complicated rules of Medicare and what additional protections you should have to stay healthy without breaking the bank.

Part 6, "What's Next for the Nest Egg," takes the journey full circle and looks at what is being done today to ensure the future of Social Security and Medicare.

Extras

I've developed a few helpers that you'll find in little boxes throughout the book:

Social Graces

The world of Social Security and Medicare can be very confusing. These boxes offer advice and information that will help you gracefully negotiate the complicated systems.

def•i•ni•tion

Social Security and Medicare use jargon with which you might not be familiar. Some of these terms are defined in these boxes.

Insecurities

Pitfalls and problems will be pointed out in these boxes.

Senior Moments

You might not be a senior yet, but you'll still find the information in these boxes enlightening.

Acknowledgments

I had lots of help cutting through the complicated rules of Social Security and Medicare and translating this book into something you can easily understand. Special thanks to Gary Goldstein and Jessica Faust for their help in getting this book off the ground and to Paul Dinas for spearheading the second edition; to Jennifer Moore for her tireless efforts to help me clarify the rough spots; to my technical editor, Richard Johnson whose astute comments and attention to detail improved the information you'll find in the book; and to Amy Lepore and Emily Garner, whose attention to detail kept the copy clean.

And of course, I can't forget to thank my husband, H.G. Wolpin, for putting up with me as I rushed to get the book done.

Special Thanks to the Technical Reviewer

The Complete Idiot's Guide to Social Security and Medicare, Second Edition, was reviewed by an expert who double-checked the accuracy of what you'll learn here. Special thanks are extended to Richard Johnson of the Urban Institute, a nonpartisan policy research organization in Washington, D.C.

Trademarks

All terms mentioned in this book that are known to be or are suspected of being trademarks or service marks have been appropriately capitalized. Alpha Books and Penguin Group (USA) Inc. cannot attest to the accuracy of this information. Use of a term in this book should not be regarded as affecting the validity of any trademark or service mark.

Part 1

Hatching the Nest Egg

Social Security as we know it today is a much different animal than when it was passed into law in 1935. It wasn't easy to build such a confusing mess of rules and regulations—it took an incredible amount of bipartisan haggling. In the following chapters, we journey back in time to learn how this nest egg was hatched and why it is such a complicated maze.

You may think it's time to throw this system out and develop a more straightforward program from scratch. After reading how we got to this point; however, you'll probably see that hatching a new egg could be more painful than repairing some of the cracks in the old one.

SHANNON WHEELER 06

Letting the Chicks Out

In This Chapter

- ◆ Putting money into the hands of the neediest
- ◆ Overcoming Social Security's detractors
- ◆ Making Social Security the law of the land
- ◆ Amending the program

If you are collecting Social Security, you probably can't live without it. If you are in your preretirement years, however, and your paycheck gets smaller each year as your money is gobbled up in FICA taxes, you're probably looking for a way to escape the obligation of paying into Social Security. You also may be wondering, "What is FICA, anyway?" It stands for the Federal Insurance Contributions Act. Does that help? Probably not. I'll describe its meaning in greater detail in the next chapter.

The good news is that one day, we will all be on the other side of the retirement fence collecting the dough. The bad news is that we don't know how much will still be there to collect. Remember that adage about counting your chickens before they hatch?

Social Security as we know it today is a patchwork of laws passed over several decades, and when you're trying to figure it out, it can feel like a maze of outdated rules that need a total rewrite. No one denies that Social

Security needs to be changed; the hard part is doing it so that we are fair to all age groups. You'll read more about the future of Social Security in Part 6. In this chapter, we're going to take a trip back in time and find out how Social Security got its start.

Roosevelt to the Rescue

If you want to place blame on someone for the current mess (or give credit to someone for coming up with the most popular social program in the United States), you can point to Franklin D. Roosevelt. Social Security was his answer to the soup kitchens and shantytowns that many seniors found themselves in after the stock market crash of 1929.

President Roosevelt wanted to be sure that this country would never again face a crisis so disastrous to so many lives. He wanted to build a safety net to ensure that every senior would stay above the poverty line and that there would be support for every worker's family after his or her death. Today, Social Security does do that, but only barely, for many folks.

Senior Moments
The tradition of Social Security stemmed from the English Poor Law of 1601. These laws helped the poor of all ages and defined the state's responsibility to provide for the welfare of its citizens. Those who had were taxed to fund relief activities for those who had not.
These laws distinguished between the "deserving" and the "undeserving" poor. The payouts were controlled locally, and almshouses were set up to shelter those on relief. The pilgrims brought this tradition with them to the colonies. This "poor law" tradition is still a part of our culture today.

A Declaration of Security

The first American to put the idea of retirement security into written form was Thomas Paine in his pamphlet *Agrarian Justice*, published in 1795. He called for the creation of a system of inheritance taxes. This tax of 10 percent on inherited property would be put into a special fund. It would be paid out as a one-time stipend to citizens just starting out at age 21, and as an annual benefit to everyone age 50 and older to protect against poverty in old age.

Paine's idea was never adopted even though inheritance taxes eventually were.

A Civil Idea

The real precursor to Social Security arrived on the scene after the Civil War and was known, not surprisingly, as the Civil War Pension Program. (The government is never very creative with its titles.) This program was passed into law in 1862. At first, benefits were linked to disabilities caused during military duty.

Widows and orphans were also entitled to pensions if their deceased soldier had been disabled. In 1890, service-connected disability was no longer a requirement for the pension. Any disabled Civil War veteran could qualify for benefits.

In 1906, the government once again tweaked the Civil War Pension Program, this time eliminating the disability requirement. Being old became the only eligibility requirement for a Civil War veteran. By 1910, Civil War veterans and their survivors had a full-fledged program of disability, survivors, and old-age benefits that was very similar to what we know today as Social Security.

> **Senior Moments**
>
> There actually was a national pension program passed in 1776 before the Civil War Pension Program. It even predated the signing of the Declaration of Independence. The program was used to help recruit soldiers. Prior to the Civil War, soldiers who served in America's various wars did get some form of pension, but none as extensive as the Civil War Pension.

In 1910, more than 90 percent of the surviving Civil War veterans were receiving benefits under this program, but they made up only .6 percent of the total United States population by that time. The pension became a great asset for these veterans in their search for young wives because a veteran's widow could inherit his benefits. Believe it or not, women were collecting Civil War pensions until as recently as 1999. Boy, talk about marrying for money!

Designing the Safety Hatch

Enough nostalgia. Let's look at how the president and Congress went about designing what we know today as Social Security.

Opponents called it a communist plot. Roosevelt's first major hurdle was to prove to his detractors that Social Security would not lead to communism. Opponents also complained that the government could never be trusted to pay benefits properly, if at all. Sound familiar? I'm sure you've heard many horror stories of folks battling to get their Social Security and Medicare payments. To be fair to the folks who run Social Security, however, they have done an incredible job. In 2005, Social Security's 70th birthday, employees of the Social Security Administration handled claims for 48 million people and paid out approximately 518 billion dollars in benefits.

This chart represents expected population growth at the time Social Security was implemented. It is from the 1937 book Social Security in America *published by the Social Security Board.*

(Source: Social Security Administration's website)

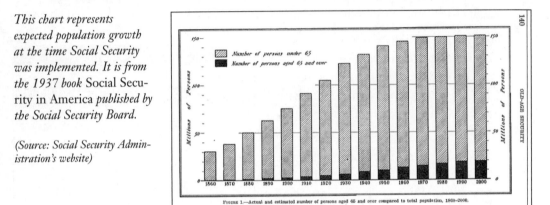

FIGURE 1.—Actual and estimated number of persons aged 65 and over compared to total population, 1860–2000.

Let's set the stage for Roosevelt's quest. The country was recovering from the 1929 stock market crash. Many people were out of work. The ratio of older folks to younger folks was steadily increasing. History does repeat itself, doesn't it? Not much different than the concerns expressed today.

What does government do when it wants to study a problem? Why, of course, it sets up a committee! Roosevelt formed the *President's Committee on Economic Security (CES)*. Today, presidents like to make such study groups sound more important, so they call them commissions.

Although they had no idea how many of us would be born between then and now, they did understand that the ratio of older to younger workers would be a major factor in being able to pay future benefits. The birth rate sharply declined starting in 1820. By 1930, 5.4 percent of the population was 65 or older, and this percentage was rising steadily. No baby boom was expected.

def•i•ni•tion

Formed in June 1934, the **President's Committee on Economic Security** was asked to devise "recommendations concerning proposals which in its judgment will promote greater economic security." Five top cabinet members made up the committee, led by Secretary of Labor Frances Perkins. It took the committee only six months to design the first comprehensive federal social insurance program in the nation's history.

The slow birth rate was expected to become more pronounced because of the tough economic times in 1934. The Committee on Economic Security also found that once a person over the age of 40 was unemployed, he or she had a very difficult time finding work because companies didn't want to retrain older workers.

These were the economic conditions the committee faced as it started to hatch the new Social Security nest egg. No visions of economic recovery were in sight.

The first thing the committee members set out to do was classify the elderly.

Senior Moments

A 1937 Social Security Board pamphlet had the following to say about life expectancy:

> The safety of life has never increased as rapidly at any time on record as in the past 40 years.
>
> Take Massachusetts, for example, where there are records over a long period. A baby born in Massachusetts in 1789 had, on the average, an expectation of a life of about 35 years. In the next century the expectation of life at birth increased about 8 years; babies born in Massachusetts in 1890 had before them a life expectation of 42.5 years for men and 44.4 years for women. But between 1890 and 1930 those averages grew to more than 59 years for men and more than 62.5 for women.

Here are the 10 classes they came up with:

- The old person who is still engaged in some occupation until age 70 or perhaps even until 80.

- The fortunate minority who can rest on their economic laurels, drawing on inherited wealth or on savings from a successful economic life.

- Those who have earned and receive a satisfactory pension from their former private or public employer.

- The large, though gradually decreasing, number of recipients of war pensions, whose number may perhaps increase if the pension principle is applied to the veterans of World War I.

- The very large (perhaps the largest) number of those who are supported by their children or other relatives.

◆ A rather limited number of persons receiving regular relief from private philan-thropic agencies.

◆ Guests or inmates of private homes for the aged, showing a very great variety of standards of comfort.

◆ The aged population of poorhouses, almshouses, or county farms.

◆ The aged in homes for incurables or insane asylums.

◆ The recipients of state old-age assistance, the latest development in the care of the aged.

Once the committee defined the classes, its next step was to figure out what to do about serving them. Many states already had some programs enacted. To beef up those programs, the committee recommended grants-in-aid to the states and territories, which were part of Title I—state welfare programs for the aged.

The committee estimated that the grants-in-aid money would make up 50 percent of the expenditures paid for noninstitutional, old-age assistance by the local governments. How it was apportioned had to be approved by the federal officials, who would tell the states and territories how to run the program and who would be eligible to collect. It's no different today. Bureaucrats are still control freaks.

Passing the Rules: 1935 Social Security Act

Now it was Congress's turn to put its stamp on the measure. The committee's proposals were introduced in Congress on January 17, 1935. The House Ways and Means Committee held hearings and killed it. Wow! What a surprise! Congress had to create its own bill.

Congress took eight months from the time the President's Committee on Economic Security first sent its recommendation to Congress to pass a law in August 1935. The law was dubbed the Social Security Act of 1935.

Congress faced its usual cast of characters—both supporters and detractors. Familiar scare tactics were used. People warned that the plan would overburden industry, reduce the purchasing power of workers, and endanger the growth of private pension plans. There were even questions about whether it was constitutional to create a national pension plan. I wonder if everyone still uses the same playbook today. The argument never seems to change, only the issues being argued.

We all know how it ended. Supporters ruled the day. The new program was intended to provide economic security for the aged using a contributory system that was paid by both the worker and his or her employer. Workers and employers paid into the system through payroll tax contributions, with each contributing one half of the tax. In 1935, the tax rate was set at just 2 percent on the first $3,000 of income.

Most of the committee's recommendations were incorporated, but Congress rejected a number of provisions and gave more decision-making control to the states. For example, it

> **Insecurities**
> All legislation that will result in some form of "raising revenue" (the founding fathers' euphemism for taxation) must be started in the House of Representatives by the Ways and Means Committee and then be sent to the Senate. The Constitution mandates this in Article 1, section 7. The House committee had primary control of Social Security's future in 1935.

rejected the requirement that a state's old-age assistance plans provide for "reasonable subsistence compatible with decency and health" once the Social Security income was added. Congress also rejected certain mandates regarding income eligibility and citizenship requirements and left more flexibility for setting eligibility standards with the states.

Congress also gave the states more flexibility in how they could spend their federal grant money. The federal government agreed to share with the states the administrative costs of running the program, but limited the costs for administration to no more than 5 percent of the total program costs for Title I.

I won't go into more details because they have been modified more than 100 times in Congress since then. We focus instead in later chapters on what is available today so you can be sure you are getting your fair share.

Senior Moments

When signing the bill into law on August 14, 1935, President Roosevelt said, "We can never ensure 100 percent of the population against 100 percent of the hazards and vicissitudes of life. But we have tried to frame a law which will give some measure of protection to the average citizen and to his family ... against poverty-ridden old age .... It is ... a law that will take care of human needs and at the same time provide for the United States an economic structure of vastly greater soundness."

Spreading the Word

Congress and the president put into place what today is one of the most extensive old-age programs in the world. They then had to tackle the challenge of figuring out how to implement the program. To get the ball rolling, President Roosevelt appointed the *Social Security Board.*

def•i•ni•tion

This massive new program was implemented by a three-member bipartisan **Social Security Board (SSB)** appointed by President Roosevelt. The Chairman was John G. Winant. The SSB's biggest challenges were informing the public, setting up field operations, and staffing those operations with trained people.

Once the board set up its offices and staff, it then faced a monumental problem. How could the board quickly register employers and workers by January 1, 1937? That was the date workers would begin to get credits toward old-age insurance benefits. Remember, there were no computers at the time!

The Social Security Board had no staff resources to accomplish this task, but at least it had money. Who should the board turn to? Why the U.S. Postal Service, of course. In the next chapter, we'll look at how the post office came to the rescue and handled this momentous task. Then we'll explore how the board began implementing the system, setting up its database, and paying out benefits.

The Least You Need to Know

◆ President Franklin D. Roosevelt came up with the idea of Social Security as an answer to the severe poverty following the stock market crash of 1929.

◆ Social Security was established in 1935 and has been changed hundreds of times since then.

◆ Social Security's precursor was the Civil War Pension Program, which provided pensions for soldiers who had served in the Civil War.

◆ Social Security's primary purpose is to serve as a safety net for all workers and their families to ensure that they are not forced to live below the poverty line when they retire.

Social Security Grows Up

In This Chapter

- ◆ Putting the plan to work
- ◆ Contacting the masses
- ◆ Expanding the program
- ◆ Experiencing growing pains

As you learned in the preceding chapter, Social Security was created in response to desperate financial times. Many people feared that the program would move the country toward communism and damage efforts to develop pension plans in the workplace. The Social Security Board needed to organize quickly to convince the public that they really would like the program, if they would just gave it a chance.

The board was starting from scratch. There was no such thing as a Social Security number. There were no centralized records of earnings. Getting the program underway was a massive task, and it had to be done manually. In this chapter, we look at how one of the most popular social experiments got off the ground.

Implementing the Plan: The Social Security Board

Not surprisingly, Social Security's first battle was for funding. Congress, in its infinite wisdom, passed the legislation to establish Social Security and the board that would run it, but at first didn't allocate any funds to pay for it.

Social Graces

Can you imagine operating without a Social Security number today? It has become such a part of our lives that it is one of the first things parents apply for after the birth of a child.

The budget bill that was slated to pay for the Social Security Board (SSB) was killed by Senate filibuster at the end of August 1935. The SSB had to borrow money from other federal agencies to begin operations. Congress finally reconvened and passed the appropriation in January 1936.

Once it had the money, the SSB could start planning its future. Its first task was to find everyone.

Senior Moments

President Roosevelt sought help from the clergy to get funding for Social Security. When Congress adjourned without passing the funding bill for Social Security, he sent a letter to thousands of clergymen around the country. It was the grass-roots effort by the clergy that aided in getting quick passage in January 1936.

Finding the Folks: U.S. Postal Service to the Rescue

The SSB contracted the U.S. Postal Service to distribute applications beginning in November 1936. Post offices around the country collected the completed forms, typed the Social Security number (SSN) cards, and returned the cards to the applicants. Imagine that kind of service today!

The 45,000 local post offices became the network of field offices for the Social Security Board. Of these offices, 1,074 were designated as typing centers to prepare the cards. It was a three-step process. Employers were given an application form, called an SS-4, beginning November 16, 1936. On this form, they indicated the number of employees they had.

Once these forms were submitted, employers then received SS-5 forms for each employee. The SS-5 form determined a person's Social Security number (SSN). People could either return the SS-5 form in person and wait at a typing center for their SSN card, or they could mail in the form. If they mailed their form, the SSN was assigned and the card was sent back to their place of business using regular mail.

The record was then sent on to the Social Security headquarters in Baltimore, Maryland, which was where the master files were kept. More than 35 million SSN cards were issued using this procedure in 1936 and 1937.

Postmen in New York City distributing SSN applications in November 1936.

(Courtesy of Social Security Administration's website)

Crafting Accounts

The post office forwarded the completed applications to the SSB's processing center in Baltimore, Maryland, where the Social Security numbers were registered and various employment records were established.

The SSB just couldn't live without designating someone as first, so Joe Fay, who was head of the Division of Accounting Operations, walked over to the stack, pulled off the top record, and declared it to be the first official Social Security record. It was number 055-09-0001 and belonged to John David Sweeney Jr., age 23, of New Rochelle, New York.

Newspapers bought the story and announced that Sweeney had been issued the first Social Security number. It's more accurate to say that the first Social Security *record* was established for John David Sweeney. The public didn't witness Fay picking out the record, and the

Insecurities

So who got the first card? No one really knows. If everyone followed instructions, the earliest date of first issue would have been November 24, 1936, but some cards did have earlier dates on them. Hundreds of thousands of SSNs were issued on that first day. No one knows whether some cards were predated when typed or actually issued early.

newspapers never questioned it, so no one knows for sure how random his selection really was. Many now suspect that it was a political, rather than a random choice. Spin doctors, those politicos who spin a story for the press, were alive and well even at the time Social Security was forming.

Senior Moments

The owner of the first Social Security number never collected a penny in benefits. John Sweeney Jr. was the son of a wealthy factory owner. He grew up in a 15-room Westchester County home and was used to being waited on by his servants. When he filled out his application for Social Security, he was working as a shipping clerk to learn his father's business from the bottom up.

It was a very political move to choose Sweeney. The Sweeneys were known Republicans who had voted against President Roosevelt and supported the Republican presidential candidate Alfred Landon in 1936. The first SSN holder died of a heart attack in 1974 at the age of 61 and never collected a penny of Social Security. His widow did receive benefits until her death in 1982.

The Social Security Board carefully crafted the Social Security numbering system, grouping the first three digits as an area number that was assigned geographically, starting in the northeast and moving westward across the country.

Social Graces

Did you know that you can tell where someone was born (or where the person first applied for a Social Security number) by the first three digits of his or her SSN? People who work regularly with SSN cards have come to recognize the states. You can see all of the geographical number assignments online at www.ssa.gov/foia/stateweb.html.

You might expect Maine to have the 001 designation, but we're talking about the government, and it was politicians who made the numbering decisions. So guess what state got 001? Why, New Hampshire, of course. Huh?

They picked New Hampshire because it was the home state of Social Security Board Chairman John G. Winant, who was a favorite son and three-time governor of the state. He declined the honor of taking SSN 001-01-0001. After attempting a couple of other honorees, who also declined, they finally just let it go to the first person in New Hampshire who randomly applied for an SSN. It went to Grace D. Owen of Concord, New Hampshire, who applied for her number on November 24, 1936, and received the first typed card in the first area number scheme.

The Social Security card was designed in 1936 by Fred Happel of Albany, New York. He was paid $60 to submit three possible designs. His most famous design was the "Flying Tigers" logo used by General Chennault's forces in World War II.

(Courtesy of Social Security Administration's website)

Today, Social Security tells us we should not make too much of the geographical code. They say the numbering was originally used to make storage of the applications in Baltimore easier so that they could be filed by region as well as alphabetically. Even though numbers are assigned centrally today, and not in local offices, your zip code at the time of applying is used to maintain the first three digits as state identifiers.

It wasn't until 1961 that the Civil Service Commission adopted the Social Security number as an official federal employee identification. In 1962, the Internal Revenue Service adopted the SSN as its official taxpayer identification number.

Once all the numbers were assigned, the board's next task was to figure out how to use the information to start paying the recipients.

Insecurities

Today, it seems as though you can't do anything financially without supplying your SSN. Consumer groups are beginning to raise concerns that the number is too easy to obtain and too broadly used. With identity theft becoming a growing problem, if you do have the option to use another identifier rather than your SSN, it's probably best to do that.

Paying the Bucks

Monthly benefits originally were supposed to start in 1942. From 1937 until that time, benefits were to be paid in a lump-sum payment.

During the time when recipients received lump-sum payments, the average payment was $58.06. You might be wondering how folks survived on that little money, but a loaf of bread cost just 11 cents at that time. The money probably went much further than it would today, but it was still not a livable income. These early recipients weren't in the program very long before collecting, so they weren't entitled to much money.

The 1939 Amendments

When Social Security became law it was intended to be exclusively a social insurance program with benefits going only to the primary worker when he or she retired at age 65.

The first batch of checks was examined by Federal Security Agency Administrator Paul McNutt at the Treasury Disbursing Center in January 1940. The Treasury machines at that time could print 7,000 checks an hour.

(Courtesy of Social Security Administration's website)

It didn't take long for Congress to realize that more benefits were needed to keep people out of the poorhouse. In 1939, Congress added amendments to the Social Security Act that expanded the program and sped up the payment of monthly benefits.

A Growing Family

Congress added two new categories of benefits to Social Security in 1939: payments to the spouse and minor children of a retired worker, and survivors' benefits to cover the spouse and children or dependent aged parents in the event of a premature death of a covered worker.

This photograph of a Visiting Nurse providing health services for a poor rural family was made possible by the welfare-like provisions of the Social Security Act of 1935.

(Courtesy of National Archives photo on Social Security website)

While the retired worker was still alive, supplementary benefits were added to that worker's monthly payment. Once the retired worker's spouse reached age 65, she got 50 percent of the worker's benefit. A dependent child was also eligible for up to 50 percent of the primary benefit. Of course, in 1939, there was no talk of a husband collecting on a wife's benefits, but the law does say "spouse."

When the worker died, his survivors continued to collect benefits. A widow aged 65 or older collected 75 percent of the primary benefit. A widow with a dependent child, even if she had not yet reached 65, was also eligible to collect 75 percent. Each dependent child was eligible to collect 50 percent of the primary benefit. If there were dependent parents and no widow or unmarried children under age 18, each dependent aged parent was eligible for 50 percent of the benefit.

Benefits were not paid for months in which a worker earned wages of $15 or more. There were no benefits for a widow under age 65 unless she had dependent children, and there were no benefits for children between 16 and 18 who were not attending school.

> **Social Graces**
>
> If a worker was eligible for $10 a month and had one dependent (an aged wife or dependent child), he collected $15. For two or more dependents, he collected $20.

Getting an Early Start

Congress also changed the start date for monthly benefits to 1940 rather than 1942, as first planned. The popularity of the program certainly made it easier to improve benefits. Once people started receiving their money, the majority of Americans no longer feared the program as a communist scheme.

The first monthly benefits were paid on January 31, 1940, to a retired legal secretary, Ida May Fuller, of Vermont. Her check totaled $22.54. She collected Social Security for 35 years and received more than $22,000 in benefits.

The original bill made no provisions to offset the erosive impact of inflation on fixed incomes. Ida May Fuller had to live on $22.54 per month for the first 10 years.

More Benefits = More Costs

Congress had to figure out how to pay for all this new spending. What did it do? Create a new tax, of course! The *Federal Insurance Contributions Act (FICA)* was born.

In 1946, Congress abolished the Social Security Board and established the Social Security Administration in its place.

def•i•ni•tion

The **Federal Insurance Contributions Act (FICA)** was established as a payroll deduction in 1939. Both employers and employees were taxed. Today, the amount of this tax is established each calendar year. The employee's portion of the tax is deducted from the paycheck. The employer matches this deduction 100 percent. All the money is paid to the federal government.

The 1950 Windfall

Congress refrained from making major changes to Social Security in the 1940s. It soon became apparent, however, that people were not able to get by on the small amounts paid under Social Security's retirement benefits. Until 1951, the welfare benefits for old-age assistance paid on Title I (state welfare programs for the aged) of the 1935 Social Security Act were higher than the retirement benefits being collected under Title II (old age benefits).

Congress realized that it needed to make major changes. In 1950, it passed an amendment that brought to life the first Cost of Living Adjustment (COLA)—a whopping 77 percent. A second COLA of 12.5 percent was passed in 1952. Fearing out-of-control spending, Congress was hesitant to make COLAs a permanent feature of Social Security benefits. COLAs were passed six more times as one-time adjustments, and it wasn't until 1972 that COLAs became an automatic feature of Social Security benefits. In addition to COLAs to adjust for increases in prices, Congress also added wage-based adjustments to correct for increases in wages.

Senior Moments

The first two COLA adjustments combined nearly doubled the monthly benefit. In August of 1951, the average Social Security retirement benefit finally exceeded the average old-age assistance grant for the first time. It took 10 years for Congress to decide it was time to wean people from the welfare aspects of Title I of the Social Security Act of 1935. Today Title I is repealed for the states, but is still in effect for Puerto Rico, Guam, and the Virgin Islands. The Commonwealth of the Northern Marianas also may decide to initiate a Title I social services program if it chooses.

Help for the Disabled

The changes just kept coming. Disability insurance was added to the Social Security package in 1954. Prior to that, disability froze workers' Social Security records, which could reduce or wipe out retirement and survivor benefits. Congress broadened the law in 1956 to provide benefits to disabled workers aged 50 to 65 and disabled adult children. Congress kept tweaking the law until it made disability benefits available regardless of age.

Supplemental Security Income (SSI) was introduced in the 1970s. It combined what the government called "adult categories," which included needy aged, blind, and disabled individuals. Because Congress deemed the Social Security Administration so good at its job, it assigned the SSA to manage these new benefits. More than 3 million people were converted from state welfare programs to SSI in the 1970s. (For more on SSI, see Chapter 14.)

Senior Moments

By 1960, 559,000 people were getting disability benefits. At that time, the average benefit was about $80 per month. By 1970, 1.7 million people were on the disability roles.

Although SSI was a huge task for the SSA, it soon had an even bigger job to tackle: health care benefits.

Medicare to the Rescue

The Medicare bill of 1965 extended health coverage to almost all Americans aged 65 or older. Nearly 20 million beneficiaries enrolled in Medicare in the first three years of the program. After signing up more than 35 million people when Social Security started, the SSA certainly had the experience to handle this massive sign up, and this time it even knew the names.

Medicare covers people who are 65 years of age and older. If they don't have enough work history to qualify for free coverage or aren't married to someone who qualifies, there are provisions for buying into it. It also covers some people who are disabled under the age of 65 and people who have permanent kidney failure that requires dialysis or a transplant.

Coverage is in two parts. Part A is for hospital insurance, and Part B is for all other medical treatments. You can get additional coverage voluntarily by paying premiums for prescription drugs (Part D) or Medicare Advantage plans such as HMOs and PPOs (Part C). In the Medicare section of the book, we'll explore these benefits more closely.

Facing a Money Crunch

All the changes in benefits, especially those related to Cost of Living Adjustments, finally created a money crunch. It became obvious with the inflation of the mid-1970s that if benefit levels continued to soar out of control, future Social Security beneficiaries could end up making more in their monthly retirement benefit than they earned while working.

Congress had to come to terms with the fact that Social Security might run out of money. It was the first sign of the political hot potato that Social Security would become—and still is—today. How do we know that money will be there when the baby boomers retire?

By 1975, the trustees of the *Social Security trust funds* reported that the trusts would be exhausted in 1979 if Congress didn't act quickly.

In 1977, for the first time ever, Congress passed amendments to actually cut back on Social Security. It split the adjustment in Social Security based on wages from the COLA adjustment, which is based on inflation, to slow the increase in benefits as well as reduce benefits being paid. It increased the payroll FICA tax from 6.45 percent to the current 7.65 percent. Officials projected that these fixes would extend the program's life by 50 years.

Senior Moments
The fix led to a campaign fought by people born between 1917 and 1921. They called themselves the "Notch Babies." They believed that the 1977 amendments discriminated against them unfairly and resulted in them getting less than they deserved in Social Security benefits. The Commission on the Social Security "Notch" Issue was formed, and its report was issued in 1994. The commission concluded, "Those born in the 'Notch' years are, in general, receiving a greater return from Social Security than will subsequent generations of beneficiaries." Notch Babies were not hurt, according to the commission.

Unfortunately, the 1977 amendments weren't enough of a fix, and in the early 1980s the Social Security program once again faced a serious short-term financial crisis. Congress enacted another round of amendments in 1983, including taxing Social Security benefits and increasing the retirement age. Also, federal employees who had been exempted from the system, were brought under Social Security and had to start paying Social Security taxes. Prior to that, they were covered by a different pension system.

Everyone knew this was only a partial fix, but no one wanted to face the full impact of the coming disaster when the baby boomers retired—it was just too big of a political problem to fix all at one time. So, we're still at it and probably will be for a long time to come, as Congress takes baby steps to get us closer to a workable solution. In the final section of this book, we'll look more closely at solutions that are under consideration today.

Yes, Social Security has become a vast and cumbersome program—much larger than anyone could have imagined when it first started in 1935. But Social Security is also the most popular social program ever designed. In the following chapters, we'll take a look at what you pay into and what you get out of this massive social experiment.

The Least You Need to Know

- ◆ Social Security started as a social insurance program solely for the worker, but it blossomed into a program that includes benefits for the spouse, children, and survivors after the death of the worker.

- ◆ Disability benefits and health-care coverage were added to the Social Security mix over the years.

- ◆ The Federal Insurance Contributions Act (FICA) was established as a payroll deduction in 1939. People who pay into Social Security are able collect benefits upon retirement.

- ◆ The problems of the future financial stability of Social Security were first recognized in the 1970s and still persist today.

Today's Security

In This Chapter

- ◆ Finding out who pays what
- ◆ Footing the bill if you're self-employed
- ◆ Discovering who doesn't pay into the system
- ◆ Trusting the trust

The Social Security Administration reported that more than 48 million Americans received more than $510 billion in Social Security benefits in 2005. About 33 million of those recipients are retired workers and their dependents. In addition, 6.6 million people receive survivor benefits and 6.4 million receive disability benefits, with 1.7 million collecting benefits as dependents of disabled workers. Mind boggling, isn't it?

In this chapter, I explain who foots the bill for all of these payments and discuss how fiscally sound the program is (or isn't). Finally, I touch on why the future of Social Security is such a hot-button issue these days.

Looking at Social Security's Bottom Line

Workers and their employers paid $553 billion toward Social Security in 2004, which is about 84 percent of the total revenue received by the system. In addition, Social Security earned $89 billion (13.5 percent) in interest on the trust fund bonds, and $16 billion (2.4 percent) from taxation of Social Security benefits.

Hmmm. That's a total of $658 billion. But they only needed $510 billion. What happened to the rest? That's what federal officials refer to as a surplus, and many people believe that it should be saved so there is enough available when the baby boomers retire. Priorities changed dramatically after the September 11, 2001 terrorist attacks, however.

Government spending increased dramatically to wage wars in Iraq and Afghanistan at the same time as government revenue was reduced by tax cuts in 2001, 2002 and 2003. This resulted in deficit government spending, which is likely to continue for the foreseeable future. Recovery from the devastating hurricanes of 2005 that destroyed New Orleans and many areas of the United States near the Gulf will add fuel to this crisis in spending. Instead of paying down the debt, to increase national saving and promote economic growth, persistent federal deficits mean that the Social Security Trust Fund is being used to pay for current government spending.

We won't know for a while how the current spending spree will impact the Social Security trust funds. We'll take a brief look at what this may mean later in this chapter and a much closer look at the entire controversy in Part 6.

For now, though, let's take a look at who pays into the Social Security system.

Paying the Bill

Social Security taxes are made in equal shares paid by workers and their employers. If you are self-employed and don't have an employer to pay part of your bill, you get stuck with the full bill.

Workers' and Employers' Bills

Every time you get a check from your employer, you see two deductions that claim a sizeable part of your check. One of the lines is variously called FICA (Federal Insurance Contributions Act), Social Security, or OASDI (*Old-Age, Survivors, and Disability Insurance*). The second deduction is identified as Medicare.

These deductions represent two types of taxes you pay toward the social insurance system called Social Security. The two lines should total 7.65 percent of your annual pay up to $94,200 in the year 2006—6.2 percent for Social Security and 1.45 percent for Medicare. If you earn more than $94,200, only 1.45 percent is taken out of the rest for Medicare. There is no cap on the salary level for which Medicare is deducted.

Your employer matches your contribution dollar for dollar, but it gets a benefit you don't: paying for employees' Social Security and Medicare benefits is a cost of doing business, so your employer gets to deduct these taxes as business expenses.

def•i•ni•tion

Old-Age, Survivors, and Disability Insurance (OASDI) is the largest social insurance program run by the Social Security Administration. It provides monthly benefits that replace lost income because of retirement, disability, or death. More than 90 percent of the jobs in the United States are covered by OASDI through mandatory payroll tax contributions.

Entrepreneurs' Payouts

If you are self-employed, you're stuck paying the full 15.3 percent on all your earnings up to $94,200 in 2006. If you earn more than that, your Medicare bill is 2.9 percent on all earnings over $94,200.

Self-employed folks can deduct half of the amount paid into Social Security and Medicare as a business expense.

Who Doesn't Pay

Some lucky folks don't have to pay these taxes, but they also can't collect any money during retirement. To avoid footing the bill, you must fit into one of these groups:

   ◆ State and local government workers who participate in alternative retirement systems

   ◆ Election workers who earn less than $1,000 a year

   ◆ Career federal employees hired before 1984 who did not choose Social Security coverage

   ◆ College students who work at their academic institutions

   ◆ Ministers who choose not to be covered

◆ Household workers who earn less than $1,100 annually

◆ Self-employed workers who have net earnings below $400

Social Graces

Let's say you netted $100,000 in 2006 as a self-employed worker. Up to $94,200, you will pay 15.3 percent toward Social Security and Medicare, or $14,412.60. In addition to that, you will have to pay 2.90 percent of the remaining $5,800, or $168.20, toward Medicare.

Some state and local government workers can opt to participate in Social Security as well as their state government pensions. If they do so, they get both their state pension and Social Security at retirement.

Career federal employees are not forced to pay into Social Security if they were hired before 1984. Federal employees then had a separate pension system called the Civil Service Retirement System. Since 1984, any newly hired federal employees must pay into Social Security.

Feeding the Trusts

You probably have read or heard reports forecasting that the Social Security trust fund will run out of money in the 2040s. You're probably wondering whether you can count on Social Security being there through your retirement.

Unfortunately, no one knows the answer to that question. If it's any consolation, Social Security is so popular and so many people are dependent on it today that it would be political suicide for any politician to say it shouldn't be saved in some form. Even if the Trust Funds run out of money, the government will still have enough revenue from the Social Security taxes to pay about 70 percent of promised benefits. So even if the worse case scenario occurred, you will still get some benefits.

Retired Americans depend heavily on Social Security. According to the Social Security Administration …

◆ Nine out of ten individuals age 65 and older receive Social Security benefits.

◆ Social Security benefits represent 39 percent of income for seniors.

◆ About two-thirds of Social Security beneficiaries who are age 65 or older receive 50 percent or more of their income from Social Security.

◆ Social Security is the only source of income for approximately 22 percent of people over 65.

♦ The poverty rate for Americans over 65 has dropped from 35 percent in 1959 to less than 10.2 percent in 2003.

♦ Without Social Security, nearly 50 percent of people over 65 would be living in poverty.

♦ An estimated 159 million workers (96 percent of all workers) are covered under Social Security. Fifty-three percent of the workforce has no private pension coverage, and 32 percent of the workforce has no savings set aside specifically for retirement.

Social Graces

If you'd like to learn more details about the rules for the Social Security trust fund and how the money is invested, check out this website for an excellent overview: www.ssa. gov/OACT/ProgData/funds.html.

Could you imagine the evening news showing elderly people out on the streets living in boxes like the public saw after the crash of 1929? I don't think so. I can't imagine any Congress or president risking that scenario.

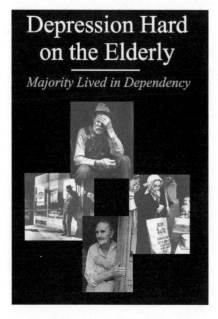

A government poster produced after the 1929 crash that showed the impact of the Depression on the elderly.

(Source: Social Security Administration's website)

That's not to say there won't be changes between now and when you and I retire. But I don't think there is any chance the program will be dismantled altogether, even if it means increasing federal debt to foot the bill. Unfortunately, the most likely scenario will probably involve a reduction in benefits and an increase in taxes.

We take a much closer look at what the future of Social Security may bring in Part 6. For now, let's look more closely at the concept of the Social Security trust fund and how it works.

Trust Money Rules

As I mentioned earlier, the Social Security system currently takes in more money than it pays out. Where does the excess money go? By federal law, the money must be invested in obligations, mostly bonds, backed by the federal government.

These bonds are essentially an I.O.U. from the federal government to Social Security. When the government starts cashing in the bonds to pay Social Security benefits, it will have to raise the money somewhere else by increasing taxes or cutting spending on other government priorities.

Trust Funds and the Budget

Social Security surpluses started to build in the 1980s and continued to build until 2001. At first, Congress used this extra money for deficit spending, but eventually the idea caught on that it makes sense to separate the Social Security surplus from the rest of the budget and put it in an imaginary "lockbox." However, the "lockbox" idea took a back seat as the country recovered from the shock of September 11, 2001, and the recession that took a strong hold on our economy shortly afterward.

Deficit spending continued to grow after the terrorist attacks, as President Bush pushed through tax cuts and waged wars in Afghanistan and Iraq. Rebuilding New Orleans and the U.S. Gulf Coast following the damage done by 2005 hurricanes Katrina and Rita, as well as the financing of the wars, will likely drive the need to continue this deficit spending into the foreseeable future.

In reality, whether the funds are put in this "lockbox" or are spent has no direct impact on the health of the trust fund. Bonds are set aside in the trust fund no matter how the government actually uses the cash. The problem is these bonds are a future debt that will have to be paid out of general tax funds. The "lockbox" idea was to pay down existing debt using the funds paid into Social Security. If Congress had been successful in keeping the lockbox in place, it would have increased national saving and domestic investment. This would make it much easier for the nation to pay the future benefits to baby boomers.

The "lockbox" is actually just a political tool being used by some to encourage less deficit spending and paying down the debt. By paying down the debt, the government doesn't have to pay as much interest. It also frees up more capital for private invest-ment.

Weathering the Baby Boom Storm

The more critical time for the budget will be when baby boomers start to retire and it becomes necessary to start cashing in on the trust fund bonds. When will that happen?

Baby boomers will begin to retire in 2008. About 70 million of them are heading toward that golden parachute.

Once boomers start retiring, the financial pressure on the Social Security trust fund will increase rapidly. Tax income will fall short in 2017 for the first time, according to projections by the Social Security trustees. That means the government will be paying more in benefits than it will be collecting in Social Security taxes.

Basically, what this means is that instead of collecting surpluses each year, the country will need to start dipping into the trust fund. By the year 2041, the trust fund is expected to be exhausted, according to the 2005 report of the Social Security trustees.

By the year 2031, there will be almost twice as many older Americans as there are today. The number of retirees will jump from 37 million today to 71 million in 2031.

Remember what I said earlier: 84 percent of what is paid out in benefits comes from workers and their employers. By 2031, there will be only 2.1 workers for each beneficiary, compared to 3.3 workers for each beneficiary today. The burden on those workers in 2031 will be much larger than it is today unless something is changed in how we foot the bill. (It should be noted that some experts doubt that the U.S. workforce will really lose that many workers by 2031. They argue that the numbers, which are solely based on current population growth, overlook the impact immigrants, who pay into Social Security, will have on the future U.S. workforce. Another unknown relates the to number of people who will decide to work longer or return to work after retiring.)

Making the burden for future workers even worse, these beneficiaries are expected to live longer than their predecessors. In 1940, when the first Social Security benefits were paid, the life expectancy of a 65-year-old was 12.5 years. Today, that has risen to 17.5 years, and it is expected to go even higher.

As you can see, there is good reason to be concerned. The Social Security trustees said in their 2005 annual report that either a permanent 13 percent reduction in benefits or a 15 percent increase in payroll tax income (or some combination of the two) will be needed to make Social Security solvent over the next 75-year period.

A 15 percent increase in the current Social Security tax rate would be .93 percent for both workers and their employers, raising the Social Security tax rate to 7.13 from 6.2 percent for workers. The gap for this shortfall could also be filled by raising the maximum income rate that is taxed for Social Security, which in 2006 was $94,200. A 13 percent decrease in the 2005 average monthly benefit of $959 would be $124.67 less per beneficiary.

In Part 6 of this book, we delve more deeply into what alternatives are being considered to survive this oncoming baby boom storm.

The Least You Need to Know

- You and your employer share the costs of Social Security and Medicare equally. Each of you pays 7.65 percent of your annual income in Social Security taxes.

- If you're self-employed, you must pay the full 15.3 percent of the Social Security tax.

◆ The Social Security trust fund must be invested in obligations backed by the U.S. government, primarily bonds, which are essentially I.O.U.'s toward future payments.

◆ When the baby boomers start to retire, it will be a major drain on the Social Security trust fund. By the year 2031, the number of retirees in this country will almost double from 37 million to 71 million.

Part 2

Getting Your Share

Now that you know how Social Security was started, it's time to look at how you get your fair share of the pot. In the following chapters, I go through the rules step-by-step, showing you what your time and money commitments will be, how much paper pushing you'll need to do to collect, and what your collection options are.

Did you know, for example, that you have some control over when you start receiving retirement benefits? I sort through the pros and cons of the various options. By the time you finish reading these chapters, you'll have a better idea of what makes sense for you—retire early, retire late, or retire right on time.

Chapter 4

It's All About Me

In This Chapter

- Figuring out your take
- Calculating your spouse's share
- Counting money for kids
- Tallying disability payments

We've wandered through the maze of legislation and regulation that got Social Security to where it is today. We've swallowed the bitter pill about what it costs us to participate. We know how much is spent and the shaky condition of Social Security's future. Now we'll turn to what you are slated to get as benefit provisions now stand.

I can't give you any guarantees as to what will actually still be there when you become eligible. All I can do is give you a snapshot of what you would receive today if you became eligible for one of Social Security's benefits.

Something to Live On

Before we get into the actual dollar amounts, we should review some basics. Social Security was intended to be social insurance, a foundation for retirement, but never a person's sole source of income. As traditional pension plans become less common in the workplace, however, more and more people are finding that Social Security could end up being their only retirement income.

In 2005, the Social Security Administration reported that Social Security benefits were the only source of income for 21 percent of its recipients. That's a 3 percent increase since 1999 when 18 percent of Social Security recipients depended solely on Social Security. Thirty-four percent of recipients depended on Social Security for 90 percent of their income in retirement, which is a 4 percent increase. In addition, Social Security benefits provided more than 50 percent of income for about 65 percent of the aged population.

The number of people depending solely on Social Security likely will continue to rise as fewer and fewer people retire from companies that offer pension benefits. In 2005, only about 15 percent of the working population can expect to collect traditional pension benefits. While companies do provide 401(k) or other retirement savings options, many people withdraw these funds when they switch jobs.

Senior Moments

The Employee Benefit Research Institute (EBRI) found that only 15 percent of working age Americans have an individual retirement account (IRA) and only 22 percent contribute to a 401(k) plan. Only 1 in 3 working Americans has saved more than $100,000 for retirement. The EBRI concludes from this information that American retirees will have $45 billion less in retirement income in 2030 than they will need to cover basic expenses.

When you read reports about how little people are saving for retirement, you can only expect that the number of people whose sole income is Social Security will increase. So what are the average amounts one can expect to collect based on today's estimates?

Just to give you an idea of benefits you might expect, here is a chart of monthly benefits for a person born on September 15, 1943 who turned 62 (the earliest age you can start to collect benefits as a retired worker) in 2005. I developed this chart using the Social Security Administration's benefit calculator.

Monthly Benefits, Based on Age at Retirement

	Age 62	Full Retirement Age	Age 70
Low-wage earner ($15,329)	$485	$669	$914
Average earner ($34,065)	$799	$1,107	$1,516
High earner ($54,503)	$1,004	$1,417	$1,976
Maximum earner ($90,000)	$1,409	$1,611	$1,926

The age for full retirement benefits is gradually increasing to age 67 depending on when you were born (see Chapter 5 for more on retirement ages). Full retirement age for the person in this example is 66, so there is a reduction in benefits for retiring four years early. Chapter 7 discusses the impact on Social Security if you decide to retire early.

Low earnings are defined as 45 percent of the national average wage index. Average earnings are equal to that index. High earnings are 160 percent of that index. A maximum earner is someone who earns the maximum amount taxed on the OASDI contributions and benefits base, which was $90,000 in 2005. The most recent national average wage index available for this chart was $34,065 (based on 2003 income levels).

Social Security payments are indexed to inflation, so the payment amount you will receive could be much higher than the numbers in the preceding chart, depending on how far you are from retirement. Another factor that impacts your benefit is the change in average wages. The cost of living will also be higher, however, so if you think you can live on the amount in the chart based on your living standards and income level today, there is a good chance that will be true when you retire.

> **Social Graces**
>
> We'll be delving deeper into how the Social Security Administration comes up with its benefit amounts in Chapter 6, but if you can't wait and want to know what your projections are right now based on your age, online calculators can be found at www.ssa.gov/planners/calculators.htm.

Unfortunately, if you quickly calculate your annual income versus what you can expect in Social Security, you'll see that it most likely means a drop in living standards unless you have additional sources of income. For example, a person earning the average wage of $34,065 can expect $1,107 monthly based on these 2005 numbers, which would mean an annual income of $13,284, or only 38.9 percent of current earnings. Now you see why it's important to beef up your savings even if Social Security is still paying at the current levels (plus inflation) when you retire.

Senior Moments

Forty-two percent of the adults receiving Social Security are men and 58 percent are women, according to the 2005 facts and figures released by the Social Security Administration. Only 1 percent of the men are collecting benefits based on their wife's earnings, while 33 percent of the women are collecting based on their husband's earnings—12 percent while their husbands are still alive and another 21 percent as survivors based on their husband's earnings record.

Maximum wage earners will have an even tougher time maintaining their pre-retirement living standards if they rely entirely on their Social Security benefits. Let's say you earn $100,000 per year and retire at age 66. Based on the 2005 numbers, your monthly benefit from Social Security would be $1,611, or $19,332 annually. That's only 19.3 percent of your current earnings. Social Security's payment scheme is skewed to give higher benefits to lower wage earners. In fact, some folks are advocating even lower benefit levels for high earners to help fix the system. We'll discuss that in more depth later in this book.

In 2006, the maximum benefit for a retiree at full retirement age is $1,939 per month. There are two components to this increase. One factor is that the maximum taxable income increases to $94,200, which means more money taxed up front (income was taxed to a maximum of $90,000, or $4,200 less). The second is an across the board Cost of Living Increase of 4.1 percent as of January 2006. Both of these contribute to the higher maximum benefit.

Money for Your Spouse

Benefits for your spouse will be 50 percent of your benefits as a retired worker, if your spouse begins collecting at full retirement age.

Many times, a worker reaches full retirement age earlier than his or her spouse. When that happens and your spouse wants to begin collecting Social Security early, the amount that can be collected is reduced, as follows:

◆ If your spouse wants to collect at age 64, the benefit amount is about 46 percent of the working spouse's full benefit.

◆ At age 63, the benefit amount is about 42 percent of the full benefit.

◆ At age 62, the benefit amount drops to just 37.5 percent of the full benefit amount.

If your spouse is eligible for benefits on his or her own work record, Social Security always pays those benefits first. Your spouse may still get some of your benefits because Social Security will make up the difference if your spouse's benefits fall short of your benefits.

For example, let's say you and your spouse retire today at age 65. Your spouse did not work for many years while raising children and then only went back part time as a low-wage earner, qualifying for just $669 in benefits. You qualify for benefits of $1,939 as a maximum wage earner. Fifty percent of $1,939 is $969.50. Your spouse would receive a combination of benefits ($669 based on your spouse's work record plus $300.50 from your benefits, totaling $969.50) from his or her own work history and yours, totaling the higher amount.

Insecurities

When you decide on an age for retirement and a benefit amount is set, there is no going back. Your basis for retirement will be that amount for the rest of your life. There is a possibility of raising that basis if you go back to work. We'll discuss that in greater detail in Chapter 16.

A person who earned $100,000 per year and retired at full retirement age could collect only $1,939 per month in 2005, or $23,268 per year. If that person were married, his or her spouse would collect 50 percent, or $11,634 annually, provided these benefits were collected starting at full retirement age. The couple's total income would then be $34,902, which would still result in a dramatic cut in lifestyle, unless the couple had saved additional funds in retirement accounts or was entitled to pension benefits from a former employer.

The 2006 increase to $2,019 monthly for a recipient entitled to the maximum won't help much. His or her spouse at 50 percent of benefits would receive $1,009. The couple's total income from Social Security would be $3,028 per month, or $36,366 per year. If both were eligible for maximum benefits based on their individual earnings history, then the couple would get total monthly income of $4,038, which is equal to $48,456 annually.

Spouses are also entitled to benefits as a survivor of a deceased worker. For example, if a husband dies, his widow can receive benefits beginning at age 60. If the widow was disabled, benefits can start as early as age 50. The amount that can be collected depends on the survivor's age when he or she begins collecting. Another factor is the amount the deceased worker would have been entitled to receive.

If the survivor begins collecting at age 60, he or she is entitled to 71 percent of the deceased worker's benefit. If the survivor waits until full retirement age, he or she can get 100 percent. The disabled survivor of a worker who begins collecting between the ages of 50 and 59 will get 71 percent of the deceased worker's benefit.

This is just a quick summary. I promise we'll take a closer look at this complicated world of survivors' benefits in Chapter 10.

Now it's time to see what benefits your children can collect when you retire.

Support for Your Kids

Your children can qualify for benefits up to age 18 or until they complete grade 12, but no later than two months after the child's nineteenth birthday. A disabled child can collect benefits throughout his or her life provided that disability started before age 22.

An eligible child can be your biological child, an adopted child, or a stepchild. A dependent grandchild may also qualify under certain circumstances.

For a child to qualify for benefits, he or she must be unmarried and be one of the following:

- ◆ Under age 18
- ◆ 18 to 19 years old and a full-time student (no higher than grade 12)
- ◆ 18 or older and disabled from a disability that started before age 22

Social Graces

When you retire, your spouse may not have to wait until age 65 to collect the full 50 percent share of your benefits if he or she is taking care of a child under the age of 16 or is taking care of a disabled child. In either of these situations, your spouse can collect 50 percent of your benefits regardless of his or her age. If you die, your spouse's benefits would increase to 75 percent if he or she is still caring for children and not yet eligible to retire.

Senior Moments

The 2000 census showed that 5.8 million grandparents live with their grandchildren. Forty-two percent, or 2.4 million of those grandparents, have the primary responsibility for raising those children. Grandmothers bear the responsibility in 62 percent of these situations, while grandfathers take the full-time duty of raising grandchildren 38 percent of the time.

Children get a monthly payment of up to one-half of your full retirement amount, but there is a limit to what can be paid to the family as a whole. The total varies depending on the amount of your benefit and the number of family members who also qualify on your record. The total amount is usually equal to about 150 to 180 percent of your retirement benefit.

Once the maximum is reached for a family, the eligible amount is divided equally among the entitled dependents. The retired worker's benefit is not reduced, but the amount collected by each of the eligible dependents may be reduced.

If the retired worker dies while the child is still eligible for benefits, the child's share rises to 75 percent. This is also the case if a worker dies before retirement and the child becomes eligible for survivors' benefits. The family maximum rules apply here, too. The total that can be paid also must be within the allowed family maximum.

There is a very complex formula for figuring a family's maximum benefit. We'll take a closer look at this in Chapter 11.

We've discussed Social Security benefits for you and your family as a worker, but what happens if you can't work?

Insecurities

Benefits usually stop at age 18 unless the child is disabled. If the child is still attending school as a full-time student in grade 12 or below, he or she can collect benefits until two months after becoming 19.

Protecting Yourself If You Can't Work

You can collect benefits if you are disabled, but there are complex criteria for qualifying. We'll visit those qualifications in Chapter 13, but we'll take a quick peek here at what you can collect if you qualify for benefits.

def•i•ni•tion

Social Security Disability Insurance is paid only if you cannot do the work you did before becoming disabled and cannot adjust to other work because of your disability. Your disability must be expected to last for at least a year or be expected to result in your death. There are no benefits for short-term disability.

def•i•ni•tion

Supplemental Security Income (SSI) provides benefits to people who become disabled but who have not worked long enough to qualify for Social Security Disability Insurance. They must also meet a financial needs test. SSI also provides benefits to people over age 65 who qualify based on financial need. It provides cash to meet basic needs for food, clothing, and shelter.

According to the Social Security Administration, disabled workers and their dependents get 14 percent of the total benefits that the SSA pays out. You may not realize it, but there is a good chance you have protection if you are or become disabled for at least a year. In fact, 80 percent of workers age 21 to 64 are covered under Social Security's disability provisions.

Two types of benefits are paid to disabled people under Social Security. *Social Security Disability Insurance* is paid if you become disabled after having worked long enough and having paid the required Social Security taxes. *Supplemental Security Income (SSI)* is paid to disabled people who haven't worked long enough.

Disability benefits are based on the age of disability as well as the number of years worked. It's a complicated formula. To simplify things here, I'll just give you an idea of the averages.

The average monthly benefit paid in 2005 for a disabled worker was $902. For a disabled worker with a spouse and one or more children, the average benefit was $1,503. This will increase in 2006 to $939 for a disabled worker and $1,567 for a disabled worker with a spouse and one or more children.

If the disabled worker and his family qualify for Supplemental Security Income (SSI), the payment in 2005 was $579 per month for an individual and $869 per month for a couple. To qualify for SSI, you must have very limited resources. The total allowed in 2005 was $2,000 for an individual and $3,000 for a couple. In 2006, the average benefit for an individual will increase to $603 per month and $904 monthly for a couple. The resource limits will remain the same in 2006.

I guess you have figured out by now you won't get rich living on Social Security, but it does serve as a safety net so you don't starve or end up homeless. For people with limited resources, additional aid options are available through your state social service offices. We discuss options for seniors with limited resources in Chapter 14.

The Least You Need to Know

♦ Social Security was intended to be social insurance, a foundation for retirement, but never a person's sole source of income.

♦ As traditional pension plans become less common in the workplace, more and more people are finding that Social Security could end up being their sole source of income.

♦ In addition to retirement benefits for the worker, there are also benefits for his or her spouse and children.

♦ Benefits are available if a worker becomes disabled or has a child who becomes disabled before age 22. There are also benefits for survivors after a worker's death.

Chapter 5

Following the Rules

In This Chapter

- ◆ Getting into the nitty-gritty of Social Security taxes
- ◆ Earning enough credits
- ◆ Finding out when you can apply for benefits
- ◆ Filing the proper paperwork

Now that you have the big picture, it's time to start breaking down the pieces into smaller, easier-to-understand bits. We're going to sort out the rules so you know what you are paying, how long you have to pay, and what sort of paper trail you should build as a future recipient. Yes, you do have a responsibility to be certain that your records are accurate. If you don't, your ultimate benefits could suffer.

Your Out-of-Pocket Costs

For most people, payments for Social Security are automatically deducted from their paycheck. As I mentioned earlier, 7.65 percent is taken out of each paycheck by your employer for Social Security taxes. Of that, 6.2 percent goes to Social Security and 1.45 percent goes to Medicare. Your employer matches that amount dollar for dollar. If you're self-employed or own a small business, you are obligated to pay the full 15.3 percent on your net earnings. You do get to deduct half of that on your 1040 tax form, however, to reduce your adjusted gross income and, ultimately, your tax bill.

The amount taxed for Social Security in 2005 stopped once a person's income reached $90,000. The amount paid into Medicare never stops, no matter how high your income goes.

How It Works If You're Employed by Someone Else

Here is how it works. Let's say you earn $100,000 a year and work for someone else. Your bill will be as follows:

$90,000 × 6.2 percent =	$5,580
$100,000 × 1.45 percent =	$1,450
	_____
Total Social Security tax =	$7,030

This is what your 2005 tax reports would show. In 2006, the maximum amount taxable will increase to $94,200. This is how your Social Security taxes will increase in 2006 if you earn $100,000:

$94,200 × 6.2 percent =	$5,840.40
$100,000 × 1.45 percent =	$1,450.00
	_____
Total Social Security tax =	$7,290.40

Maximum wage earners will pay $260.40 more in Social Security taxes in 2006 than they did in 2005.

All of this will be taken out of your paycheck by your employer. Once you fill out your *W-4 form* when you are hired, your reporting obligation is over. The responsibility for paying the bill is solely on your employer's shoulder.

def•i•ni•tion

The **W-4 form (Employee Withholding Allowance Certificate)** gives your employer the information needed to withhold the correct federal income tax from your pay. If your financial situation changes or you get married or have a child, it is good to revisit what you told your employer on this form because the amount of tax being taken out of your check may need to be adjusted.

How It Works If You're Self-Employed

It's not so simple if you are self-employed or run a small business. In these cases, the onus is on you not only to pay the bills but to report the earnings.

As you learned in Chapter 3, the tax bill for self-employed folks is much higher. They must pay both the employee and the employer obligations. Here's how that works for someone whose net earnings are $100,000:

$90,000 × 12.4 percent =	$11,160.00
$100,000 × 2.9 percent =	$2,900.00
	———————
Total Social Security tax =	$14,060.00

As mentioned above, maximum earnings for Social Security tax purposes were raised to $94,200 in 2006. Let's take a quick look at how the increase will impact self-employed folks.

$94,200 × 12.4 percent =	$11,680.80
$100,000 × 2.9 percent =	$2,900.00
	———————
Total Social Security tax =	$14,580.80

Self-employed folks will pay $520.80 more in Social Security taxes in 2006. Remember that you get to deduct half of this Social Security tax on IRS Form 1040 on line 30. This amount is subtracted from your gross income, thereby reducing your adjusted gross income and your overall tax bill.

You report your earnings from self-employment when you file your federal income tax return. You must prepare a Schedule SE form for Social Security purposes as long as your net earnings are $400 or more in any year.

Now that you know how much you must pay, let's look at how long you must pay it.

Social Graces

If you own a small business and want more information about your obligations as an employer, here is an excellent place to start: www.ssa.gov/employer.

Your Time Commitment

From the day you start working, and for as long as you work, you must pay into Social Security and Medicare unless you are in one of the exempt categories. There is no time off for good behavior.

Once you start paying into Social Security, you start earning credits so you can collect some money on the other side—when you retire or become disabled. The credits are based on the amount you earn.

Senior Moments
You may have heard that credits were earned by the number of quarters worked. That used to be true. Before 1978, employers reported your wages every three months. You earned one credit for each quarter worked, provided you earned at least $50 in a three-month quarter. Starting in 1978, employers changed to reporting earnings just once a year. Credits today are based on your total wages and self-employment income during the year, no matter when you did the actual work. You don't have to work a full year to earn four credits. If you can earn the minimum required (in 2005, it was $920 per credit, or $3,680 for four credits) in one month, you've met your earning obligation for the year.

Retirement Requirements

Each year that you work, your wages are posted to your Social Security record. Your credits are based on the wages posted. These credits are used to determine your eligibility for retirement or disability benefits. They are also used to determine what benefits your survivors will get if you become disabled or die.

The amount of earnings needed to get credits increases as the average earnings levels increase, based on the national average wage index. In 2005, a person earned one credit for each $920 of earnings up to a maximum of four credits per year. Once earned, these credits stay on your record even if you lose a job and have no earnings for a while.

How many credits do you need to collect Social Security? Well, as with everything else, that depends. Your date of birth is a critical factor in determining your retirement benefits.

If you were born after 1929, you need 40 credits to be eligible for retirement benefits. Prior to that time fewer credits were needed, with the least amount required for someone born in 1924—35 credits. As discussed in Chapter 2, when Social Security payments first started, those closest to retirement could earn as few as six credits to qualify for benefits.

Disability Dues

The number of credits needed to qualify for disability benefits varies according to the age when you become disabled. The rules are very specific for each age.

If you become disabled before age 24, you will need to have earned six credits during the three-year period before your disability begins. If you are disabled between the ages of 24 and 30, you will need to have earned credit for half of the number of years between age 21 and when you become disabled. For example, if you become disabled at age 25, you could have worked fours years between age 21 and 25 and earned 16 credits (four credits can be earned in each year of work). In order to qualify for disability, you would need to have earned half of that number, or eight credits. If you're disabled at age 31 or older, the number of credits needed is shown in the following table from the Social Security Administration:

Disabled at Age	Credits Needed
31 through 42	20
44	22
46	24
48	26
50	28
52	30
54	32
56	34
58	36
60	38
62 or older	40

At least 20 of these credits must have been earned within the 10 years prior to your claiming disability.

Survivors and Benefits

Survivors of a deceased worker may qualify for benefits even if the worker didn't earn all the credits needed for retirement benefits. If the deceased worker was born in 1929 or before, one credit is needed for each year after 1950 and prior to the year of death. If the deceased worker was born during or after 1930, one credit is needed for each year after age 21 and prior to the year of death. In both cases, the maximum number of credits needed is 40.

Social Graces

A person born in 1955 who dies at age 50 would need 29 credits for his or her family to qualify for benefits. Those 29 credits would represent the one credit needed for each year between the ages of 21 and 50.

Dependent children can get survivors' benefits if the deceased worker had six credits in the three years before his or her death, regardless of when the worker was born. The children would continue to collect benefits until they reached age 18 (or age 19 if they are attending school up to grade 12). A widow or widower caring for dependent children who are under age 16 or disabled may also be able to get benefits.

Meeting Medicare Requirements

Your Social Security credits also count toward Medicare, which is an automatic benefit when you reach age 65 as long as you or your spouse have earned 40 credits. You may also become eligible for Medicare at an earlier age if you are entitled to disability benefits for 24 months or more.

Dependents or survivors may be eligible for Medicare at age 65 or if they are disabled. People who have permanent kidney failure or need kidney dialysis may also be eligible for Medicare at any age.

If you don't have enough credits for Medicare, you can buy into the system. I'll cover that in more detail in Chapter 19.

Credit Poor

Some workers don't earn credits toward Social Security. The following are the most common groups of people who don't:

◆ Most federal employees hired before 1984. (Federal employees did start paying into Medicare on January 1, 1983.)

◆ Some state and local government employees who choose not to participate in Social Security.

In all these cases, other types of retirement plans are available.

Now that you know your time commitments, let's look at how old you need to be before you can begin to collect your benefits.

 Social Graces

The Social Security Administration recently developed a site for state and local government employers to help them understand how their retirement plan decisions impact their employees. If you'd like to learn more, go to www.ssa.gov/slge.

Admitting Your Age: When Older Is Better

You may not like to admit to your age. In fact, you may have spent many years telling people that you are younger than you really are. But when it comes to reporting to the Social Security Administration, it's time to come clean. This is definitely a time in your life when older is better.

You can start getting Social Security benefits as early as age 62, but your benefits will be reduced if you apply for benefits earlier than your full retirement age.

There are some exceptions to this rule. For example, a widow or widower can start collecting at age 60 on his or her spouse's record, or even as early as age 50 if disabled.

Retiring earlier than 62 can have a negative impact on the amount you will ultimately collect. As we'll discuss in greater detail in Chapter 6, Social Security benefits are computed on a 35-year average. If during some of those years you earn no income, this could have a significant negative impact on your final benefit amount.

Senior Moments
When President Ronald Reagan signed the Social Security Amendments of 1983, which included extending the retirement age, he said, "We're entering an age when average Americans will live longer and live more productive lives. And these amendments adjust to that progress. The changes in this legislation will allow Social Security to age as gracefully as all of us hope to do ourselves, without becoming an overwhelming burden on generations still to come." In passing these amendments, Congress said that improvements in the health of older people and increases in the average life expectancy were the primary reasons for increasing the full retirement age.

It used to be that 65 was the full retirement age for all workers. Congress amended the law in 1983, however, and now the year of your birth determines when you actually reach full retirement age. Here is a chart you can use to figure out when you will reach this age:

Year of Birth	Full Retirement Age
1937 or earlier	65
1938	65 and 2 months
1939	65 and 4 months
1940	65 and 6 months
1941	65 and 8 months
1942	65 and 10 months
1943–1954	66
1955	66 and 2 months
1956	66 and 4 months
1957	66 and 6 months
1958	66 and 8 months
1959	66 and 10 months
1960 and later	67

If you were born on January 1 in any year, the SSA requires you to use the previous year to determine your full retirement age.

Now that you know what your money and time commitments are, let's look at how to make sure Social Security is aware that you have met those commitments.

Starting the Paper Trail

You hope that your employer is diligent about reporting your income to Social Security. You also hope that when Social Security gets the information from your employer, it promptly appears on your personal record. Unfortunately, things do not always turn out the way we hope they will.

It is your responsibility to make sure your Social Security paper trail is accurate, so you can be sure that when it's time to start receiving your benefits you get your fair share. Each year, beginning when you reach age 25, the Social Security Administration sends you a report of your Social Security payments. The report shows the earnings on which you have paid Social Security during your working years and provides a summary of the estimated benefits you and your family may be eligible to receive based on those earnings.

I'll bet you've gotten those statements, taken a quick look at them, and tossed them into a file. Maybe you considered them junk mail, and they ended up in the garbage. If you haven't been paying attention to them, it's time to change your habits.

> **Insecurities**
>
> If you ignore your Social Security statements year after year and wait until you are near retirement to start worrying about them, it could be too late to correct any errors. For example, a former employer could have gone out of business, and you could have a difficult time trying to prove your earnings.

Correcting Errors

The first thing you should check when you get your statement is whether your earnings have been properly reported. It is much easier to get the record corrected when the mistake is only a couple years old rather than waiting several years.

If you find that your record is not complete, you can call the Social Security Administration at 1-800-772-1213 to reach specialists who can help you sort out the problem and correct it. You'll need to provide them with your name, Social Security number, the year or years that are not correct, and the business name and address of your employer in those years. If you have your *W-2 forms* available for the incorrect years, that's even better.

> **def•i•ni•tion**
>
> Your employer provides the **W-2 form (Wage and Tax Statement)** at the end of each year, usually by January 31 of the following year, to report your earnings and the taxes paid on those earnings. This is the form you send in with your tax returns each year.

If you are now living outside the U.S. and cannot use the toll-free number, you can correct a statement by mail by writing to the following address:

Social Security Administration
Office of Public Inquiries
Windsor Park Building
6401 Security Blvd.
Baltimore, MD 21235

The information needed for a mail request is the same as that needed by phone. Again, W-2s showing your earnings for the missing years will help solve the problem more quickly, but the Social Security Administration can research the information using the business name and address of your employer during the missing years.

If the missing earnings are for last year, your record might not have been updated yet. Current year earnings are reported the following year.

The Social Security Administration will send you a letter after any correction has been made. The correction should show up on your next annual statement, but you can ask for a new statement immediately after getting the correction letter.

Social Graces

You can speed the process and get the information in two to four weeks by ordering a statement online at www.ssa.gov/mystatement. If you do stop by online, you'll find it is also a good spot to get more details about what is in a statement and what it means to you.

Getting Your Statement

Statements are sent out automatically once you reach age 25, but you can request one at any time. You can order a statement request form by calling 1-800-772-1213, or you can download a request form online at www.ssa.gov/online/ssa-7004.html.

It takes four to six weeks to get the statement after you have mailed your request.

In 1997, the Social Security Administration tested the possibility of allowing you to get a statement immediately using an online, interactive process. The test was stopped when questions about privacy and confidentially were raised.

Didn't Get a Statement?

Statements are not sent to people under age 25 or to people who are already receiving benefits on their own record or on someone else's record. In addition, the SSA doesn't send an automatic statement for 11 months after a requested statement has been sent.

If you haven't received a statement in a while, it could be that the Social Security Administration doesn't have a current address for you. You can order one online at www.ssa.gov or call Social Security at 1-800-772-1213.

You now know how Social Security collects its money based on your earnings and that you are the one responsible for making sure Social Security builds an accurate earnings history for you. In the next chapter, I detail how the SSA uses your earnings history to calculate your benefit amount.

The Least You Need to Know

♦ Social Security taxes are taken out of your paycheck automatically. If you are self-employed, you must report earnings yourself and pay Social Security taxes as both the employee and the employer.

♦ You can earn up to four credits a year and must earn 40 credits to qualify for Social Security retirement benefits.

♦ Eligibility for disability benefits is also based on the number of credits you earn. For disability, however, the number of credits needed varies by your age at the time your disability begins.

♦ Monitor your annual Social Security statements very closely to be sure you are getting proper credit for all the money you've earned.

Chapter 6

Counting Your Cash

In This Chapter

- ◆ Making sense of the payout policies
- ◆ Estimating your take
- ◆ Understanding why you might get less
- ◆ Applying for benefits

Although the government makes it very easy for you to pay into Social Security, I bet you won't be surprised to find out that it's not as easy to get your fair share when the time comes. In this chapter, you'll find out how the government figures your fair share and, even more important, how you go about getting your money.

Let's start by looking at how Social Security calculates your benefits.

Cracking the Payout Rules

When it's time to get your money, the first thing you want to know is how much will you get. The payment is called your *Primary Insurance Amount (PIA)*.

def•i•ni•tion

The **Primary Insurance Amount (PIA)** is the amount you will receive at your full retirement age. As long as you were born before 1938, that age is 65. Beginning with people who were born in 1938, that age gradually increases to 67 for people born after 1959. See the chart in Chapter 5 to find out your full retirement age. The SSA pays disability and survivor's benefits based on the worker's PIA.

If you have a pension plan at work and have looked at your future estimated benefits, you may have noticed that those benefits are calculated based on your last five years of earnings or on your three highest years of earnings. That is common for most pension plans, but it is not true for Social Security.

Social Security uses a four-step process to determine your PIA, and calculates an average based on your 35 highest years of earnings. This is not a typo. Your PIA is figured based on earnings over 35 years of your working life.

Social Graces

You can get an estimate of your benefits online using one of the interactive calculators at www.ssa.gov/planners/calculators.htm.

Ready? We're now going to work through the four-step process so you can understand how your PIA is calculated. By the way, if you don't like math, you'll be relieved to learn that you never have to calculate your PIA on your own. Interactive online calculators can do it for you, or you can call Social Security at 1-800-772-1213 and someone will crunch the numbers for you.

Even though you don't have to do it yourself, it's important to understand how Social Security calculates your PIA. When you start getting into the more complicated questions about when to retire, whether to work or not, and whether to collect on your earnings record or on your spouse's, knowing the calculations will help you make the right choices. Bear with me, I know this can be confusing. I'll do my best to clarify for you:

1. Social Security first determines how many years to use as a base. If you were born after 1928 and will retire after 1990, your base number is calculated using your 35 highest years of earnings. If you were born in 1928 or earlier, fewer years are used.

2. Next, Social Security adjusts your earnings for wage inflation. This is called indexing. As I'm sure you are well aware, inflation eats away at your earnings

each year. This step uses the national average earnings level to adjust your earnings based on inflation. Your age is also considered in this calculation.

3. Your average adjusted monthly earnings amount is then calculated based on the number of years determined in step 1. For example, if you were born after 1928 and don't have earnings in 35 different years, some years will have $0 used to figure this average amount. Parents who stay home to raise a family can be hurt by this step.

4. Now comes the hard part. Social Security uses a complicated formula to finally determine your PIA. Social Security multiplies your average adjusted monthly earnings using a formula set by law. I'll give you the official wording, and then we'll work through a couple of examples. These are the three steps used to calculate PIA:

   a. Take 90 percent of your first $627 of average monthly earnings.

   b. Then take 32 percent of the amount between $627 and $3,779.

   c. Finally, take 15 percent of everything over $3,779 to give you your full retirement benefit amount. (Remember, if you start your benefits before you reach full retirement age, this amount will be reduced.)

If you are a high wage earner, you will be only taxed on the first $94,200 of income in 2006. It was even less than that in prior years. When Social Security calculates the PIA, the maximum PIA is based on the maximum amount of salary taxed.

Senior Moments

Your earnings record can be hurt if you don't have regular earnings every year. For example, let's say your average earnings were $30,000 for each of 25 years. The rest of your adult life you did not work; you stayed at home to raise children or to care for a family member who was sick. Ten of your 35 years would be calculated at $0 rather than an average of $30,000 over 35 years; the average would actually be reduced to $21,439. That represents 25 years at $30,000 and 10 years at $0.

In Chapter 16, we talk about how going back to work in retirement may help offset some of this loss.

Let's look at two wage earners and see what happens. One has an average monthly wage of $1,000 ($12,000 annually) during his 35 highest years of earnings. The second has an average monthly wage of $10,000 ($120,000 annually) over his 35 years of highest earnings. Remember that, in 2005, Social Security taxes were only paid on the first $90,000 of earnings.

We'll use the formula to calculate benefits for these two examples.

Scenario 1: Average monthly wages of $1,000

90 percent of first $627 =	$564.30
32 percent of next $373 =	$119.36
	————
Primary Insurance Amount =	$683.66

In this scenario, the worker's monthly benefit of $683.66 is 68.4 percent of earnings.

Scenario 2: Average monthly wages of $10,000

90 percent of first $627 =	$564.30
32 percent of next $3,779 =	$1,209.28
15 percent of $5,594 =	$839.10
	————
Primary Insurance Amount =	$1,612.68

In this scenario, the worker exceeded the maximum PIA that was allowed in 2005, which was $1,611. His benefit amount is $1,611, or 16.1 percent of earnings. Remember, this high income earner only paid Social Security taxes on the first $90,000 of income in 2005 and will pay taxes on the first $94,200 in 2006.

You've probably noticed from these two examples that lower wage earners get a much higher percentage of their earnings. That's true. Social Security is set up to replace about 42 percent of earnings for people who had average earnings during their working years. (Average earnings were $34,065 in 2003, the most recent calculation of the national wage index used in 2005 by the Social Security Administration.) A low-wage earner actually gets more than 42 percent of his or her average earnings, while a high-wage earner gets considerably less. The Social Security benefits formula is weighted in favor of low-income workers. In designing this payout scheme, lawmakers believed that low-income workers, who most likely will have less opportunity to save and invest during their working years, need more retirement insurance. Remember that Social Security is a social insurance program, not a retirement program.

Why You Might Get Less

If you had jobs that weren't covered by Social Security for part of your career, you may find that you are not entitled to full Social Security benefits. Your benefits could be cut in one of the following two ways:

◆ **The Government Pension Offset.** This affects the benefits of a spouse or widow(er). We'll look more closely at these provisions in Chapters 9 and 10.

◆ **The Windfall Elimination Provision.** This provision primarily affects people who earned a pension while working for a government agency but were not required to pay Social Security taxes. In addition, they worked at other jobs during their career and paid Social Security taxes long enough to qualify for retirement or disability benefits. You could also be impacted by this provision if you earned a pension in any type of job in which you didn't pay Social Security taxes.

If you will receive both a government pension (or another pension based on work not covered by Social Security) and Social Security, the formula used to figure your PIA is modified.

Earlier in this chapter I told you that in step 4 the first $627 of average monthly earnings is multiplied by 90 percent. If your benefits are to be reduced by the Windfall Elimination Provision, that 90 percent factor is reduced to 40 percent, as long as you reached retirement or disability in 1990 or later.

If you worked in a job that places you under this provision, all may not be lost. Remember, we're dealing with the government, so there are exceptions to every rule ever written. When it comes to this provision, the 90 percent factor is not reduced if you have more than 30 years of "substantial" earnings in a job in which you did pay Social Security taxes, and it is reduced on a sliding scale if you have between 21 and 29 years of substantial earnings.

You can review two charts to determine how you may be affected by the Windfall Elimination Provision. The first chart shows what qualifies as substantial earnings for each year. The second chart shows how much of the 90 percent factor will be reduced based on the number of years you had substantial earnings. Both charts are from the Social Security Administration.

Amount Needed in Substantial Earning Each Year

Year	Substantial Earnings
1937–50	$900
1951–54	$900
1955–58	$1,050
1959–65	$1,200
1966–67	$1,650
1968–71	$1,950
1972	$2,250
1973	$2,700
1974	$3,300
1975	$3,525
1976	$3,825
1977	$4,125
1978	$4,425
1979	$4,725
1980	$5,100
1981	$5,550
1982	$6,075
1983	$6,675
1984	$7,050
1985	$7,425
1986	$7,875
1987	$8,175
1988	$8,400
1989	$8,925
1990	$9,525
1991	$9,900
1992	$10,350
1993	$10,725
1994	$11,250
1995	$11,325
1996	$11,625

Year	Substantial Earnings
1997	$12,150
1998	$12,675
1999	$13,425
2000	$14,175
2001	$14,925
2002	$15,750
2003	$16,125
2004	$16,275
2005	$16,725

Credited earnings from 1937 through 1950 are divided by $900 to get the number of years of coverage (maximum 14 years).

Reduction of 90 Percent Factor

Years of Substantial Earnings	Percentage
30 or more	90%
29	85%
28	80%
27	75%
26	70%
25	65%
24	60%
23	55%
22	50%
21	45%
20 or fewer	40%

The modified formula does not apply if you are collecting survivors' benefits. It only impacts the worker's benefit. You also may be exempt if you fall into one of the following categories:

◆ You are a federal worker first hired after December 31, 1983.

♦ You were employed on December 31, 1983, by a nonprofit organization that was exempt from Social Security, and it became a mandatory coverage under Social Security on that date.

♦ Your only pension is based on railroad employment.

♦ The only work in which you did not pay Social Security taxes was before 1957.

♦ Your earnings were "substantial," as previously discussed.

If this has totally confused you and you fall into the category of people with both covered and noncovered years of earnings, your best bet is to call the Social Security Administration and ask someone to review your personal earnings history.

Now that you have the tools to figure out what your monthly benefits will be, you're ready to consider your retirement options.

Planning Your Strategies

The benefit figures calculated in the preceding section are based on you retiring at the full retirement age. You don't have to wait until you are 65 (or older if you were born after 1938) to start receiving Social Security benefits. You can retire as early as age 62 and apply for benefits. Of course, there's a catch—your monthly benefits will be permanently reduced.

Insecurities

If a person becomes disabled or dies before reaching full retirement age, it is possible that fewer than 35 years will be used to calculate monthly earnings. Otherwise, the same basic formula is used to determine disability and death benefits. We take a closer look at disability benefits in Chapter 13.

If you're one of those folks who says you'll never retire, holding off on applying for Social Security benefits will help you, but only to a point. Your benefit amount does increase for each year in which you don't collect, until you reach age 70. At that point, there is no reason to delay collecting Social Security any longer. Your benefit amount will not increase. And, if you really do want to work, you can do so without losing any benefits. It's a no-brainer. Collect your dough.

We look more closely at your retirement options in the next chapter. It's an important decision that you should make only after considering all of the choices. Social Security does have trained claims representatives who can explain your options to you.

It is best to set up an appointment and meet with them in the year before you plan to retire. They can help you sort out your options and, using your own earnings records, let you know how each choice affects the amount of benefits you will collect.

Collecting Your Stash

Finally, it's time to talk about the rules for actually getting the money. Social Security recommends that people apply for retirement benefits about three months before they want their benefits to begin.

Even if you are not entitled to Social Security, you should sign up for Medicare three months before age 65. We sort through Medicare and its benefits in Part 5.

Social Graces

You can get the location of the Social Security office nearest you by using the online locator at www.socialsecurity.gov/locator. All you need to do is enter your zip code.

Making Contact

You can apply to collect your benefits in three ways. You can complete an application online. Go to www.ssa.gov/applytoretire and click on "Apply to Retire" near the top of the page to enter the secure connection.

You can also apply by phone, or you can make an appointment to apply in person at a local Social Security office. Call 1-800-772-1213 to apply by phone or to set up an appointment.

Social Graces

Are you living or traveling outside the United States? You are not cut off from services. Here's information about where to get help when you are outside the country: www.ssa.gov/foreign/index.html.

You can reach Social Security by phone between 7 A.M. and 7 P.M. Eastern Standard Time, Monday through Friday (recorded information is available 24 hours a day, 7 days a week). The Social Security Administration has a toll-free "TTY" number for people who are deaf or hard of hearing; it's 1-800-325-0778 and is available between 7 A.M. and 7 P.M. Monday through Friday.

You can also get answers to your questions by mail. Send your questions to the following address:

Social Security Administration
Office of Public Inquiries
Windsor Park Building
6401 Security Blvd.
Baltimore, MD 21235

Now that you know how to contact Social Security, let's take a look at what documents you need to apply.

Gathering the Right Documents

You need a number of documents to apply for Social Security benefits, but most of them should be readily accessible in your files at home. Here's the list of what you will need:

◆ Your Social Security number.

◆ Your birth certificate. (If you don't have a birth certificate, you can get one from the state where you were born. You can quickly find out where to write for vital records in each state at www.cdc.gov/nchs/data/misc/07-26-05.w2w.pdf.)

◆ Your W-2 forms or self-employment tax returns for last year.

◆ Your military discharge papers if you served in the military.

◆ Your spouse's birth certificate and Social Security number if he or she is applying for benefits based on your earnings at the same time.

Social Graces

The Social Security Administration needs to see original documents or a copy certified by the issuing office when you apply for benefits. You can mail or bring the documents to a Social Security office. Your documents will be photocopied and returned to you.

◆ Your children's birth certificates and Social Security numbers, if they're applying for children's benefits based on your earnings at the same time.

◆ Proof of U.S. citizenship or lawful alien status if you (or a spouse or child applying for benefits) were not born in the United States.

◆ The name of your bank and your account number so that your benefits can be directly deposited into your account.

A claims representative can help you with questions you may have about securing the proper documentation when it comes time to retire.

As you can see, the Social Security Administration makes it very easy for you to pay into the program, but requires you to jump through a lot of hoops to collect your benefits. About six months before you plan to retire, I encourage you to set up an appointment with a Social Security claims representative to review your individual work history and be certain you understand your benefits and any options you might have.

The Least You Need to Know

- The benefit amount you collect is called your Primary Insurance Amount (PIA), and it is calculated using a four-step process.

- Your benefits could be reduced if you worked a combination of jobs that were and were not covered by Social Security. If your earnings history is mixed, be sure you understand the Windfall Elimination Provision and how it could affect your benefits.

- You can apply for benefits online, by phone, or by mail. However you decide to apply, make sure your application is turned in at least three months before you want to start collecting.

Chapter 7

Timing Your Exit

In This Chapter

- ◆ Freedom from work
- ◆ Leaving early
- ◆ Staying late
- ◆ Timing it just right

Are you counting the days until you can finally escape from the day-to-day drudgery of work? Or are you the type who wants to die at your desk? Maybe you fall somewhere in between these two extremes and just want to figure out what makes the most sense financially.

Whatever your plans, now that you know how to apply for your well-deserved benefits and how the Social Security Administration figures out what you get if you retire at full retirement age, it's time to look at how your payout varies depending on when you decide to apply for benefits.

As you already know, you can begin collecting benefits as early as age 62. You can also decide never to quit work, but you shouldn't put off collecting your benefits past the age of 70.

Your Date to Escape

It's totally up to you to decide when to retire. Before you do, however, you should figure out when you can *afford* to retire.

Senior Moments

AARP (formerly the American Association of Retired People), in which membership is automatic upon your 50th birthday, found in a recent survey that 80 percent of baby boomers plan to work at least part time during retirement and only 16 percent plan to not work at all.

Does everyone who plans to work want to work? According to the AARP, 35 percent say they will be working because of personal interest or enjoyment, 23 percent because they will need the income, 17 percent want to start their own business, and 5 percent want to try out a new career.

Generally, financial planners assume you will need at least 70 percent of your current income to live approximately the same lifestyle as you do today. People are living longer, many even 30 years or more after retirement. In fact, many planners separate retirement into three phases. The length of each phase is based on your life expectancy, your health, and your desired level of activity. The three phases are as follows:

- **Initial retirement phase.** In the early retirement years, planners expect most people to be very active, travel, and do things they have always put off doing while they were too busy working. In this first stage of retirement, many experts recommend that you plan a retirement budget closer to 90 percent of your current income level.

- **Mid-retirement phase.** In the mid-retirement phase, the retiree is expected to be active but slowing down. Health problems are creating the need to stay closer to home or do less. In this phase, a retiree may need only 50 to 60 percent of their current income to maintain a similar lifestyle.

- **Late retirement phase.** In the later years, it is expected that the retiree's budget will be eaten up by medical and assisted-living costs, possibly even in a nursing home or other facility. In this case, budget figures could be back up to 70 percent of your current earning needs. It all depends on how well you've planned for this phase of life and whether you have long-term-care insurance or other protections in place to make your later years more comfortable.

This is not a retirement planning book, so I won't go into any more detail about how to plan for these phases. It's important, however, for you to start thinking about your needs so you can better understand the financial impact of starting your Social Security benefits early, late, or at full retirement age.

Your Lifespan Determines Your Income

When deciding how much to reduce benefits for early retirees, *actuaries* try to figure out how to make sure that an early retiree and a retiree who waits until full retirement will end up with the same amount in total benefits if they live what the actuary thinks is a normal lifespan.

def•i•ni•tion

Actuaries analyze the financial consequences of risk. They use mathematics, statistics, and financial theory to study uncertain future events, such as how long people will live and collect payments from Social Security.

Currently, the Social Security Administration actuaries project that the average male aged 65 can expect to live until age 78. Women are expected to live until age 82. A man is expected to receive benefits for 13 years after retiring at age 65, and a woman is expected to get benefits for 17 years.

The attempt to equalize benefits among retirees who retire early or late with those who retire at the full retirement age can sometimes backfire if people die much earlier or much later than the actuaries expect. If both an early retiree and an on-time retiree die at age 70, the early retiree, who collected money for a longer time even if it was a bit less, will have collected more in total benefits.

Social Graces

If you want to take a closer look at your retirement needs, Choose to Save offers an excellent ballpark calculator at www.choosetosave.org/ballpark.

Let's look at two retirees, Early Edna and On-time Otto. For this example, we'll use the 2005 benefits for an average-wage earner. Early Edna started collecting $799 per month in benefits at age 62, while Ontime Otto waited until age 65 and got $1,107 per month in benefits. Both Edna and Otto died at age 70. Early Edna, who began collecting benefits at age 62, collected benefits for 96 months, while poor Ontime Otto, who retired at age 65, only collected benefits for 60 months. Who collected more in total benefits?

Early Edna (retired at age 62)

$799 × 96 months = $76,704

On-time Otto (retired at age 65)

$1,107 × 60 months = $66,420

In this case, Edna beat the system and got more in total benefits before her death. Otto would have gotten more in total benefits, though, if he had lived considerably longer than the actuaries expected. Here is what would have happened to the same two people if they had both died at 90:

Early Edna

$799 × 336 months = $268,464

On-time Otto

$1,107 × 300 months = $332,100

You can see that in this scenario, Ontime Otto ended up with more in total benefits. Another factor in all of this is the benefits that could be collected by the retiree's spouse and children. Don't worry. I'm not going to bore you with a series of calculations for these scenarios. I just wanted to alert you to the fact that it gets a lot more complicated once you start considering survivors' benefits and even more complicated if disability becomes a factor.

Now that we know a bit about the impact of retiring at various ages, let's look at the specifics of what could happen to your benefits if you decide to retire early.

Senior Moments

None of us know how long we will live, but we can look at our family history and try to determine an average lifespan based on how long our parents, grandparents, aunts, and uncles lived. A good retirement planning program will ask you to estimate your lifespan before calculating how much you will need to save. Without some estimate of lifespan, it is not possible to figure out how much you will need for retirement.

Early Arrival

The earliest age at which you can begin collecting Social Security is 62. You can retire earlier than that, of course, but you won't get money from Social Security.

So how much do you lose if you retire at age 62? It depends. When you were born becomes a big factor in this answer. If you were born before 1937, the calculation is much simpler. Your full retirement age is 65. The reduction in benefits would be as follows:

- ♦ At age 62, your benefits would be reduced 20 percent.

- ♦ At age 63, your benefits would be reduced about 13⅓ percent.

- ♦ At age 64, your benefits would be reduced about 6⅔ percent.

Insecurities

If you stop work before age 62, it could have a negative impact on how much you will collect. Remember that the SSA uses your highest 35 years of income to come up with your average benefit. If you stop working at age 50 and don't have 35 years of earnings, some of your earnings years will end up being $0, and your benefit could be lower than it would have been if you had worked a full 35 years.

If you were born after 1937, it's a different story. You may recall previous discussions about the retirement age gradually increasing to age 67. No change was made in the age at which you can retire early, but there is a change in the amount of the reduction that will be required for early retirement. In fact, the reduction could be as high as 30 percent if you were born in 1960 or later.

You can use the following table, from the Social Security Administration, to calculate your reduction based on the year you were born. The first column shows the year you were born. The second column shows the age at which you can retire and receive your full benefit. The third column shows the number of months early you will be retiring if you retire at age 62. The fourth column is the percent reduction for each month that you retire early. This column can be used to figure your reduction if you want to retire between age 62 and your full retirement age. The last column shows the total reduction if you retire at age 62.

Social Security Full Retirement and Reductions by Age*

Year of Birth	Full Retirement	Age 62 Reduction (in Months)	Monthly % Full	Total % Reduction
1937 or earlier	65	36	.555	20.00
1938	65 and 2 months	38	.548	20.83
1939	65 and 4 months	40	.541	21.67
1940	65 and 6 months	42	.535	22.50
1941	65 and 8 months	44	.530	23.33
1942	65 and 10 months	46	.525	24.17
1943–1954	66	48	.520	25.00
1955	66 and 2 months	50	.516	25.84
1956	66 and 4 months	52	.512	26.66
1957	66 and 6 months	54	.509	27.50
1958	66 and 8 months	56	.505	28.33
1959	66 and 10 months	58	.502	29.17
1960 and later	67	60	.500	30.00

Monthly percentage and total reductions are approximate due to rounding. The actual reductions are .555, or ⁵⁄₉ of 1% per month for the first 36 months and .416, or ⁵⁄₁₂ of 1% for subsequent months.

I warned you that it was going to get confusing. As you can see, in trying to tweak this to be fairer to those who are going to have to retire later, the SSA lowered the percentage after the first 36 months of early retirement. You can see from the footnote that for the first 36 months, the reductions are .555, or ⁵⁄₉ percent per month. After that, the reductions are less. The percentage for each month from the thirty-seventh month until full retirement age is .416, or ⁵⁄₁₂ of 1 percent for each subsequent month.

Let's try an example using the data in this table. Let's say you were born in 1945. Looking at the chart, you see that your full retirement age is 66. The number of months for early retirement at age 62 is 48. The reduction percentage per month is .520.

You can figure the percentage by which your benefit amount will be reduced as follows:

48 months × .520 = 24.96 percent

If you wanted to retire at 63, you would use 36 months to calculate your reduction:

36 months × .520 = 18.72 percent

You may be asking why this doesn't jump back to the .555 percentage since it falls within the first 36 months calculation. The reason for the difference is that the law states that benefits are reduced by .555 for the first 36 months and then by .415 for each of the next 20 months. Social Security simplified your calculations by publishing this chart, but since rounding is involved the numbers are slightly different when you do the math.

Once you figure out your reduction percentage, you can multiply that amount times the projected full retirement age given on your Social Security statement to guesstimate what you could expect in benefits if you choose to retire early.

Deciding whether or not to retire early can be very confusing and complicated. In addition to worrying about how your Social Security benefits will be affected, you need to consider how your other retirement plans will be impacted. You also need to remember that you cannot count on Medicare until you reach age 65. There is no way to tap into those benefits early. If you are planning to retire early, you need to figure in medical insurance and other medical expenses, which can eat up your savings very quickly and unexpectedly.

Social Graces

If you want to try a few calculations based on your expected benefits at various ages, use the online interactive calculator to get your estimated benefit amount for full retirement: www.ssa.gov/planners/calculators.htm.

You can get the estimate based on today's dollars or based on inflated future dollars.

Let's now take a look at what happens when you put off collecting Social Security benefits.

Late to the Party

The good news is that if you wait to retire, your benefits go up. The amount of the increase, as you found out with early retirement, varies by the year of your birth.

Once you reach age 70, there is no benefit to waiting any longer. You can collect Social Security without any penalty, and the benefits will not increase. The monthly increase in the following table is only applied up to age 70.

Increase for Delayed Retirement

Year of	Yearly Rate of Increase	Monthly Rate Birth of Increase
1930	4.5%	⅜ of 1%
1931–32	5.0%	$\frac{5}{12}$ of 1%
1933–34	5.5%	$\frac{11}{24}$ of 1%
1935–36	6.0%	½ of 1%
1937–38	6.5%	$\frac{13}{24}$ of 1%
1939–40	7.0%	$\frac{7}{12}$ of 1%
1941–42	7.5%	⅝ of 1%
1943 or later	8.0%	⅔ of 1%

Note: Persons born on January 1 of any year should refer to the rate of increase for the previous year.

Insecurities

No matter what age you decide to retire, don't forget to apply for Medicare three months before your sixty-fifth birthday. There is no benefit to waiting. In fact, it could cost you more if you wait. We'll cover this in more detail in Chapter 19.

Once you have reached the age of 70, you've maxed out on how much you can increase your benefits. Just bite the bullet three months before your seventieth birthday and fill out the application for Social Security. It's time.

Now that you know the impact of retiring early or late, how should you decide what works best for you? Although I can't give you an answer, I will try to review the issues you should think about as you make that decision.

What Timing Is Best for You?

You are the only one who can decide when to retire. There are many factors to consider, but the two most important questions you need to answer are as follows:

- ◆ What can you afford to do financially?
- ◆ How long do you think you'll live, and how active will you be?

According to today's statistics from Social Security's actuaries, a 20-year-old faces roughly a 20 percent possibility of dying before reaching retirement age. There is a greater chance—roughly 30 percent—of becoming severely disabled and unable to work before the age of 67.

Once you beat the odds and make it to retirement, you need to consider how long you think you will live in retirement and how active you will be. If you are healthy and still able to travel, you'll probably want more funds to work with so you can enjoy your retirement years. If you are unable to get around easily, you may look for a retirement community that provides assistance with everyday living needs. Depending on how much assistance you need, this can actually be more expensive than living an active life.

If you find that you want or need to keep working, once you reach full retirement age, you can start collecting Social Security and continue working at least part-time as well. New legislation called the Senior Citizens Freedom to Work Act of 2000 lets seniors work after reaching full retirement age without risking a reduction in benefits. We'll look more closely at the provisions of this law in Chapter 16.

The SSA has rules about everything. Even the day of the month you will receive your benefits is carefully planned by your birth date. If your birthday falls on the first through the tenth day of the month, monthly benefits are paid on the second Wednesday of the month. People born from the eleventh to the twentieth day of the month get their money on the third Wednesday of the month. The fourth Wednesday of the month is payday for folks born between the twenty-first through thirty-first days of the month. People who started getting benefits before May 1997 get their checks on the third day of the month, earlier if the third falls on the weekend.

Once you are ready to take the plunge, you should contact a claims representative to figure out what the best month is for you to retire. If you have earned some money for the year, a monthly test is used to consider the impact of those earnings. Also, if you were born after 1937, the increase in retirement age begins to vary greatly. For example, someone born in 1939 reaches full retirement age at age 65 and 4 months.

I wish I could give you a simple formula to help you decide when to retire, but Social Security is like life in that there are few simple decisions. I hope I have helped you to understand all the variables you must think about before taking the plunge. Once you decide to apply for benefits, there is no going back. Your Social Security benefit is set for life (except for COLA increases) once you start collecting.

Social Graces

To help you sort out some of the issues, the Social Security Administration offers a retirement planner at www.ssa.gov/r&m1.htm.

Oh, here's one final word of advice: once you *do* start collecting your Social Security benefits, enjoy your freedom!

The Least You Need to Know

◆ You can begin collecting Social Security at age 62, but your monthly benefits will be permanently reduced if you retire before your full retirement age.

◆ Your monthly benefit amount will increase if you hold off on retiring until past your full retirement age, but there is no increase in benefits once you reach age 70.

◆ The timing for your retirement is a very personal decision based on many variables. The two most important are your financial resources and how healthy you are.

Part 3

Cracking Open Your Nest Egg

Sometimes cracks might appear in your nest egg before you are ready to open it. Divorce, one of these cracks, is becoming more and more common. One in six people die before they reach retirement age. Others are disabled and have to quit working before they are eligible to retire.

All these setbacks in life can impact your efforts to build a strong retirement nest egg. The Social Security Administration provides benefits to help you through each of these unexpected bumps in the road. In this part, you'll learn about the benefits for widows, ex-spouses, children, dependent parents, and the disabled.

WHEELER

Chapter 8

Picking Up the Pieces

In This Chapter

- ◆ Relying on Social Security to get through a loss
- ◆ Insuring your assets
- ◆ Making the right decisions after a loss
- ◆ Avoiding identify fraud

So far, we've primarily looked at collecting Social Security benefits for those who make it to retirement at the time of their own choosing and with their family intact. Life throws us many curves, though, and not everyone makes it to retirement before needing Social Security.

In this chapter, we consider what happens when things don't go as planned. Although everyone hopes he or she will never face the problems we'll be outlining here, it's best to be ready to face them anyway.

Dealing With a Loss of a Spouse, Divorce, or Disability

When dealing with Social Security, losses can involve not only the death of a spouse. Divorce is becoming more common, and disability can also be a major factor in losing expected earnings. We'll take a quick look at how these losses can affect you, but we'll delve more deeply into each loss in later chapters.

It's a fact that women live longer than men—an average of seven to nine years longer. In fact, according to the National Center for Women and Retirement Research (NCWRR), the average age for widowhood in the United States is 56. In 1996, 71 percent of the nation's 4 million elderly poor were women, and 48 percent of these women were widows. Even when a woman does get a pension of her own, it is likely to be only half of what a man gets.

The NCWRR believes that, among women who are 35 to 55 years old today, between one third and two thirds of them will be impoverished by age 70.

Divorce has tripled in the United States, according to the U.S. Bureau of Census. In 1970 the number of divorced adults was 3.2 per 1,000. By 1996 that number jumped to 9.5 per 1,000. The number of divorced people has quadrupled according to the Census Bureau. In 1970, there were 4.3 million divorced people. In 1996, the number of divorcees jumped to 18.3 million. The 2000 Census revealed that divorce rates leveled off in the 1990s.

The NCWRR found that one year after divorce, the average midlife woman is still single and is earning only $11,300. More than 58 percent of female baby boomers have less than $10,000 saved toward their retirement, while male boomers have saved three times that amount.

Insecurities

The NCWRR found in its 1996 baby boom study that the average female born between 1946 and 1964 is at risk of the following:

♦ Having to remain in the workforce until at least age 74 because she does not have adequate financial savings and pension coverage.

♦ Having inadequate resources to maintain the same standard of living as prior to age 65.

Why do women tend to save less than men? The NCWRR found that for every year a women stays home to care for a child, she must work five extra years to recover the lost income, pension coverage, and career setbacks. Women on average also earn less. The average woman earns 74 cents for every dollar a man earns. All these factors result in lower pensions and Social Security benefits. According to the Social Security Administration, women received on average only $798 per month compared to $1,039 for men in 2005.

Your future retirement plans can also be affected by disability. As mentioned in the preceding chapter, the Social Security Administration estimates that 30 percent of today's 20-year-olds will become disabled before they reach their full retirement age of 67.

The U.S. Census Bureau found that the number of disabled people, which they define as having "limitations in activity due to chronic health conditions and impairments," is steadily increasing. In 1970, 11.7 percent of the population faced disability. That rose to 18.6 percent by 2000. The trends for men and women are about the same.

You can do numerous things to avoid the most devastating aspects of the losses discussed here. One of the first things to do is protect your resources.

Protecting Your Assets

We all hate to think about sitting through an insurance presentation, but one of the first things to do when you think about protecting your assets is to review how much insurance protection you have. If you don't already have good insurance coverage, check into the following options:

◆ **Life insurance.** *Term life insurance* is the best life insurance option in most situations because you can get much more coverage for the same money. Rather than saving your money in a *whole life* policy, it makes more sense to invest it in a vehicle from which you can earn better returns. Be sure to seek information from several insurance professionals and be certain you understand your options before signing up for any insurance.

def•i•ni•tion

Life insurance pays your beneficiary a set amount when you die. **Term life insurance** is coverage based on a set period of time and has no cash value. At the end of the term, there is no residual value to the policy. **Whole life insurance** is permanent coverage for your entire life and includes the build up of a cash value.

◆ **Disability insurance.** The SSA found that 70 percent of the workforce has no long-term disability insurance. The SSA provides disability coverage for a worker with a spouse and up to two children that is equivalent to a $233,000 disability policy, but as you'll learn in Chapter 13, there are limitations to that coverage and it can be hard to qualify for it. Your best bet is to consider private coverage for disability in the same way you have a private pension plan or other savings toward your retirement.

Insecurities _____

Don't expect much in the way of life insurance from Social Security. The death benefit for a survivor is $255. That would make barely a dent in funeral costs alone.

◆ **Long-term care insurance.** For most people, the best time to purchase long-term care insurance is between the ages of 55 and 60 to get the best rates. If you consider applying for it earlier than that, you may be paying for it much longer than necessary. If you apply for it later than that, you could end up with astronomical monthly premiums. We'll talk about all this medical stuff in much greater detail in Part 5.

Making the Right Moves

When you are faced with a tragedy or an economic shock, the first thing to do is nothing. That may sound strange, but many people make the mistake of wanting to get things done quickly and end up doing things that later turn out to be huge errors. In many cases, the wrong move could result in paying more taxes than necessary or permanently receiving less in Social Security or other benefits for the rest of your life.

If you don't have a good planning team (including an accountant, lawyer, and financial planner) before a death or divorce, it probably would be well worth it for you to find one before making any moves—to be sure you are doing the right thing.

Social Graces _____

The Board of Standards for certified financial planners is a good place to start if you don't know how to find a planner: www.cfp-board.org/search.

So far, we've been looking at risks that involve something related to your life—death, disability, or divorce. There also are risks related to unsavory folks out there who want to try to get your money using scams or fraud.

Protecting Yourself from Scams and Fraud

Even before you reach retirement, you can be a victim of a scam or fraud. In the case of Social Security abuse, the most likely problem you will run into is someone using your Social Security number and assuming your identity for financial gain.

I'm sure you have noticed that your Social Security number is used for almost everything related to finances today—opening a bank account, applying for credit, applying for a mortgage, and so on. There is very little you can do relating to money that doesn't involve the use of your Social Security number.

There are folks out there who know how to get a hold of your Social Security number and then pretend to be you in order to get their hands on your money either by cashing checks fraudulently or by opening bank or credit accounts. This is known as *identity theft*.

If you are an unfortunate victim of identity theft, it can wreak havoc with your life. Here are just a few of the things that can go wrong, according to the Federal Trade Commission:

def•i•ni•tion

Identity theft occurs when a criminal uses another person's personal information to take on that person's identity. Identify theft can include credit card and mail fraud.

- A credit card account can be opened in your name using your name, date of birth, and Social Security number. After the imposter uses the card and doesn't pay the bills, you are the one stuck with the delinquent account on your credit report.

- An imposter can call your credit card issuer and, pretending to be you, change the mailing address on your credit card account. The thief then runs up charges on your account. The bills are sent to the new address but are not paid. It could take you a while to realize that it has even happened. Although you might like missing a bill now and then, always check with your credit card company if your monthly bill doesn't arrive.

- Cellular phone service can be established in your name.

- A bank account can be opened in your name. Bad checks can be written against that account, and you won't even know it exists until someone tries to collect from you after tracking you down.

It's surprisingly easy to find personal information about other people, especially for someone who is a professional scam artist. Here are some key ways in which identity thieves can get a hold of your personal information:

- Stealing your wallet or purse or your mail (which may contain bank and credit card statements, preapproved credit offers, telephone calling cards, and tax information)

- Stealing personal information that you provide to an unsecured site on the Internet, from business or personnel records at work to personal information in your home

- Rummaging through your home or business trash for personal data

- Posing as someone who legitimately and legally needs information about you, such as employers or landlords

- Buying personal information from "inside" sources

If you always carry your Social Security number around with you, stop it. The Social Security Administration recommends that, to prevent theft, you should show your card to your employer when you start a job to be certain your records will be correct, and then put it in a safe place at home or in a safe-deposit box.

Suspicions of Theft

Are you finding unexplained charges on your phone bill or credit card? Was your wallet or purse recently stolen? These could be signs that someone is using your number.

Social Graces

The Federal Trade Commission has an excellent website about identity theft and what you should do: www.consumer.gov/idtheft.

If you suspect that someone is using your Social Security number, one sure way to find out is to ask for your Social Security statement. If someone is using your number, you may find missing or incorrect earnings. You also could find out that your name or date of birth is listed incorrectly. Unfortunately, the onus will be on you to prove that something is wrong. You will have to produce a birth certificate and current identification to get a correction.

If you suspect that someone is using your identity, call the Social Security fraud hotline at 1-800-269-0271. If appropriate, an investigation will be started by the Office of the Inspector General. You can also contact Social Security by mail or fax as follows:

Social Security Fraud Hotline
P.O. Box 17768
Baltimore, MD 21235
Phone Number: 1-800-269-0271
Fax: 410-597-0118

Congress made identity theft a federal offense in October 1998. Violators can be investigated by the U.S. Secret Service, the FBI, and the U.S. Postal Service. They can be prosecuted by the Department of Justice. That makes things tougher for the criminal, but you are still left with the job of cleaning up the mess.

Fixing the Mess

Unfortunately, once the nightmare starts, it's up to you to fix it. The biggest problem most likely will be correcting damage to your credit. The Social Security Administration can't do that for you.

The first thing you will need to do is contact your creditors by phone and then follow up with a letter. You'll also need to file a police report.

If you suspect fraud, you should also contact the major credit bureaus as quickly as possible. They can put a flag on your record, which will require creditors to contact you personally before approving additional credit using your name and number. Be sure to ask these bureaus how long they will put the flag on your record and what you need to do to extend it, if necessary.

In addition to the flag, you can add a victim's statement to your report. In this statement, you should include your name, describe the problem you are experiencing, and give a telephone number where you can be reached.

You should also get copies of your credit report from each of the major credit bureaus to check for signs of fraudulent activity.

As of September 1, 2005, consumers have the right to one free credit report per year from each of the major credit bureaus. You can order that free report at www.annualcreditreport.com. You will find links to each of the credit bureaus, but pay close attention when you get there—the pages primarily advertise paid services. You have to read the material very carefully to find the free service.

Insecurities

Many consumer advocates recommend that people check their credit reports yearly, or even quarterly, to catch any suspicious activity as quickly as possible. An annual check is probably sufficient unless your pocketbook, wallet, or other identification is stolen.

Here is contact information for the major credit bureaus:

Equifax
www.equifax.com
Report fraud: 1-800-525-6285
Order a credit report: 1-800-685-1111
P.O. Box 740241
Atlanta, GA 30374-0241

Experian
www.experian.com
Report fraud: 1-888-397-3742
Order a credit report: 1-888-397-3742
P.O. Box 9532
Allen, TX 75013

Trans Union
www.transunion.com
Report fraud: 1-800-680-7289
Order a credit report: 1-800-916-8800
Fraud Victim Assistance Division
P.O. Box 6790
Fullerton, CA 92834-6790

If you do find a problem, be sure to keep a log of all phone calls you make to correct the problem. Also keep copies of all letters and other documents you use to prove your identity and any other efforts to correct the misuse of your identity. Unfortunately, victims of identity theft have found that this problem can follow them, or even reoccur, for years after they first notice it.

Changing Numbers

You may think the easiest way to correct this mess is to just get a new Social Security number. Wouldn't it be nice if life were that easy? Although that might sound like a good idea, it can only be used as a last resort. Before Social Security will even think about assigning you a new number, you will have to prove that you have done everything you can to fix the problem and that you are still being disadvantaged by the problem.

Getting a new Social Security number won't happen quickly, and it won't happen at all if the Social Security Administration determines any of these to be true:

◆ You are trying to avoid the law or your legal responsibility.

◆ You intend to avoid disclosure of a poor credit or criminal record for which you are at fault.

◆ You have no proof that someone else caused the problem.

◆ You have lost your Social Security card or it was stolen, but there is no evidence that your Social Security number is being misused or that you are being disadvantaged.

If you think you qualify for a new number, you can start the process by going to your local Social Security field office to request a new number. If the SSA believes you are eligible, no fee will be charged.

Ah, that reminds me of another scam. If someone comes to you and says he or she can get you a new number for a fee, it is most likely another type of fraud. In fact, the number you receive could be fraudulent, and you could even get caught up in a criminal offense.

The Least You Need to Know

◆ Death, divorce, and disability can have a major impact on your Social Security benefits. Be certain to act with caution at the start of a crisis and learn your options to be sure you protect your share.

◆ Insurance salesmen may not be your favorite people to invite to a party, but they can help you protect your cash and other assets. Be certain to seek information from several people and to understand all options thoroughly before making a choice.

◆ Identity theft can wreak havoc on your life. Know how to avoid it and what to do if it happens to you.

Chapter 9

Partings Not So Sweet

In This Chapter

◆ Getting your fair share after a divorce

◆ How remarrying might affect your benefits

◆ Filing a name change with the SSA

◆ Getting a new Social Security number if you've suffered from domestic violence

We all hope when we take the plunge and marry that it will be for life. Unfortunately, the reality is that 43 percent of first marriages end in separation or divorce within 15 years, according to a 1995 survey of family growth released by the Centers for Disease Control and Prevention's National Center for Health Statistics in May 2001.

In the l990s, 10 percent of U.S. adults were divorced, a sharp increase from 1970 when only 3 percent of adults were divorced.

These are shocking numbers. Divorce was very rare when Social Security was first implemented in the 1930s. As divorce numbers increased, Congress realized it needed to do something to protect divorced spouses who never worked outside the home.

Social Security and Divorce

In 1965, the first Social Security benefits for divorced people were enacted. At that time, the spouse had to be married for 20 years to collect benefits on his or her estranged spouse's work record. In 1977, eligibility was extended to those married at least 10 years. Ex-spouses are entitled to both retirement and disability benefits, as appropriate.

If you are divorced and are wondering what kind of benefits you qualify for, this chapter will help you make sense of the rules.

Timing Is Everything

Social Security's coverage for a divorced spouse is very rigid. If you were married for 10 years or more, you may be entitled to full spousal and survivor benefits, but if you divorced your spouse after 9 years, 11 months, and 27 days, you get nothing.

Timing is everything when you are in the midst of a divorce, especially if your soon-to-be ex-spouse is a much higher wage earner than you are.

Insecurities _____

You are entitled to benefits on your own earnings, and they may be better than your benefits as an ex-spouse. We are only looking at the option of collecting on a former spouse's benefits in this chapter.

Spousal Benefits

As a divorced spouse who was married for at least 10 years, you are entitled to 50 percent of your ex-spouse's benefits, just as a spouse who is still married would be. Here's the catch: in most situations, you cannot be remarried. There are some exceptions to this rule, and they are covered later in this chapter.

The earliest an ex-spouse can collect on his or her former spouse's work record is at the age of 62. If the ex-spouse applies for benefits before his or her full retirement age, the benefits will be permanently reduced. The following table shows the percentage of the worker's full benefit the spouse will receive based on year of birth:

Year of Birth[1]	Full Retirement Age	Age 60 Reduction Months	Monthly % Reduction[2]
1939 or earlier	65	60	.475
1940	65 and 2 months	62	.460
1941	65 and 4 months	64	.445
1942	65 and 6 months	66	.432
1943	65 and 8 months	68	.419
1944	65 and 10 months	70	.407
1945–1956	66	72	.396
1957	66 and 2 months	74	.385
1958	66 and 4 months	76	.375
1959	66 and 6 months	78	.365
1960	66 and 8 months	80	.356
1961	66 and 10 months	82	.348
1962 and later	67	84	.339

[1]If you were born on January 1st of any year you should refer to the previous year.

[2]Monthly reduction percentages are approximate due to rounding. The total % reduction for anyone who receives benefits at age 60 is always 28.50.

If the couple is divorced before the worker turns 62, the divorced spouse must wait at least two years before he or she can receive benefits on the ex-spouse's work record. However, if the worker was already receiving benefits, the divorced spouse can apply for them immediately. If the worker wants to continue working but the ex-spouse wants to collect benefits, he or she does not have to wait until the worker stops working, provided the ex-spouse is at least 62 years old.

Insecurities

When a divorced spouse applies for benefits based on his or her ex-spouse's records, a divorce decree must be shown at the time of application.

Spousal benefits end when the worker dies (unless the ex-spouse is taking care of a child under the age of 16 who belongs to the worker or is eligible for benefits because of a disability; in this case survivors' benefits will be possible for the ex-spouse and the children), but the ex-spouse may then be entitled to *survivors' benefits* in the form of widow or widower's benefits.

def•i•ni•tion

Survivors' benefits are benefits paid after the death of a worker. They can be paid to a widow or widower, unmarried or disabled children, or surviving dependent parents. The rules for each vary and will be discussed in greater detail throughout this part of the book as we cover benefits for each type of recipient.

Survivors' Benefits

After your ex-spouse dies, you are entitled to survivors' benefits based on widow's (or widower's) benefits, which are 100 percent of the ex-spouse's actual retirement benefit, provided you apply for benefits at full retirement age. (Remember from earlier chapters that full retirement age is gradually increasing to age 67.) You can choose to apply for benefits as early as age 60, but your benefits will be decreased. A widow or widower's survivor benefits range from 71 percent of the deceased spouse's benefit (even if the deceased is an ex-spouse) if they begin at age 60 to 100 percent at full retirement age. If you are disabled, you can begin collecting as early as age 50 on your ex-spouse's work record.

Senior Moments

If a woman divorces a man after 10 years of marriage, once she reaches retirement age (and provided she isn't remarried), she is entitled to the spousal benefit, which is one half of the ex-husband's (the worker's) benefit. When the ex-spouse dies, her spousal benefits end, but she then qualifies for a survivors' benefit, which is equal to the ex-spouse's full benefit. So a person's take actually doubles upon the death of the ex-spouse.

If you skipped over the information about late and early retirement options, you may want to go back to Chapter 7 to review how it works. Before making a final decision, discuss your options with a Social Security representative. You can review the options based on your individual record and that of your ex-spouse to be sure you are making the choice that would be to your greatest advantage.

What happens to your spousal or survivor benefits when you die? That's it. The benefits don't get passed on to anyone else.

No Peeking

If your ex-spouse is still living, privacy rules prohibit the Social Security
tion from giving you your ex-spouse's work record, but they can tell you what benefits
you may be entitled to receive. They will need documentation to prove your relationship to the worker, such as a divorce decree.

> **Senior Moments**
>
> If your ex-spouse is deceased, there are a few things to weigh when considering
> whether to collect on your work history or that of your ex-spouse. If you are entitled to
> benefits on your own work record, you can take reduced retirement payments on your
> own record at age 62 and then receive full widow's benefits at age 65. Or you can
> reverse that and take reduced widow's benefits until you are age 65 and then file a
> claim for full retirement benefits on your own record. You can also delay and apply for
> one of these benefit options when you reach age 70. That way, you could take advan-
> tage of the increase in benefits.

Multiple Marriages

What happens if you were married to and divorced from more than one person, each
for 10 years or more? You are eligible for benefits from both workers' records, but
you will be able to collect only one benefit check. Obviously, you should pick the one
that offers the highest benefit.

The Remarriage Trap: Why So Many Seniors Just Live Together

To avoid being cut off, many couples
who meet later in life decide simply to
live together rather than remarry. If they
wait to marry until they reach age 60, the
surviving divorced spouse is not prevented
from collecting benefits on a prior deceased
spouse's Social Security earnings record.

A divorced spouse who is collecting disability
benefits based on his or her ex-spouse's work
record has a little more leeway when it comes

Insecurities

Although Social Security
is a big factor in deciding
whether to remarry or just live
together, it is usually not the only
one. There can be other compli-
cations related to wills and inheritance provisions involving children
from previous marriages.

to getting remarried. A divorced spouse who is collecting disability benefits can remarry as early as age 50 and still collect survivors' benefits.

If you do get married before the age of 60, you still might be able to collect on your ex-spouse's work record. If your second marriage ends, whether by death, divorce, or annulment, you can collect on the record of your first spouse as long as you were married 10 years before the first divorce.

Changing Numbers

Sometimes you may want to avoid your first spouse altogether, especially if domestic violence was a reason for the divorce. It may be that the best way to evade abuse and avoid further violence is to relocate and establish a new identity. If that occurs, you may even want to get a new Social Security number to make it harder for your abusive ex-spouse to find you.

Social Security will help you change your identity if you show evidence that you are being harassed, abused, or endangered. If you have been the victim of spousal abuse, you will need to apply in person at any Social Security office. You'll need to supply a statement explaining why you need a new number as well as fill out an application for the new number.

You will need to provide the Social Security office a number of documents:

- Original documents establishing your age, identity, and U.S. citizenship or lawful alien status, such as a birth certificate and a driver's license.

- One or more documents identifying you by both your old and new names if you have changed your name (as the Department of Justice recommends).

- Evidence showing that you have custody of children for whom you are requesting new numbers.

- Any evidence you may have that documents the harassment or abuse. The SSA will help you obtain additional evidence that is needed.

The best type of evidence is statements about the abuse from third parties, which can include police, medical facilities, or doctors. The information should describe the type of harassment, abuse, or life endangerment.

Additional evidence that can be helpful includes court restraining orders and letters from shelters, family members, friends, counselors, or others who have knowledge of the domestic violence or abuse. If you do get a new number in this manner, it is important to restrict how many people know this number.

Changing Names

Many women decide to change their name after getting divorced. If you do decide to do that, be sure you file the proper paperwork to change your name with the Social Security Administration.

There is no charge to change your name with Social Security. To get a new Social Security card, you will need to show identification that includes your old name and a second piece of identification that shows your new name. A driver's license can be a very good source along with a marriage certificate or a divorce decree. If you were born outside the United States, you will need proof of U.S. citizenship as well.

Divorce is a painful process, but just because you want to forget about your ex-spouse and the pain, there is no reason to forgo the benefits you deserve. When you're negotiating a divorce, always keep in mind the value of your and your spouse's retirement benefits, including Social Security benefits, pensions, or other retirement income.

Many people are not aware of their rights regarding their husband or wife's retirement package after divorce. Be sure you discuss this with your attorney before signing the final divorce papers. You could lose some valuable rights if retirement assets are not properly handled as part of a divorce decree.

Social Graces

You can make arrangements to change your name at any local Social Security office or by calling 1-800-772-1213.

The Least You Need to Know

- If you are divorced, you are still entitled to your ex-spouse's Social Security benefits, provided you were married at least 10 years and did not remarry before age 60.

- If your ex-spouse is alive, you are eligible for 50 percent of his or her Social Security benefit, just as a spouse would be. After your ex-spouse dies, that increases to 100 percent as a survivor benefit.

◆ If you remarry before the age of 60, you will not be able to claim benefits on your first spouse's work record in most situations, but you can regain survivor benefits if the second marriage ends by death, divorce, or annulment.

◆ If your marriage ended because of spousal abuse, you can change your identity to avoid future violence. To apply for a new Social Security number, you'll need to show evidence that you were being harassed, abused, or endangered.

Hard Choices After the Death of a Spouse

In This Chapter

- ◆ Applying for Social Security upon the death of a spouse
- ◆ Calculating your survivor benefits
- ◆ Remarrying and other life changes
- ◆ Understanding why women benefit more

About 6.6 million survivors of deceased workers collect Social Security benefits. These survivors account for 13 percent of the total benefits paid, and their average monthly benefit is $925, according to the Social Security Administration.

Only 1 percent of men receive survivors' benefits. Most men collect on their own work record. To simplify the discussion in this chapter, I address survivor benefits primarily for women, or widows. Men, or widowers, can expect the same benefits if they want or need to collect on their deceased wife's record.

Forty-five percent of all elderly women in the United States are widows. Social Security's survivor benefits are crucial for the vast majority of these women, with Social Security being the only source of income for 29 percent of elderly women. Without Social Security benefits, the elderly poverty rate among widows would jump from its current rate of 19 percent to a whopping 60.6 percent, according to a study done in 1998 by the National Economic Council Interagency Working Group on Social Security.

Social Graces

There isn't much to collect as a death benefit. SSA makes a one-time payment of $255 to the surviving spouse. That won't go very far, but survivor benefits can last a lifetime.

Dealing with the loss of a spouse is difficult for everyone, but after taking the time to grieve, there are a number of things you must do as quickly as possible. This chapter will walk you through those steps.

Timing Your Actions

After the death of a spouse, you must contact the Social Security Administration as quickly as possible to inform them of the death if your spouse was collecting benefits. A call to 1-800-772-1213 is sufficient to start the process. If your spouse wasn't already collecting benefits, you should contact the SSA as soon as you get a chance so that you can start the process of applying for benefits if you qualify. A spouse with young children who will need the benefits to get by will probably want to start the application process for survivors' benefits quickly.

Insecurities

Under no circumstances should you use the benefits of a deceased beneficiary. You will have to pay the money back to Social Security.

If your spouse was receiving monthly benefits and they were directly deposited into a financial account, notify the bank (or other financial institution) that accepts the payment about the beneficiary's death. Ask the bank to send any funds received during the month of the death and later back to the SSA.

If monthly benefits were paid by check, do not cash the check for the month in which the beneficiary died or any after that. Instead, return the checks to the SSA as soon as possible.

The period of time between the spouse's death and when survivors' benefits begin can be a real financial hardship for a spouse. Unless she has other sources of income, she will only be collecting 50 percent of her husband's benefits until all the paperwork is done to change over the records. Many times, a bank can assist widows in the short term with a loan until the Social Security benefits are changed. Don't hesitate to contact your banker for help through this period of transition.

If your husband's Social Security benefit is higher than your own, you will be able to switch and collect the higher benefit.

We'll now take a look at your benefit options and how you collect them.

Your Benefit Options

To be eligible for widows' benefits, a deceased spouse must have met the required number of credits to collect benefits during his working years. As noted in a previous chapter, these credits should total 40. In some situations, the number of credits can be fewer. To review the rules, reread the section "Your Time Commitment," in Chapter 5.

Widows are entitled to 100 percent of the retirement benefits of their deceased spouse if they apply at full retirement age, or they can collect reduced benefits as early as age 60. You'll recall from Chapter 7, that this reduction is a permanent reduction.

This reduction could be on top of a reduction that your deceased spouse has already taken. For ex-ample, if you and your spouse decided to collect benefits when your spouse reached age 62, your spouse's payment would have been reduced by 20 percent or possibly even more if your spouse was born after 1937. If your spouse dies and you decide to apply for survivor's benefits at age 60, the reduction will be applied to the already-reduced benefit.

> **Senior Moments**
>
> Unmarried women over age 65 get 52 percent of their income from Social Security. Pensions account for 15 percent of their income, and income from other assets make up 20 percent. Some women go back to work, but only about 10 percent of income after age 65 comes from earnings, according to a study by the National Economic Council Interagency Group on Social Security.

> **Social Graces**
>
> Social Security pulls together all the details about women and Social Security at www. socialsecurity.gov/women. You'll find details about what to do after the loss of a spouse and your benefit options.

Let's take a look at how this works. Mary and Mark are a married couple; Mary is 62, and Mark is 62. They decide to retire early. Mark's full Social Security retirement benefit is $1,200 per month. That is reduced by 20 percent because he started to collect his benefits early. With the 20 percent reduction, Mark's monthly benefit is $960. Mary collects the 37.5 percent spousal benefit, which totals $450 per month. The total collected by the couple is $1,410 per month.

If Mark dies at the age of 64, Mary's spousal benefits will stop, but she can begin collecting survivor benefits. Because she is now 64, her reduction will be 82.5 percent of the benefit Mark was collecting, or $990. Her monthly income will be just over half of what the couple had together. Now you can see why so many elderly single women are living in poverty, unless the couple has substantial savings or other pension benefits.

Mark and Mary's situation was a relatively simple example. If you are thinking of early retirement, you may want to review the rules in Chapter 7. Also, don't forget that full retirement age is gradually increasing to 67. The reduction for women will vary depending on the year in which they were born.

If you are a disabled woman, you can begin collecting benefits as early as age 50. We talk more about disability benefits in Chapter 13.

Senior Moments

In 2002, the median income for elderly unmarried women, which includes women who are widowed, divorced, separated, or never married, is $11,406. The median income for elderly unmarried men was $19,436. Elderly couples fared much better, with a median income of $32,592. This translates to much higher poverty rates for women. The poverty rate for elderly women is 13.1 percent, whereas only 7 percent of elderly men face poverty. Unmarried elderly women fare the worst, with a poverty rate of about 19 percent.

Married with Children

If you have unmarried children under the age of 16,, you will be eligible for survivor benefits even if you have not reached age 60. The benefit will be 75 percent of your deceased spouse's benefit. If you reach full retirement age while still caring for children, your benefit will increase to 100 percent. Once the children are past school age, survivor benefits will end for the spouse until he or she reaches retirement age. At that point, they will start again, provided he or she hasn't remarried before the age of 60.

Children can receive benefits, too. We talk about that in greater detail in the next chapter.

Remarriage Hurts

As noted in the previous chapter, you can lose your right to collect benefits if you remarry before the age of 60. After the age of 60 (50 if you are disabled), you can remarry without losing the right to a deceased spouse's benefits. If you do remarry and the marriage ends, whether by death, divorce, or annulment, you can regain the rights to collect on your first spouse's records.

Benefit Options

Your benefit amount will be based on the earnings of the person who died. The more your spouse paid into Social Security, the higher the benefits will be. If you worked as well, you can decide to collect on your own benefits. As a single woman, however, you will only be able to collect on one person's record, whether it is your own or your spouse's. Obviously, the best choice is the record that will result in the higher payment. You can review your options with a Social Security claims representative to be sure you are making the right choice.

Sometimes your benefit is reduced for reasons other than age. If you worked for the government, your Social Security benefits could be reduced. If neither you nor your spouse worked for a government entity, you can skip the following section.

Government Pension Offset

You could be subject to the *Government Pension Offset* if you receive a pension from a job in which you did not pay Social Security taxes. For many widows, this is true if they or their spouse worked for the federal government or as a teacher who received benefits from a local or state government. For a more detailed discussion of this topic, read Appendix C.

The offset can be very substantial. It can reduce your Social Security benefit as a widow by two-thirds of the amount of your government pension. Let's revisit Mark and Mary to see how this works. In this scenario, when Mark dies at age 64, Mary is eligible to collect on her state pension as a teacher as well as her benefits as a widow. She never paid into Social Security when she was working. She became eligible for teachers' pension benefits at the age of 62.

def•i•ni•tion

The **Government Pension Offset** is a law that impacts widows, or widowers who worked for federal, state, or local government agencies in which they did not pay Social Security taxes. Spouse's benefits are also impacted by this provision. The pension received from that agency may reduce any Social Security benefits for which the widow or widower would otherwise be qualified.

Her pension benefits as a teacher are $600. Two-thirds of that amount, or $400, must be used to offset the Social Security widow's benefit. As we previously figured, Mary's benefit after Mark's death is $990. With the $400 offset, Mary's Social Security benefit is reduced to $590. She is still better off, though, because she'll be collecting both the teacher's pension of $600 and the Social Security benefit of $590, which totals $1190.

This government pension offset would have impacted Mary's pension even if Mark survived. Her 50 percent Social Security benefit as a wife would have been reduced under this offset provision as well.

def•i•ni•tion

Double dipping is collecting pensions from two sources. It can also refer to collecting a pension from one source and an income from another. This is less common today with the passage of the Government Pension Offset, which affects widows and widowers, and the Windfall Elimination Provision, which impacts workers. Double dipping is only a problem when government pensions are involved and no money was paid into Social Security.

This may sound unfair, but before the offset was enacted, many government employees qualified for a pension from their agency plus a spouse's benefit from Social Security. This was called *double dipping* when government employees collected government pensions plus Social Security, even though they did not pay into Social Security while working. It was unfair to the many people who had paid FICA taxes on all of their earned income.

Let's take a quick look at how double dipping might work. If Mary had not been subject to the Government Pension Offset, her total benefits would have been $990 plus $600, or $1,590. In this scenario, Mary would actually end up with a monthly benefit higher than she and Mark were getting. But if Mary had worked in a job in which she had paid Social Security taxes, she would have had to choose between the Social Security benefits based on her work record and the benefits based on her husband's. She would not have been able to collect both. She could collect a private pension plus Social Security without an offset as long as she had paid Social Security on the income earned to qualify for the private pension.

As with any government program, there are always loopholes, and this offset rule is no exception. Some people are exempt from the rules. Here are the escape clauses from the Social Security Administration:

◆ Any state, local, or military service employee whose government pension is based on a job in which he or she was paying Social Security taxes for the last 60 months of government employment. (Some government entities were not initially covered by Social Security but chose to participate in Social Security at a later date.)

♦ Anyone whose government pension is not based on his or her own earnings.

♦ Anyone who received or was eligible to receive a government pension before December 1982 and who meets all the requirements for Social Security spousal benefits in effect January 1977.

♦ Anyone who received or was eligible to receive a federal, state, or local government pension before July 1, 1983, and was receiving one-half support from her or his spouse.

♦ Federal employees, including Civil Service Offset employees, who are mandatorily covered under Social Security. (Civil Service Offset employees are federal employees rehired after December 31, 1983, following a break in service of more than 365 days, and who had five years of prior Civil Service Retirement System [CSRS] employment.)

♦ Federal employees who chose to switch from CSRS to the Federal Employees' Retirement System (FERS) on or before December 31, 1987, as well as those employees who were allowed to make a belated switch to FERS through June 30, 1988. Employees who switched outside of these periods, including those who switched during the open season from July 1, 1998, through December 31, 1998, need five years under FERS to be exempt from the government pension offset.

Insecurities

Widows' benefits vary from 50 to 67 percent of the Social Security benefits received by a married couple. This is not enough. The National Economic Council Interagency Working Group on Social Security found that, based on its poverty studies, a widow needs 79 percent of the income the couple received prior to the death of her spouse.

A lot of these exemptions probably seem like gibberish to you. If they do, most likely you or your spouse have never worked for a government entity, and you can ignore the entire discussion. If you have worked for a government entity and you still are not sure, call the Social Security office and speak with a claims representative about your specific situation. He or she can help you sort out your benefits based on your individual situation.

Making Changes

If you are collecting on your own work record when your spouse dies, you will want to switch to your spouse's record if his or her benefits were higher. You should definitely talk with Social Security about changing your benefits after the death of a spouse if you were collecting only 50 percent of your spouse's benefit while he or she was alive.

As a survivor, you are now entitled to 100 percent of your spouse's benefits, provided you are at full retirement age. Even if you are not at full retirement age, your check should increase as long as you are at least 60 years old.

Things get even more complicated for widows who have not yet applied for benefits. When you reach the age of 60, you will become eligible to apply for benefits on your spouse's record. You cannot collect on your own record until you reach 62.

At age 60, you are entitled to 71.5 percent of your deceased spouse's benefits. It might make sense for you to live on those benefits for as long as possible and let your own work record benefits continue to build. Your Social Security benefits might be reduced based on the retirement earnings test, which I discuss in Chapter 16. If you wait until age 70 to collect on your own benefits, your benefits will increase each year after age 65 by 6 to 8 percent, depending on when you were born. You may want to review the rules of late retirement in Chapter 7 to understand how all this works.

You have probably figured out by now that widows face some significant challenges in living on Social Security. We'll take a closer look at these challenges now.

Women's Differences

Women tend to live longer than men. A woman who is 65 years old today can expect to live to age 85. A 65-year-old man can expect to live to age 81. In addition to living longer, women often have lower lifetime earnings than men. These lower earnings usually result in lower pensions and fewer assets than men.

Social Security does offer some benefits that pensions might not. The biggie is the Cost of Living Adjustments (COLAs) for inflation. These make Social Security an inflation-protected benefit. Many pensions do not have COLAs.

Since women tend to live longer than men, they are at greater risk of outliving their other forms of income; fortunately, you cannot outlive your Social Security benefit.

Social Graces _____

You can find out more information about women and retirement online at the Women's Institute for a Secure Retirement (WISER): www.wiser.heinz.org.

WISER was created by the Heinz Family Philanthropies in 1996. This nonprofit institute was created to improve the long-term economic security of millions of American women and men.

Women's Bigger Benefit

Women also tend to get a bit more of a benefit from Social Security. Because the formula is a progressive benefit, workers with lower earnings get a higher percentage of their average lifetime earnings than those with higher earnings.

Remember the complex formula in Chapter 6 that explained how benefits are calculated? In step 4 of that formula, 90 percent of your first $627 of average monthly earnings is included in your final Social Security benefit. This is especially helpful to women who tend to have lower earnings.

In fact, the National Economic Council Interagency Working Group on Social Security found that for the median female retiree, Social Security benefits replace 54 percent of her average lifetime earnings. The median male employee receives only about 41 percent of his earnings in Social Security benefits. So women do get some benefit for their lower earnings.

Even with the advantage in the calculation, women still tend to choose to receive their husbands' benefits rather than their own when they become widowed. In fact, 74 percent of elderly widows receive benefits based on the earnings of their deceased spouse.

Women's Future Benefits

Social Security will continue to be important to women in the future, but because more women are in the labor force, their earnings history at retirement may increase. Social Security expects that the number of women with their own earnings history will rise from 37 percent today to 60 percent in 2060.

We don't know whether this will translate into more women collecting on their own records. According to Census Bureau figures, women are still making significantly lower salaries than men. The median income for men in 2002 was $39,429. Women's median income was $30,203, which is only 76.6 percent of men's income. If this trend doesn't change, women most likely will still be looking to collect on their husband's work record. Only time will tell.

The Least You Need to Know

- ◆ The surviving spouse's benefits can double after the spouse's death if the surviving spouse is at full retirement age.

- ◆ The surviving spouse can collect benefits on his or her deceased partner's work record as early as age 60, but the benefits will be reduced for life.

- ◆ If the surviving spouse worked in a government job in which he or she did not have to pay Social Security taxes, his or her survivor benefits may be reduced by the Government Pension Offset law.

- ◆ You have the option to collect on your work record or the work record of your spouse. Obviously, whichever record will get you the greater benefit is the one you should choose.

Chapter 11

Children's Share

In This Chapter

◆ Understanding the various Social Security benefits available for children

◆ Applying for disability or survivors' benefits for a child

◆ Arranging for benefits for a disabled child

◆ Supplementing aid to children

When most people think about Social Security, they primarily think of benefits for the elderly. However, Social Security is an important source of income for many children.

More than 5.3 million children under the age of 18 received Social Security payments in 2002, according to the Social Security Administration. About half of these children received them as children of deceased workers, but children of retired or disabled workers also received payments.

Coverage is also available for blind and disabled children in low-income homes under the provisions of Supplemental Security Income.

Dough for Kids

Your unmarried children under the age of 18 (or up to age 19 if they are attending an elementary or secondary school full time) are eligible for benefits if their parent is a retired, disabled, or deceased worker who has met Social Security eligibility requirements. An eligible child can be your biological child, an adopted child, or a stepchild. A dependent grandchild may also qualify.

Children are eligible for Social Security benefits in the following ways:

◆ As a dependent of a retired, disabled, or deceased worker.

◆ As a child disabled before reaching the age of 22.

◆ As a blind or disabled child in a low-income home. These children qualify for a benefit called Supplemental Security Income, which is administered by the Social Security Administration and is discussed later in this chapter.

Children of deceased workers generally receive a higher average monthly payment than children of disabled or retired workers because they are entitled to 75 percent of the worker's Primary Insurance Amount (PIA). Children of retired or disabled workers get 50 percent of the PIA.

The average monthly benefit for children of deceased workers is currently $627.80, according to the SSA. Children of retired workers receive an average of $469.90 per month. Children of disabled workers get checks averaging $266.10 monthly.

> **Senior Moments**
>
> In 2002, 5.3 million children were living in families that received Social Security and/or Supplemental Security Income. Without Social Security, about 1 million of these children would be living below the poverty level.

There is a limit to the total amount a family can receive on a worker's benefit. The limit varies depending on individual circumstances but is around 150 to 180 percent of a worker's Social Security benefit. If the total for dependent family members is greater than the family limit, the amount each family member receives is reduced proportionately. The worker's benefit is not affected by this adjustment.

Getting Kids' Money

When you apply for Social Security benefits as a retired or disabled worker, you can apply for your children's benefits at the same time. If you die and the children are under age 18 (or 19 if a student), the benefits for the children will automatically be increased to survivors' benefits after the death is reported to Social Security. Remember that a dependent child gets 50 percent of a retired or disabled worker's benefit, but 75 percent of a deceased worker's benefit. If additional information is needed to adjust a child's benefits after the death of a worker is reported, someone from the Social Security administration will contact the family.

If you are applying for survivors' benefits for a child after the death of a parent, you need to do so as quickly as possible. You can apply by telephone or at any Social Security office. You can apply for both spousal and children's benefits at the same time.

Social Graces

The Social Security Administration pulled together all the key information that parents need to know about benefits for their children at www.ssa.gov/kids/parent1.htm.

Here is the information that the SSA requires when applying for children's benefits:

- Proof of death, either from the funeral home or a death certificate

- The child's Social Security number as well as the worker's

- The child's birth certificate

- The deceased worker's W-2 forms or federal self-employment tax return for the most recent year

- The name of your bank and your account number so that benefits can be directly deposited into your account

These benefits usually stop when a child reaches age 18 (or 19 if the child is an elementary or secondary school student), but if the child is permanently disabled, he or she can continue getting benefits as long as the disability began prior to age 22.

You might be wondering why benefits s top at age 18 or 19 but continue for children whose disability began prior to age 22. As long as the parent is still working, the disabled child does not collect benefits. It is only when a worker begins collecting benefits or dies that a disabled child is eligible to apply for benefits directly from Social Security.

In most cases, "adult children" are much older than 22 when they apply for benefits on their parent's record. Waiting this long before applying for benefits can create all kinds of problems, especially finding proof of the medical condition prior to age 22. If you think your child may need disability coverage in the future, be sure to collect medical records so he or she will be able to prove when the disability started.

When Congress first added the disability coverage for children in 1956, its intent was to cover children with congenital conditions or conditions that existed since early childhood. Initially, the disability had to occur prior to age 18. In 1972, the age for eligibility was raised so children with disabilities starting before age 22 were covered.

This allowed children who became permanently disabled between the ages of 18 and 21 to apply for benefits once their parents retired, died, or became disabled.

> **Senior Moments**
>
> Most of the people getting benefits under the child disability provision are in their 20s and 30s or even older, but the benefit is still considered a "child's" benefit because it is paid on the basis of a parent's Social Security earnings record.

Let's say a worker who retires at age 62 has a 40-year-old son who was disabled from birth with cerebral palsy. The son will begin collecting a disabled child's benefit on his father's record at the age of 40 and will be able to collect for the rest of his life, as long as his disability continues to meet eligibility requirements.

Benefits for a Disabled Child over Age 18

Once a child reaches 18, he or she must meet the same disability tests as an adult. To qualify for disability benefits once a child reaches 18, the physical or mental impairment (or combination of impairments) must keep the child from doing any substantial work for at least a year or be expected to result in death.

> **Insecurities**
>
> What is substantial work according to Social Security? For Social Security purposes, any job that pays more than $830 a month is considered substantial in 2005. Could you live on that?

When a child applies for disability benefits, his or her condition is compared to a list of impairments that are considered to be severe enough to prevent an individual from working for a year or more. If the child's impairment meets or equals a condition on the list, the child is considered disabled for Social Security purposes.

If there isn't a match for the child's impairment on the list, Social Security will do an assessment of the child's ability to work. If the child has worked in the past, the Social Security Administration will first assess the child's ability to do that work. If the child has never worked, Social Security will look at his or her ability to do any kind of work based on age, education, and experience. After the SSA completes this assessment, if they find that the child is unable to do any substantial work, he or she would qualify for disability benefits from the SSA.

Reviews don't stop once the child qualifies for disability benefits. The law requires the SSA to review all disability cases to verify that individuals continue to be disabled. The frequency of the review depends on whether the child's disability is expected to improve, might improve, or is not expected to improve. The process for reviews is spelled out on the disability award notice.

Disability payments can be supplemented for some disabled kids based on economic need.

Supplemental Income for Disabled Kids

Supplemental Security Income (*SSI*) is a program that helps disabled kids in low-income families. We'll discuss the program in detail in Chapter 14, but here we look briefly at the benefits children can expect.

Children can apply for this program if they meet the definition of disability and if their income and assets fall within eligibility limits. This program is intended to supplement a person's income to a certain economic level. The level varies from state to state because some states choose to supplement the federal benefits. To find out the levels in your state, contact your local Social Security office.

def•i•ni•tion

Supplemental Security Income (SSI) makes monthly payments to people with low income and few assets who are 65 or older, blind, or disabled. SSI is run by the Social Security Administration, but the money for the program does not come from Social Security taxes or Social Security trust funds. SSI payments are financed by the general revenue funds of the U.S. Treasury.

Meeting the Criteria

When determining payment levels for a child under the age of 18, the parents' income and assets are considered whether the child lives at home or is away at school, provided the child is subject to parental control. After the age of 18, the parents' income and assets are no longer considered.

Sometimes a child who was not eligible before the age of 18 becomes eligible after the age of 18 because the parents' income and assets are not considered. Before the age of 18, the disabled child may have been rejected because the parents' income or assets were too high. If the child continues to live at home after age 18 and does not pay for food or shelter, the SSI payment could be based on a lower rate.

def•i•ni•tion

The **Disability Determination Service** is a state-based team of specialists that includes a disability evaluation specialist and a doctor. Each applicant's case is reviewed by this team to determine whether he or she meets the Social Security Administration's definition of disability.

The local Social Security office determines whether a child is eligible for SSI benefits by looking at the parents' or child's income and assets. *The Disability Determination Service (DDS),* a state-level agency, determines whether the child meets the disability requirements.

When you apply for SSI based on a child's disability, the DDS team will review available medical records. If the team finds that the records are not thorough, you may be asked to take your child to a special examination that will be paid for by the Social Security Administration. You must agree to this examination and be certain that your child puts forth his or her best effort during the examination. If you fail to go to the examination or if the examining doctor determines that your child did not put forth his or her best effort, you could end up with an unfavorable decision.

The disability requirements for children under 18 are laid out by law. A child will be considered disabled if he or she has a physical or mental condition (or combination of conditions) that results in "marked and severe functional limitations." The condition causing the disability must be expected to last at least 12 months or be expected to result in the child's death. The child cannot be working at a job that is considered by Social Security to be substantial work.

Social Graces

Some of the most common types of disabilities include cerebral palsy, mental retardation, and muscular dystrophy.

In making the decision about disability, the first thing the disability evaluation specialist checks is whether the child's disability can be found on a special list of impairments in Social Security's regulations. This list contains descriptions of symptoms, signs, or laboratory findings for more than 100 physical and mental problems.

It is not mandatory that the condition appear on the list for a child to be considered disabled for SSI purposes. It is only mandatory that the symptoms, signs, or laboratory findings of the child's condition be the same as, or medically equal in severity to, a listed impairment. In addition to these tests, a child can also be considered disabled if the functional limitations from his or her condition (or combination of conditions) are the same as the disabling functional limitations of any listed impairment.

Primarily, the DDS team is looking for evidence of how the disability affects your child's ability to function on a day-to-day basis. The team will seek out a wide variety of sources who are familiar with your child's condition and how it impacts your child. Some of the people Social Security could contact, in addition to doctors and health professionals, include teachers, counselors, therapists, and social workers.

The evaluation for disability usually takes several months. If your child's condition is so severe that the disability counselor taking the application determines a presumption of disability, benefits can start immediately and be paid for up to six months while you await a formal disability decision, provided the child meets the income and assets eligibility requirements.

Here are some of the disability categories for which Social Security presumes the child is disabled and may make immediate SSI payments:

- HIV infection

- Blindness

- Deafness (in some cases)

- Cerebral palsy (in some cases)

- Down's syndrome

- Muscular dystrophy (in some cases)

- Significant mental deficiency

- Diabetes (with amputation of one foot)

- Amputation of two limbs

- Amputation of leg at the hip

Social Graces

Children with HIV usually acquire the infection in different ways than adults and also face a different course of disease than adults. DDS disability examiners and doctors have extensive guidelines to follow when evaluating claims for children with HIV infection.

A child with HIV infection may not have the conditions specified in the current guidelines used by the SSA to evaluate the infection, but he or she could have other signs and symptoms that indicate an impairment that results in marked and severe functional limitations. If you think there could be evidence that would help show that your child is disabled for SSI purposes, be sure to pull that together for the examiners.

If the SSA approves these special payments and then later decides the child's disability is not severe enough to qualify for SSI benefits, you will not be obligated to pay the benefits back.

Continuing Reviews

Once a child starts to receive SSI, reviews don't stop. The law requires that Social Security review a child's disability to verify whether he or she is still disabled. These Continuing Disability Reviews must be done every three years for children under 18 if their condition is expected to improve. If the disability is based on low birth weight, it must be done in 12 months.

During the reviews, parents must provide evidence that the child is receiving treatment that is considered medically necessary and available for the child's disabling condition. In some cases, it could be determined by the Social Security Administration that this medical evidence is not necessary.

New Rules at 18

When the child turns 18, he or she must go through a disability redetermination to continue to collect SSI benefits. This reevaluation is required if the child was receiving benefits at least one month before turning 18.

The redetermination process can take up to a year, beginning on the child's eighteenth birthday. The child will be subject to the rules for adults filing new claims during this redetermination process.

Applying for SSI Benefits

To apply for SSI benefits for your child, call or visit your local Social Security office. You will need your child's Social Security number and birth certificate. You will also need to provide records that show your income and assets as well as those of your child.

You can speed the medical evaluation by providing your child's medical records or assisting Social Security with getting them. You will need to give the Social Security interviewer the names, addresses, and telephone numbers of all doctors, hospitals, clinics, and other specialists your child has visited.

In addition to medical evidence, you will be asked to describe how your child's disability affects his or her ability to function on a day-to-day basis. You may also be asked to provide names of teachers, daycare providers, and family members who are familiar with your child's ability to function. In addition, bring any school records with you to the interview.

Most DDSs have professional relations officers who work with medical providers, social services agencies, and schools to help facilitate the process of getting your child's records. Anything you can do to help get information to the DDS will help speed the claims process.

Medical Care

In most states, children who get SSI benefits qualify for Medicaid, which is a health-care program for people with low incomes and limited assets. In many states, Medicaid coverage is automatic once SSI eligibility is determined. If you are a resident of one of these states, you'll have to apply for Medicaid separately. Some children qualify for Medicaid even if they don't qualify for SSI. Check with your Social Security office or your local state or county social services office for more information.

Once a child with disabilities turns 20 years old, he or she may qualify for Medicare coverage, which is primarily a federal health program for people aged 65 or older. We review Medicare coverage in great detail in Part 5.

Medicare is a government program, so of course we have an exception: children with chronic renal disease who need a kidney transplant or maintenance dialysis can get Medicare sooner if a parent is getting Social Security or has worked enough to be covered by Social Security even if the child is younger than 20.

Children who are disabled and eligible for SSI also can receive health care services under the Children with Special Health Care Needs (CSHCN) provisions of the Social Security Act. These programs are usually run by state health agencies.

CSHCN programs vary state by state, but most provide specialized services through arrangements with clinics, private medical offices, hospital-based out- and inpatient treatment centers, or community agencies. These services may be provided even if your child is not eligible for SSI. Check with your local health department, social services office, or hospital if you think your child may qualify for these medical services. Many times, you can find out about these services through the hospital's social services office when your child is in the hospital.

The Least You Need to Know

- ◆ Children of a worker qualify for benefits if the worker is retired, disabled, or deceased, provided that the child is under the age of 18 (or age 19 if the child is in high school or elementary school).

- ◆ Children who become disabled before the age of 22 may qualify for disability benefits on their parents' work record.

- ◆ Disabled children in homes that meet income and asset requirements may also qualify for Supplemental Security Income.

- ◆ Medical care for disabled children may be available through Medicaid. Disabled children may also qualify for medical services under the Children with Special Health Care Needs (CSHCN) provisions of the Social Security Act.

Chapter 12

Dependent Parents' Slice

In This Chapter

◆ Arranging for benefits for dependent parents upon the death of their child

◆ Caring for sick parents

◆ Taking advantage of the Family Medical Leave Act

◆ Handling your parents' finances

As people live longer, more and more parents are living with their adult children. Sixty-seven percent of elderly people who are not institutionalized live in a family setting, according to a recent study from the U.S. Bureau of Census.

At the time of the survey, there were about 10.8 million older men and 10.7 million older women living in family settings. About 13 percent of these older folks lived with children, siblings, and other relatives. That's a lot of elderly people who may be dependent on their children for their living expenses.

What happens if the child dies before the elderly parent? The Social Security Administration has made provisions for exactly this situation. Once the dependent parent reaches the age of 62, he or she can apply for benefits on the child's work record if the child is deceased.

In this chapter, I tell you how benefits for dependent parents work. We also take a quick look at financial and health-care considerations for elderly parents.

Learning the Rules

It's every parent's worst nightmare to lose a child. If that parent is financially dependent on the child, dealing with the loss of the child as well as the financial crisis can be a double whammy.

Parents who were dependent on their deceased child for at least half of their support can apply for Social Security benefits as survivors on that child's work record, provided they are at least 62 years old. Parents are entitled to 82 percent of a child's Primary Insurance Amount. If both parents apply for benefits, they can each receive 75 percent. The percentage paid does not increase if the dependent parent waits until they reach full retirement age. For Social Security purposes, a parent can be the natural parent or someone who became the worker's stepparent or adoptive parent before the worker reached 16 years of age.

Senior Moments
Dependent parent benefits are rarely paid, but they do exist. The average monthly parents' benefits paid in 2000 were $910.30 for eligible folks, according to the SSA.

If the parent was receiving a Social Security benefit that was lower than the child's benefit, the parent's benefit will be adjusted upward based on the child's earnings history. The parent will receive the higher of the two amounts but will not receive two benefit checks. This works the same as it does for a spouse who could get benefits on his or her own work record but chooses instead to collect based on his or her spouse's record because the benefits will be higher.

Dependent parent benefits are subject to the total amount payable to a family, which is 150 to 180 percent of the worker's benefit. The actual amount received could be lower when the benefit is apportioned among dependents.

In addition to meeting the age requirements, the child must have met full eligibility requirements for Social Security at the time of his or her death. When the parent applies for dependent parent benefits, he or she will have to prove that more than half of his or her living expenses were paid by the deceased child. To do this, a dependent parent must show canceled checks, bank statements, credit card payments, or other evidence that half of their bills were paid by their dependent child.

Caregiving Resources

Caring for an elderly parent can be both emotionally and financially draining. A lot of resources are available to help families with these difficult times.

One of the best first stops to make if you have Internet access is the National Family Caregiver Support Program at www.aoa.dhhs.gov/prof/aoaprog/caregiver/ caregiver.asp. If you don't have Internet access, you can reach them at the following address:

> Family Caregiver Support Program
> Administration on Aging
> 330 Independence Ave.
> Washington, D.C. 20201
> Phone: 202-619-0724

The center also offers its services toll free for people with hearing impairments using TTY devices at 1-800-877-8339.

One of the most difficult aspects of caring for an elderly parent who is sick is the need to balance work requirements with your caregiving responsibilities. Fortunately, the Family and Medical Leave Act, which took effect in 1993, made this juggling act much easier.

> **Social Graces**
>
> If you would like to find out more about the Family and Medical Leave Act, go to www.nationalpartnership.org and use the "Quick Jump" drop-down menu to download the FMLA Guide. You can also contact the National Partnership for Women & Families at the following address:
>
> 1875 Connecticut Ave., NW, Suite 650
> Washington, D.C. 20009
> Phone: 202-986-2600
> Fax: 202-986-2539

Taking Leave from Work

More than 50 million Americans have balanced their work and family needs without harming their business relationships using the Family and Medical Leave Act (FMLA. The FMLA guarantees people who work for companies with 50 or more employees up to 12 weeks of unpaid leave each year to care for seriously ill family members, including spouses and parents. The most frequent use of FMLA has been for parents after the birth of a child.

What are the chances you will need to take advantage of the FMLA for a sick relative? According to studies by the National Partnership on Women and Families …

◆ Nearly two-thirds of American women and men under the age of 60 expect to be responsible for the care of an elderly relative in the next 10 years.

◆ One in four Americans have eldercare responsibilities.

◆ Almost half of all caregivers provide care for at least 8 hours per week, and 21 percent spend between 9 and 20 hours per week caregiving. A majority of caregivers are employed full-time (52 percent).

The FMLA gives caregivers job-protected family leave. Leave does not have to be taken as a lump of time. Rather, time can be taken as needed—in blocks of several hours, a half-day, a full day, a week, four weeks, or as much as 12 weeks at once. A company cannot fire you for taking family leave time.

In addition to caregiving responsibilities, children taking care of dependent parents often have financial concerns. Although an extended discussion of this issue is beyond the scope of this book, the following section reviews some of the key issues to help you get you started thinking about them.

Finances and Your Dependent Parents

One of the hardest things to think about when you are caring for a dependent parent is how to take control of his or her finances, especially if your parent is experiencing difficulties related to senility or Alzheimer's disease.

def•i•ni•tion

A **durable power of attorney** allows you to make legal and financial decisions. How much control you have depends on how the document is written. Sometimes broad power of attorney arrangements allow you to set up trusts and other similar financial arrangements.

You will need to seek legal help to obtain *durable power of attorney* from your parent so you can access his or her assets to pay for doctor, nursing home, or hospital expenses in the event that he or she will no longer be able to do it alone. If your parent has sizeable assets, you will also need to seek help to be certain the proper estate planning is in place.

In the past, people used a strategy of transferring the parent's assets to other family members, so he or she could qualify for Medicaid. This means the parent must be left with no more than $2,000. New government regulations make this much more difficult to do.

Your best bet, if you are faced with this situation, is to work with a financial planner or attorney who specializes in eldercare issues and who can advise you on various types of federal and other assistance for which your parent may qualify. These services vary state by state.

Last but not least, be sure your parents have a will. Estimates are that three quarters of Americans don't have wills. If your parents die without one, the state gets to decide how your parents' estate is distributed. I'm sure neither you nor your parents want that to happen.

The Least You Need to Know

♦ Parents who depend on their child for more than half of their expenses are eligible to apply for Social Security benefits on their child's work record if the child dies before they do.

♦ Caregiving can be a very difficult burden for a family. The Family and Medical Leave Act provides job protection for people who must take time off to care for a sick family member.

♦ Getting your parents' finances in order is critical when caring for dependent parents, especially if you will need to make arrangements for medical care.

13

Collecting Disability

In This Chapter

- ◆ Following the rules
- ◆ Determining the size of your benefit
- ◆ Making sense of the appeals process
- ◆ Keeping benefits
- ◆ Returning to work

No one likes to think that he or she might become disabled, even though the United States Census Bureau says there is a one in five chance of an American becoming disabled. In a study the Census Bureau released in 1997, it was found that more than 152 million people in the United States between the ages of 21 and 64 had some form of disability. Not all of these people had a disability that was severe enough to qualify for Social Security disability benefits, but even the Social Security Administration states that 30 percent of the current generation of 20-year-olds will face disability at some point in their lives. In 2005, 6.4 million disabled workers were receiving benefits from Social Security. The average monthly benefit was $902 and is expected to rise to $939 in 2006.

Hopefully, this is one chapter you will never need, but in case you do, we walk through the process of applying for, getting, and keeping disability benefits.

Passing the Test

Some disability insurance programs consider you disabled if you can't continue to work in your own field. Others cover partial or short-term disability.

The SSA's definition of disability is far more strict. Not only must you be unable to continue working in your own field, you must also be unable to adjust to other types of work because of your medical condition. Furthermore, your disability must be expected to last at least 12 months or until you die.

Establishing a Work History

To qualify for disability from the SSA, you will need to have earned enough credits. Most people need to have earned at least 20 credits in the 10 years before becoming disabled. (Remember that you can earn up to four credits per year. In 2005, you had to earn $920 per credit, or $3,680 for the maximum of four credits. See Chapter 5 for more on credits.) In 2006, you will need to earn $970 per credit or $3,880 to earn four credits in a year.

> **Senior Moments**
>
> If your disability started before the age of 22, you may be eligible to apply on your parents' record. See Chapter 11 for more details about children's disability rules.

If you become disabled at a young age, there is some leeway in the number of credits you need to qualify. If you become disabled before the age of 24, you will only need to have earned six credits in the three-year period before your disability started. Between the ages of 24 and 31, it is possible to qualify for disability if you have worked half the time between age 21 and the age at which you became disabled. For example, let's say you became disabled at age 29. There were eight possible work years. You would need to have worked for four years, earning 16 credits.

Once you reach age 31, Social Security has a table you can use to figure out how many credits you need to be eligible for disability benefits based on your own work record.

Disabled at Age	Credits You Need
31–42	20
44	22
46	24
48	26

Disabled at Age	Credits You Need
50	28
52	30
54	32
56	34
58	36
60	38
62 or older	40

* The table applies only to people born after 1928.

If you have enough work credits, your next step is to apply for benefits.

Applying for Benefits

You can apply for disability benefits as soon as you become disabled, but the actual payment of disability benefits can't begin until five months after the onset of your disability. You should apply for benefits at your local Social Security office as soon as you become disabled. You can apply by phone, by mail, or in person. The Social Security Administration will take at least 60 to 90 days to process your claim, and it can take even longer. The best way to speed up the claim is to bring all of the required documentation when you apply. After the appointment, continue to help the SSA get any other information they request as quickly as possible.

Insecurities

The actual payment of disability benefits starts during the sixth full month after the onset of your disability.

Here is a list of the things you'll need to apply:

- Social Security number and proof of age for each person applying for benefits, including your spouse and children

- Names, addresses, and phone numbers of doctors, hospitals, clinics, and institutions that treated you as well as the dates of treatment

- Names of all medications you are taking

- Medical records from your doctors, therapists, hospitals, clinics, and caseworkers

- ◆ Laboratory and test results

- ◆ A summary of where you worked and the kind of work you did

- ◆ A copy of your W-2 form (Wage and Tax Statement) or, if you are self-employed, your federal tax return for the past year

- ◆ Dates of prior marriages if your spouse is applying

If you don't have all this information handy, start the process anyway. Once you get it started, you can always add documents to your records as soon as you get them. The SSA will also help you get records.

Determining Disability

The first thing the SSA will do once it gets your application is make sure you meet the basic requirements for disability benefits. If you earn what the SSA considers to be substantial income, which in 2006 is more than $860 a month, you will not be eligible for disability.

The only exception to this is if the SSA determines that your disability requires certain equipment or services to be able to work. The cost of that equipment or those services can be subtracted from your paycheck when calculating eligibility. We discuss this in greater detail later in this chapter, when we talk about going back to work.

In addition to looking at earnings, the Social Security interviewer will make sure you have earned enough credits in the time period required to qualify for benefits. The interviewer will also check your age and your relationship to others for whom you are seeking benefits.

def•i•ni•tion

The **Disability Determination Service** (DDS) is a state-based team of specialists that includes a disability evaluation specialist and a doctor. Each applicant's case is reviewed by this team to determine whether he or she meets the Social Security Administration's definition of disability.

The Social Security interviewer will then send the information to the *Disability Determination Services* (*DDS*) in your state. These are the folks who will determine whether you are disabled based on current Social Security law.

The DDS will collect information about your medical problem, including when it began and how it limits your activities. They will also review what was found in the medical tests and what treatment you have received. Your doctors and others providing your medical treatment will be asked to comment on your ability to do work-related activities (such as walking, sitting, lifting, and carrying) and your ability to remember instructions.

If not enough medical information is available, the DDS may ask you to go to a special examination called a "consultative examination." This can often be done by your doctor or at the medical facility where you have already received treatment. If Social Security requests the examination, it will pays for it as well as for certain travel costs related to the examination.

The DDS uses the consultation examination to determine whether your condition is severe enough to interfere with basic work-related activities—not just in the job you were doing but in any work for which you are qualified based on your education and experience.

Insecurities

Even if you have a Ph.D., you could end up working at a fast food restaurant if your disability prevents you from being able to do the complex work you were trained to do. As long as the Social Security examiner determines that you can be gainfully employed, even if it is for a much more menial job than the one for which you were trained, you will not get benefits. If you want disability coverage that protects you based on your line of work, you will need to buy a private disability insurance plan. When you do buy private disability insurance, be certain you understand how that policy defines disability.

Your condition will be compared to a list of impairments developed for each major body system that are considered so severe that they automatically mean you are disabled. If your condition isn't on the list, then the DDS must decide if your condition is equal in severity to one that is on the list. According to Social Security's Blue Book for physicians …

> … *a medically determinable physical or mental impairment is an impairment that results from anatomical, physiological, or psychological abnormalities which can be shown by medically acceptable clinical and laboratory diagnostic techniques. A physical or mental impairment must be established by medical evidence consisting of signs, symptoms, and laboratory findings—not only by the individual's statement of symptoms.*

You probably get the idea—this is all very cut and dried. There isn't much room for flexibility in the Social Security Disability Determination process, but there is some variability in how the rules are applied in each state.

If the DDS determines that your condition is severe, but is not the same or of equal severity as an impairment on the list, they will then try to determine whether your individual impairment interferes with your ability to do the work you previously did.

Social Graces

You can review a list of impairments for adults online at www.ssa.gov/disability/professionals/bluebook/AdultListings.htm.

If the DDS determines that you cannot do the work you did in the past, they will then consider whether you can adjust to other work based on your medical condition and your age, education, past work experience, and any transferable skills you may have. You will only be awarded disability benefits if they determine that there is absolutely no work you can do.

Special Rules If You Are Blind

The SSA has special rules for blind people who apply for disability benefits. Folks are considered blind for the purpose of getting disability if their vision cannot be corrected to better than 20/200 in their better eye or if their visual field is 20 degrees or less, even with corrective lenses.

The monthly earnings limit for blind people to qualify for benefits is higher than for nonblind disabled workers. In 2005, the earnings limit for blind people who collected disability was $1,380 versus $830 for nonblind people. In 2006, the disability earnings limit for blind people increases to $1,450 per month versus $860 for nonblind people. Any costs for impairment-related work expenses (such as paying for a sighted reader or a guide dog) can be deducted from income and is not considered part of substantial earnings.

If you have vision problems but don't meet the strict definition of blindness, you still could qualify for disability benefits if your health problems prevent you from working. If you think you might qualify, it doesn't hurt to apply. The worst that can happen is that you get rejected.

Collecting Your Money

Let's say you've made it through the medical examination process and get a letter stating that you qualify for benefits. When will the benefits start, and how much will they be?

The earliest that benefit payments can start is six months after the onset of your disability. Earlier I said there is a five-month waiting period, but benefits are paid in the month following when they were due, so if your benefits were to start in May, you would receive the May payment in June.

Your monthly disability benefit is based on your lifetime average earnings covered by Social Security. The formula is complex, and it's not worth it for you to spend the time trying to figure it out yourself. You can get your earnings record and an estimate of your disability benefit by requesting a Social Security statement. If you don't know where your most recent statement is, you can request a copy from the SSA by phone. This statement also includes estimates of retirement and survivor benefits that your family may be eligible to receive now and in the future.

In addition to disability payments, you will be automatically enrolled in Medicare once you get disability benefits for two years. We talk about Medicare benefits in greater detail in Part 5.

Insecurities

Your disability payment could be reduced if you are eligible for workers' compensation or another type of public disability payment. Other types of public disability payments include civil service disability, military disability, state temporary disability, and state or local government retirement benefits that are based on disability. The general rule is that your combination of disability payments cannot exceed 80 percent of your average earnings while working.

What If You Are Rejected?

Given the strict criteria for qualifying for disability benefits, not everyone who applies for benefits gets approved to receive them. What if you are denied benefits, but you believe you really do qualify?

If your benefits are rejected, you can appeal the decision. You have 60 days from the date on which you receive your notice of denial of benefits to file an appeal. Your appeal must be submitted in writing, but you don't have to do it alone. You can ask for help from a lawyer, a friend, or someone whom you think may be a good advocate for you. You appoint this person to be your representative, and he or she will receive copies of any written notifications that are sent to you.

Insecurities

If you wish to have a representative, your representative cannot charge or collect a fee from you without getting written permission from the SSA.

Essentially, there is a four-step review process. With each level, you have 60 days to file an appeal with any Social Security office if you disagree with the decision made. All appeals must be in writing.

1. **Request for reconsideration.** The first step in the appeals process is called reconsideration. Essentially, during this step, someone who was not involved in the first decision reviews the claim. If you disagree with the reconsideration, you again have 60 days to file an appeal.

2. **Administrative law hearing.** The next level of appeal is a hearing before an administrative law judge. At the hearing, the judge will ask you to explain your case in person. You can review the information in your file and bring new information if you think it will help you to make your case. The judge will question you and any witnesses you bring.

   You don't have to go to the hearing. If you decide not to go, you must notify Social Security in writing that you will not be attending. However, it is usually advantageous to go to the hearing. After the hearing, the judge's decision will be sent to you in writing by Social Security. If you disagree with the judge's decision, you can again appeal the decision in writing within 60 days.

3. **The Appeals Council.** The next level of appeal is the Appeals Council. The Appeals Council will look at your request for review, but if it believes the administrative law judge was correct, it may deny your request for that review. If the Appeals Council decides to review your case, it can decide the case itself or return it to the administrative law judge for further review. You will receive a copy of the council's decision or an order sending it back to the judge. Again, you have 60 days to appeal the council's decision in writing.

4. **Federal Appeal.** Your final level of appeal is in federal district court. For this step, you will need to file a lawsuit.

Avoiding Benefit Loss

Everyone who gets disability has to face periodic reviews by Social Security. The frequency of the reviews depends on your medical condition. This information will be stated in your letter awarding you disability benefits. There are three different frequencies of reviews, depending on the likelihood that you will recover from your disability:

1. If medical improvement is "expected," a review will likely be in 6 to 18 months.

2. If medical improvement is "possible," you can expect a review no sooner than in three years.

3. If medical improvement is "not expected," you will usually have at least seven years before a review.

Insecurities

> You must report to the SSA if you go back to work. Failure to do so could result in having to repay benefits if it is determined that you should not have been collecting them after the change in status. You are entitled to a trial work period, so benefits are not cut off immediately upon returning to work. See the section "Staying in Touch" for more details.

Two things will cause you to lose your benefits after your review. One is if your average earnings are above $860 a month, which means they will be determined to be substantial. The second is if your medical condition has improved enough that you are no longer determined to be disabled. You are required to promptly report any improvement in your condition.

When you get a letter alerting you to an upcoming review, you will be asked to provide information about your medical treatment and any work you might have done or been doing. The evaluation team will include a disability examiner and a doctor. You could be asked to go for a special examination as part of the review process.

Once the team makes a decision, the SSA notifies you in writing. If the team determines that you are still disabled, your benefits will continue. If they decide you are no longer disabled, you can go through the appeals process previously outlined. If you don't appeal, your benefits will stop three months after it is determined your disability ended.

If you are denied continuing benefits, you have two special appeals rights. You can have a disability hearing, in which you meet face-to-face with the person reconsidering your case to explain why you think you are still disabled. You can submit new evidence or information, and you can bring someone who knows about your disability. This step occurs before you have a hearing before the administrative law judge.

If you decide to appeal your discontinuation of benefits, you can also submit a written request for a continuation of benefits during the appeals process. You must request this continuation within 10 days of receiving the notice that you have been denied benefits. If your appeal is not successful, you could be ordered to repay the benefits.

Staying in Touch

Once you get benefits, you must keep the Social Security office informed of any changes in your life. These changes include …

- **Moving.** You must call Social Security with your new address and phone number as soon as you know them. Your benefits will be stopped if the SSA tries to contact you and cannot reach you. You should also let Social Security know about any family members who receive benefits who will be moving with you.

- **Changes in condition.** You must notify the SSA if your condition changes for the better. If you fail to do so, you may get benefits that were not due to you and could be ordered to repay them.

- **Going to work.** You must inform the SSA if you take a job or become self-employed, even if you are making very little money. There is something called a "trial work period" in which you can still collect benefits for up to nine months. We'll talk more about that later in this chapter.

- **Traveling outside the United States.** You can travel or live outside the United States and continue to collect benefits. The Social Security Administration actually has offices in 60 countries. You must notify the administration of your plans to be outside the United States and provide an address if you will be traveling for more than 30 days. There could be special rules related to traveling outside the United States.

- **Receiving other disability benefits.** You must let the SSA know if you apply for another type of disability benefit, if you begin receiving a disability benefit or get a lump-sum settlement, or if the amount you are currently receiving for another disability benefit changes.

- **Getting married.** In most cases, you must report to the SSA if you get married and are changing your name. If you are collecting disability benefits on your own record, your payments will not change. In fact, unless you are changing your name, you don't need to report the marriage. If you are collecting benefits on your spouse's record as a disabled widow or widower, you must report the name change. If your new spouse dies, you may be eligible for higher benefits on your previous spouse's work record. If you are an adult who was disabled before age 22 and you are getting benefits on a parent's or grandparent's record, your benefits will generally end. They can be started again if your marriage ends.

◆ **Becoming unable to manage your own funds.** If you become unable to manage your own funds, someone should notify the SSA. In these situations, the administration will arrange for an organization or person called a "representative payee" to receive and use benefits on behalf of the beneficiary. Social Security will ask for periodic reports on the use of the funds.

◆ **Being convicted of a criminal offense.** You must notify the Social Security Administration if you are convicted of a crime. Benefits are not generally paid for the months a person is in prison, but eligible family members can continue to collect benefits. This is also true of persons found to be mentally ill who commit a crime and are confined to an institution by court order and at public expense.

◆ **Death of the beneficiary.** You must notify the SSA when the beneficiary dies. No payment is made in the month of death. If the deceased beneficiary receives a check during the month of death, you should return it. Family members will be switched over to survivors' benefits after Social Security is notified.

All these changes can be reported to the SSA by calling 1-800-772-1213. You can also report changes by mail or in person at a Social Security office. In addition to reporting the new information, you will need the beneficiary's Social Security claim number, the name of the person about whom the report is made, your own Social Security number, your Social Security claim number (if you are getting benefits), and the date of the change.

Going Back to Work

After staying home for a while with a disability, you may decide you've had enough and want to try to go back to work. With the Ticket to Work and Work Incentives Improvement Act of 1999, Congress made it easier for people receiving disability benefits to go back to work. The bill expands opportunities for people with a disability by providing Social Security disability beneficiaries with improved access to employment services, vocational rehabilitation services, and related support services.

Today the program is available in all 50 states. Qualified Social Security and Supplemental Security Income (SSI) recipients get a "ticket" in the mail. This ticket can be used to obtain vocational rehabilitation, employment, or other support services to help them go to work. An individual who is using a ticket will not be subjected to regularly scheduled disability medical reviews, but their benefits can be terminated if they earn more than the maximum earning limit of $860 per month ($1,450 per month if blind).

Congress established a panel to advise the Social Security Administration about the progress of this program and then report back to Congress periodically. The panel is called the Ticket to Work & Work Incentives Advisory Panel. Members include a cross section of people with experience and knowledge as beneficiaries, consumer advocates, providers, researchers, legal advocates, and employers. You can find out more about the panel and its activities at www.socialsecurity.gov/work/panel.

How Going Back to Work Affects Benefits

For anyone who decides to use the ticket, a big question, of course, is, "What will happen to my benefits if I go back to work?" The SSA has a number of incentives to make it easier for you to try. These work incentives include cash benefits as well as Medicare or Medicaid while you work, help with any extra work expenses you may incur as a result of your disability, and help with education, training, and rehabilitation to start a new line of work. The specifics of these work incentives are detailed in the following sections.

Trial Work Period

You will be able to try working over a nine-month period without affecting your Social Security benefits. The nine months do not have to be consecutive. If the nine months do not fall within a 60-month period, you may have even more time to test your ability to work.

Senior Moments
The Ticket to Work program was phased in over three years beginning in 2002 and is now available in all 50 states. You can find out more about the Ticket to Work Program at www.ssa.gov/work.

In 2006, if you earn at least $620 in any month, it counts as a trial work month. If you are self-employed, that $620 is after expenses. It also counts as a trial month if you spend more than 80 hours in your own business. The SSA adjusts these earnings limits each year.

Extended Period of Eligibility

After the trial work period, for at least 36 months, you can receive a benefit for any month in which your earnings fall below the "substantial gainful activity" level. For 2006, that level is $860 per month for people with disabilities and $1,450 for people who are blind.

If a periodic review of your condition is scheduled, it will be delayed if you are in a trial work period until the trial ends.

Expedited Reinstatement of Benefits

If your medical condition makes you unable to work again within 60 months of the end of the extended period of eligibility, you can request that your benefits be reinstated without having to file a new disability application.

Continuation of Medicare

If you have premium-free Medicare hospital insurance and start working, you can have at least eight years of extended coverage. After that time, you can buy Medicare coverage by paying a monthly premium.

Impairment-Related Work Expenses

Expenses for things you need to work because of your impairment can be deducted when counting earnings to determine whether you meet the substantial work test. These impairment-related work expenses can include a seeing-eye dog, prescription drugs, transportation to and from work (under certain conditions), a personal attendant or job coach, a wheelchair, or any specialized work equipment.

Recovery During Vocational Rehabilitation

If you are likely to benefit from rehabilitation, training, or education, you will likely be referred to a state rehabilitation agency or a private organization for rehabilitation services. If your medical condition improves while you are participating in a vocational rehabilitation program that could lead to your becoming self-supporting, benefits may continue until the program ends. For example, if someone is taking a vocational training program to learn a new skill and during that program his or her medical condition improves to such a great extent that he or she is no longer disabled, benefits will continue to be paid until the retraining program is completed.

Social Security disability coverage is a great safety net, but you must be severely disabled to take advantage of this coverage. If you are a professional and want disability coverage for your specific type of work, you should consider getting private coverage.

The Least You Need to Know

- ◆ The Social Security Administration has a strict definition of disability. Not only must you be unable to continue working in your desired field, you must also be unable to adjust to other types of work because of your medical condition. Your disability also must be expected to last at least 12 months or until you die.

- ◆ If you are denied disability coverage, you can appeal the decision.

- ◆ While on disability, the maximum you can earn in 2006 is $860 per month ($1,450 if you are blind).

- ◆ The SSA has created incentives that make it easier for you to try working again without losing your disability benefits.

Chapter 14

Supplementing Income

In This Chapter

- ◆ Understanding how SSI helps low-income and disabled people get by
- ◆ Finding out how to apply for assistance
- ◆ Calculating your benefit amount
- ◆ Making sense of the appeals process
- ◆ Returning to work

If you are faced with a disability (or are over age 65) and have a low income and few assets, you might qualify for Supplemental Security Income (SSI). This program, which is administered by the Social Security Administration, is designed to help people who are 65 or older, blind, or disabled and who don't own much or have a lot of income.

SSI is not just for adults. Monthly benefits can be paid to disabled and blind children as well. Even though the program is administered by the SSA, the benefits are not paid out of the Social Security trust fund. They are funded out of the general U.S. treasury.

SSI: Assisting the Poor and Disabled

In September 2005, 7.1 million people were getting payments from SSI, totaling about $3.3 billion. The average monthly payment was $437.10. These amounts included about $362 million in state supplements, which are available only in certain states.

Social Graces

You can get more details about SSI at the Social Security website. The main page for SSI is www.socialsecurity.gov/notices/supplemental-security-income/index.htm.

More than 80 percent of SSI recipients are disabled and almost 6 out of every 10 are mentally retarded or have another mental disorder. More than half of them (55 percent) have no income other than their SSI payment. If SSI recipients do have an income, 36 percent of the time that income is in the form of Social Security benefits.

Obviously, this is a program that you hope you will never need.

Rules for Supplementing Income

Your eligibility for SSI depends on what you own and how much income you have. Income can include wages, Social Security benefits, and pensions. In addition, non-cash items you receive (such as food, clothing, or shelter) are also included in the income calculations. If you are married, the income of your spouse and the assets he or she owns also becomes part of the equation.

Insecurities

Social Security will need to verify your wages or self-employment income. To do this, they will ask for copies of your pay slips and, if self-employed, your completed federal and state income tax forms. Be sure to keep good records of your earnings.

Income limits vary by state. You can call your local Social Security office to find out what they are in your state of residence.

Income that is counted, according to Social Security, includes the following:

- Wages from your job, whether in cash or another form
- Net earnings from your business if you're self-employed
- The value of food, shelter, or clothing that someone gives you or the amount of money you get to help pay for these items
- Department of Veterans Affairs (VA) benefits

- ◆ Railroad retirement and railroad unemployment benefits

- ◆ Annuities, pensions from any government or private source, workers' compensation, unemployment insurance benefits, black lung benefits, and Social Security benefits

- ◆ Prizes, settlements, and awards, including court-ordered awards

- ◆ Proceeds from life insurance policies

- ◆ Gifts and contributions

- ◆ Support and alimony payments

- ◆ Inheritances in cash or property

- ◆ Interest earned, including interest on savings, checking, and other accounts

- ◆ Rental income

- ◆ Strike pay and other benefits from unions

Not all income is counted. The first $65 per month earned from working is not counted, as well as half of the amount over $65. (If the person has no other income during the month, such as interest earned, pensions, or stock dividends, then the first $85 earned is not counted.) The maximum a person can earn in a month before SSI payments are stopped is $1,291 in 2006 ($1,243 in 2005).

Food stamps are not figured into the equation, and shelter received from a private, nonprofit organization also is left out. In most cases, home-energy assistance also does not figure into the income eligibility calculations. If you are a student, some wages and scholarships received also may be left out of the eligibility calculations.

Other things not counted as income include medical care and services; social services; receipts from the sale, exchange, or replacement of things you own; income tax refunds; Earned Income Tax Credit payments; payments made by life or disability insurance on charge accounts or other credit accounts; proceeds of a loan; bills paid by someone else for things other than food, clothing, or shelter; and replacement of lost or stolen income.

In addition to your income, Social Security will consider how much you own. They will review your real estate holdings, bank accounts, cash, stocks, and bonds. The most you can have on hand is $2,000 if you are single and $3,000 if you are a married couple.

People who are blind or have a disability have a little more leeway when collecting SSI. They can earn more money, but their SSI payment could go down. They also may be permitted to set aside money for a work goal or to go to school. If you are on SSI and want to do this, you must coordinate it with SSI first. Some states also provide special services to SSI recipients, including counseling, job training, and help in finding work. Going back to work when on SSI will be discussed in more detail later in this chapter.

To collect SSI, you must live in the United States or Northern Mariana Islands. You must also be a U.S. citizen or national.

Senior Moments

Not everything you own is counted when you apply for SSI. The SSA doesn't count the home you live in or the land it is on. In most cases, they will not count your car. Burial plots and funds set aside for burial up to $1,500 for you and $1,500 for your spouse are left out of the equation, as are life insurance policies with a face value of $1,500 or less.

If you live in a city or county rest home, halfway house, or other public institution, you probably cannot qualify for SSI. As we've learned time and time again, however, there are exceptions to almost every federal rule. People in publicly operated community residences that serve no more than 16 residents may be able to qualify for SSI. If you are in a public institution primarily to attend an approved educational program or for job training that could help you get a job, you may be eligible for SSI benefits. Also, people living in a public emergency shelter for the homeless may qualify for benefits.

Social Graces

Some noncitizens can qualify for SSI. For more information on noncitizen qualifications, go to www.ssa.gov/pubs/11051.html.

Now that we know the eligibility rules, let's take a look at how you apply for SSI benefits.

Applying for Help

You can go to any local Social Security office to apply for benefits. You can make an appointment in advance by calling 1-800-772-1213. Parents or guardians of a blind or disabled child under the age of 18 can apply for that child.

You've probably already guessed a lot of paperwork is involved in the application process. Here is what the SSA asks you to bring:

- ◆ Your Social Security card or a record of your Social Security number

- ◆ Your birth certificate or other proof of your age

- ◆ Information about the home in which you live, such as your mortgage or your lease and landlord's name

- ◆ Payroll slips, bankbooks, insurance policies, burial fund records, and other information about your income and the things you own

- ◆ If you're signing up for disability, the names, addresses, and telephone numbers of doctors, hospitals, and clinics that have seen you

- ◆ Proof of U.S. citizenship or eligible noncitizen status

In addition to these items, you'll need your checkbook or other papers that show your bank, credit union, or other financial institution account number. This information will be used to deposit benefits directly into your account. Social Security prefers to deposit benefits directly to prevent loss, mail delay, or theft.

If you are applying for benefits based on a disability, the application process is the same to be considered disabled under both programs. I won't cover the disability rules again here. If necessary, review Chapter 13. Chapter 11 contains more information about children, disability, and SSI.

Collecting Benefits

Each year, the Social Security Administration sets a maximum amount that someone can collect from the federal government under SSI. This amount increases with the same automatic cost-of-living increase that applies to Social Security retirement and disability payments.

Senior Moments

The maximum amount that a single person can receive in SSI benefits in 2006 is $603 per month. A couple can get $904 per month. These amounts are adjusted downward if the recipient has countable income. Annual income on SSI is $7,236, which is still below the government's poverty line of $9,800 for an individual. A couple's annual SSI income of $10,848 is also below the government's poverty line of 13,200 for a couple.

If you qualify for SSI benefits, you will receive a letter that spells out the amount of benefits you will receive and when those benefits will begin. The monthly amount could vary each month, depending on your other income and living arrangements.

The SSA usually makes the first two months' payment based on your first month's income. After that, the amount of your payment is usually based on the income reported two months prior to the benefit being paid. If you get a check that is for more money than usual, you should call your Social Security office. You will have to return any extra money you receive, even if you were not the one who made the mistake.

Appealing the Decision

If you disagree with a decision made by the SSA about your SSI claim, you have 60 days to appeal the decision. After 60 days, you lose your right to appeal.

If you appeal, you can do so alone or be represented by an attorney or another person of your choosing. If you choose to have a representative, you have to inform the SSA in writing and provide the name of the person you are appointing. You can do this by filling out Form SSA-1696, "Appointment of Representative," which you can get by calling the SSA. If your representative is not an attorney, he or she will also need to sign the form, accepting the appointment as your representative.

Your representative can charge you a fee, but it must be approved by the SSA. If he or she overcharges you, your representative could be suspended or disqualified from representing people before the Social Security Administration and may face criminal prosecution. Fees can be no more than 25 percent of the past-due benefits or $4,000, whichever is less. You and your representative must file a fee petition stating the charges.

Appeals for SSI are fairly similar to those for disability claims, as described in Chapter 13.

1. **Reconsideration.** The first step is a reconsideration, which is done by someone who was not part of the initial application process. SSI reconsiderations can be done in two different ways—either a *case review* or an *informal conference*. If the question is about a medical determination, your only option will be a case review.

def•i•ni•tion

A **case review** is a reconsideration of your application for SSI without the reviewer meeting with you personally. You do have the right to review your file before the reconsideration. If you feel that additional information may help your appeal, you can provide that information before the case review.

def•i•ni•tion

An **informal conference** allows you meet with the person who will be reviewing your case and tell him or her why you disagree with the decision. You can bring witnesses to this informal conference to talk about your case. You can also bring a representative if you choose to have one. You will be able to review your file before the conference, and if you think it would be helpful, you can bring new information to the conference.

2. **Hearing.** If you disagree with the decision of the reconsideration, you can appeal the decision and ask for a hearing. As with each step in the appeals process, you will have to request a hearing within 60 days of getting notification of the reconsideration decision.

   The hearing will be before an administrative law judge. The judge will notify you of the time and place for the hearing, which must be within 75 miles of your home. The SSA may request additional information before the hearing, and you are obligated to provide it as soon as possible.

   You can attend the hearing and bring your representative if you have one. You'll be given an opportunity to review your file, and you can give the judge new information. The judge will ask you questions and will question any witnesses you bring to the hearing. You or your representative can also question the witnesses. You don't have to go to the hearing in most cases (unless the judge requires it), but it is probably best for you to be there.

   Social Security will send you a copy of the judge's decision in writing, and again, you will have 60 days to decide whether you want to appeal if you disagree with the decision.

3. **Appeals Council.** If you do disagree, the next level of appeal is the Appeals Council. The council reviews all requests but can decide to deny a case for further review if it agrees with the administrative law judge. If it decides the case should be reviewed, it will either review the case itself or send it back to the administrative law judge for further review.

   You'll receive a letter from Social Security informing you of the Appeals Council's decision. If you disagree, you will have one more option for appeal. Again, you will have to ask for the appeal within 60 days or lose your right to appeal.

4. **Federal lawsuit.** The final level of appeal is to file a lawsuit in a federal district court.

Reporting Changes

Once you start collecting from SSI, you will find that you must stay in constant contact with the SSA and report any changes in your life. These changes include …

♦ **Change of address.** If the SSA can't find you, your SSI payments will stop.

♦ **Change in the number of people living with you.** You must inform Social Security when someone moves in or out of your home, when someone who lives with you dies, or when someone living in your home has a baby.

♦ **Change in income.** You must report any income you receive other than SSI. If the income you have already reported increases, decreases, or stops, you must report that as soon as possible. This includes any change in the income of family members as well.

♦ **Change in possessions.** You must report any changes in what you own. Remember that you can only own items worth up to $2,000 if you are single and $3,000 if you are married.

♦ **Change in help with living expenses.** If you were getting help with money, food, clothing, or housing and you lose that help, you need to report it to SSI. You also must report if you get new help with these expenses.

♦ **Enter or leave an institution.** If you enter or leave an institution, hospital, skilled nursing facility, nursing home, intermediate care facility, halfway house, jail, prison, public emergency shelter, or any other kind of institution, you must report it to the SSA. It is particularly important to report if you enter a medical institution right away because there are different rules for a stay in a medical institution under 90 days.

♦ **Marriage, separation, or divorce.** Any change in your marital status must be reported as soon as possible.

♦ **Leave the United States.** If you leave the United States or the Northern Mariana Islands for more than 30 days, you will not be eligible for SSI. People who move to Puerto Rico also are no longer eligible for SSI. If you are outside the United States for more than 30 days, your benefits cannot start again until you are in the United States for at least 30 straight days.

♦ **Start or stop school.** If you are under the age of 22 and start or stop school, you must report it to SSI.

◆ **Not able to manage funds.** If you are no longer able to manage your funds, it must be reported to the Social Security Administration. They will appoint a representative payee, who can be a relative or someone else who agrees to manage the funds.

◆ **Death of a recipient.** If someone receiving SSI dies, Social Security must be informed as soon as possible. If there is a surviving husband or wife, the amount received may change. Any SSI benefits sent in the month after death must be returned.

There are also special rules for people in certain states. In California or New York, for instance, you must report to SSI if you are eating your meals in a different place. In Hawaii, Michigan, or Vermont, you must report any changes in your level of care if you live in a facility such as a nursing home. In Massachusetts, you must report a significant change in your living expenses.

All changes must be reported within 10 days after the month in which it happened (for example, if someone dies on June 14, you'd have until July 10th to report it). If you fail to report a change, you could end up getting less money than you deserve. You also could end up getting more money and having to pay it back. Failure to report a change or to repay money could result in a fine or even imprisonment.

> **Social Graces**
>
> You can report changes by calling the SSA toll free at 1-800-772-1213 or by mail. You'll need to include the name of the person about whom you are reporting, the name and Social Security number of the SSI beneficiary, and the change and the date it happened. You'll also need to sign the report and give your address and phone number.

Reviewing Your Case

When you're approved for benefits, it doesn't end there. Your case will be reviewed periodically. The review can be done by mail, by phone, or in person. Essentially, the information you will be asked to provide will be similar to when you first applied. It is a good idea to keep copies of any pay slips and bank, savings, or other financial account statements in case the SSA asks for them.

If you are on SSI because of a disability-related claim, the review process for your disability is the same as for people receiving Social Security disability. You can review that process in Chapter 13.

Going Back to Work

As with Social Security disability, there are incentives for you to go back to work. SSI payments will be continued for blind or disabled recipients who go back to work until their countable income exceeds SSI limits. Those limits are set on a state-by-state basis.

If you do go back to work, it doesn't mean SSI payments stop immediately. As you begin to earn more, your SSI benefits will gradually decrease and eventually stop. Even if SSI stops, you may still be eligible for medical care under Medicaid, which will be discussed later in this chapter.

Some people can deduct special work expenses because of their disability. Items needed so that you can work with a disability (such as wheelchairs, attendant care services, Braille devices, certain drugs, and medical services) are deducted from your income to reduce your countable income. You will need to keep copies of receipts for any work-related expenses.

Getting a PASS

As an SSI recipient, you may also be eligible for a PASS if you decide to go to work. This stands for "plan for achieving self-support." A PASS permits you to set aside money to help you become more fully employed. This can include help with education, vocational training, work-related equipment, or starting a business.

A PASS usually allows SSI recipients to keep more of their SSI benefits because they can save money without lowering the SSI amount. You need to work with the SSA to develop a PASS before you try to implement a plan.

Insecurities _____

If you are collecting SSI because of a disability, you may be contacted by your state's vocational rehabilitation agency and offered help in getting back to work. This help can include job training, education, and job placement. If you are offered this help and refuse it, you can lose your SSI benefits.

Other Help You Can Get

SSI beneficiaries are also eligible for other help from their state or county. Some of the services for which you may qualify include Medicaid, food stamps, or other social services. To find out about services that may be available in your community, call your local social services department or public welfare office.

If you are over the age of 65 with low income and few resources, you may also be eligible for assistance from your state to pay your Medicare premiums. In some cases, the state even pays for Medicare expenses such as deductibles and coinsurance. Only your state can determine whether you qualify for such assistance. To find out if you are eligible, contact your state or local welfare office or Medicaid agency.

We all hope we will never need Supplemental Security Income and other related assistance programs, but it's comforting to know these programs are available if we are faced with a crisis.

Social Graces

Social Security puts out a publication about assistance with medical payments. Call and ask for *Medicare Savings for Qualified Beneficiaries* (HCFA Publication No. 02184).

The Least You Need to Know

◆ If you are 65 or older or you are disabled or blind at any age, you may qualify for Supplemental Security Income. To qualify, your income must be low and you can't own much.

◆ When you start collecting SSI, you have to report changes in your life including changes in income, marital status, and living arrangements.

◆ You can appeal any decision made by the SSA regarding your Supplemental Security Income, but you must do so within 60 days of receiving the decision or you lose the right to appeal.

◆ SSI recipients who want to improve their work situation can apply for something called a PASS, which is a plan that lets you save for a goal to enable your self-sufficiency.

Part 4

Living Right

Congratulations—you've made it through the roughest part of the book! It's no fun considering all the things that can go wrong as you work your way to retirement.

In the following chapters, I help you figure out how to make the most of your Social Security retirement benefits. Hopefully, you have additional assets to supplement your SS income. Among the topics I tackle are budgeting issues, returning to work after retirement, using assets wisely, and minimizing the tax bite.

Making Ends Meet

In This Chapter

◆ Living on a fixed income

◆ Making sense of Cost of Living Adjustments

◆ Getting aid from others

◆ Understanding how two can live cheaper than one

You've probably realized by now that making ends meet if you are solely dependent on Social Security income will be a difficult task. Yet, in 2003, 90 percent of older people reported that Social Security was their major source of income. Fifty-five percent did have some income from assets. Twenty-nine percent received money from private pensions, and 22 percent from earnings.

This chapter takes a look at how people live on a fixed income, the impact of Cost of Living Adjustments (COLAs), what type of assistance you may be able to get from state or local governments (as well as private agencies), and how you might be able to live on less by sharing your home.

Senior Moments

The median income of older people in 2003 was $20,363 for males and $11,845 for females. Households headed by a person 65 or older reported a median income of $35,310 in 2003. Almost one of every nine family households headed by an elderly person had an income of less than $15,000.

Keeping Your Head Above Water

The most important thing you can do when you start living on a fixed income—an income that has no chance of increasing with raises or job changes—is to have a good handle on your budget. You need to know what you are spending money on and whether there is any way to cut those expenses further to give you a bit more leeway with your money.

One of the biggest drains on the budget of an elderly person is health-care costs. Older Americans average $3,741 annually in out-of-pocket health-care expenditures in 2003, a 45 percent increase since 1992.

Senior Moments

If you are a man, there is a 71 percent chance that you will be living with your spouse between the ages of 65 and 84, but if you are a woman, there is only a 41 percent chance that your spouse will be around to share the burden of living on a fixed budget. After the age of 85, 53 percent of men are still living with their spouse, but only 12 percent of women are.

People under age 65 spend much less on health care, an average of $2,416 annually in out-of-pocket costs. This translates into older Americans spending 12.7 percent of their total income on health, which is three times the proportion spent by younger folks. These numbers come from a report titled "A Profile of Older Americans: 2004," which was prepared by the Administration on Aging of the U.S. Department of Health and Human Services.

Insecurities

The poverty rates are much higher for elderly women than elderly men. Almost 12.5 percent of women 65 and over are living in poverty, whereas 7.3 percent of men fall into that category.

Financial planners find that most retired people need about 70 percent of their previous income to live at the same standards they've grown to expect before retirement. In actuality, people face three stages of retirement. In the first stage, when they initially retire, they are active and may actually spend close to 90 percent of their previous levels. They usually feel well enough to travel and do things they always wanted to do, but didn't have time for when they were working.

In the second stage of retirement, people tend to slow down as their health begins to fail. Spending can sometimes drop to as low as 50 percent of their costs before retirement. They often cut down on the use of their cars (or maybe sell one), travel less, and live a more sedentary lifestyle.

The third stage of retirement, and the one that can be almost as costly as the first stage, is when health fails and medical costs take over.

Even a well-planned budget can quickly be thrown out of whack in retirement with healthcare expenditures, but there are things you can do to make these expenses fit better with a fixed income.

> **Senior Moments**
>
> About 40 percent of baby boomers will end up needing 24-hour care in either an assisted-living situation, a nursing home, or another medical setting. Costs for this will be tremendous and will quickly eat up life savings.

Getting COLAs

You may be thinking that you won't be living on a fixed income because Social Security offers Cost of Living Adjustments (COLAs). Well, don't get too excited about those. Let me tell you the truth about how much you'll get from them.

The Cost of Living Adjustments are based on the *Consumer Price Index* (*CPI*). The amount of the increase is actually equal to the increase in the average costs of consumer goods. As we all know, the necessities of life, such as food and health costs, frequently go up faster than the CPI.

def•i•ni•tion

> The **Consumer Price Index (CPI)** is one of the tools used to measure inflation. It measures the change in the cost of a group of products and services, including housing, electricity, food, and transportation. This index is published monthly by the federal government. You may also have seen it called the cost-of-living index.

The automatic COLA increase in 2005 was 4.1 percent. Here is a table from the SSA that shows you how that translated into dollars in people's pockets on a monthly basis:

Type of Benefit or Family	Before COLA	After COLA	Increase
All retired workers	$963	$1,002	$39
Aged couple	$1,583	$1,648	$65
Widowed mother and two children	$1,992	$2,074	$82
Aged widow(er) alone	$929	$967	$38
Disabled worker, spouse, and one or more children	$1,506	$1,571	$65
All disabled workers	$902	$939	$37

You can see that even a widowed mother with two children, the category with the highest increase, only received $82 more in her monthly check. Food and medical costs alone probably ate up most of that increase.

If you think that this was an unusually low year because inflation rates were so low, take a look at what the COLAs have been since the automatic increases became permanent in 1975. Here is a table from Social Security:

Automatic Cost of Living Adjustments

Year	COLA
1975	8.0%
1976	6.4%
1977	5.9%
1978	6.5%
1979	9.9%
1980	14.3%
1981	11.2%
1982	7.4%
1983	3.5%
1984	3.5%
1985	3.1%
1986	1.3%
1987	4.2%

Year	COLA
1988	4.0%
1989	4.7%
1990	5.4%
1991	3.7%
1992	3.0%
1993	2.6%
1994	2.8%
1995	2.6%
1996	2.9%
1997	2.1%
1998	1.3%
1999[1]	2.5%
2000	3.5%
2001	2.6%
2002	1.4%
2003	2.1%
2004	2.7%
2005	4.1%

1 The COLA for December 1999 was originally determined as 2.4 percent based on CPIs published by the Bureau of Labor Statistics. Pursuant to Public Law 106-554, however, this COLA is effectively now 2.5 percent.

As you can see, there are more adjustments under 5 percent than over 5 percent. If you remember your financial history, the inflation rates were very high in 1980 and 1981 when the COLAs were over 10 percent.

COLAs will not help keep your head above water if you are already drowning in bills you can barely pay and you have to use a large share of the COLA just to pay for the increase in Medicare premiums.

Social Graces

You might want to consider taking out an insurance policy (such as Medigap or long-term care insurance) to minimize the money surprises. We'll talk more about these policies in Chapters 21 and 22.

Stretching Your Bucks

The best thing you can do before retirement is get control of your money. Be sure you know how much money you are spending and how you are spending it. If you already know that, you are way ahead of the game, but I'll give you some steps you can take if you are like some Americans and don't have a good idea of where the money goes.

Track and Rate Your Expenses

Your first step is to get a good handle on where the money goes. Getting a grip on that can be a tedious task, but it's one worth taking the time to do. For the next month, keep track of every penny you spend. Total your spending and see whether this is more than you expected, less than you expected, or about the same. Next, take a look at your debt situation. Do you owe a lot on credit cards but are only able to make the minimum payment? If so, I'm sure you've figured out by now that you will never pay off the debt that way. If you don't pay off that debt before retirement, how will you pay it on a fixed income that will likely be even less than you are now earning? Here are a few steps you can take now to start getting things under control.

> **Senior Moments**
>
> According to a survey released by Champion Mortgage in 2001, only about three out of four (77 percent) Americans know off the top of their head how much they budget each month for household expenses and how much they owe on their credit cards. A slightly smaller number (72 percent) knows how much they owe on all of their personal debts.

When the month is over, look at your spending and rate it. Give it a 1 if it was crucial spending you could not live without, such as food or housing. Give it a 5 if you now think the spending was frivolous and that you could have done without it. Rate the others between 1 and 5 depending on how close they are to necessary versus unnecessary spending.

Add up all your 1s, 2s, 3s, 4s, and 5s. You may be surprised how many 5s you have. Just think how much money might have been available if you hadn't used it on the 4s and 5s. It's time to take action, cut at least the 5s out, and use that money to pay down your debt faster.

One successful strategy is to put the extra money you save toward the debt with the highest interest and pay minimum payments on all other debt. When the highest interest debt is paid, you then move on to the next highest debt, increasing the amount on that second debt payment by the total paid monthly on the debt you just paid off plus the minimum you were paying on the current debt. Using this strategy, you'll be amazed at how it snowballs into debt payoff and freedom from charge cards. For this to work, though, you need to limit your new charges.

Learn to Live Frugally ... Before You Need To

I know it is hard. You may want to get some help to learn how to live frugally. There are many books available on the subject. A good way to test out which strategy works best with your lifestyle is to go to the library and borrow a few books about living frugally. Find one that matches your style, buy it for your home library, and follow its suggestions. *The Pocket Idiot's Guide to Living on a Budget* (Alpha Books, 2005) and *The Budget Kit: The Common Sense Money Management Workbook* (Kaplan Publishing, 2004) are two good books you might want to check out.

Find out which money-saving techniques work best for you and keep trying to improve your money-saving skills. Get creative with new ways to save money.

Let's look at your food budget, for example. How often do you use prepared foods or go out to eat? Both are more expensive alternatives to preparing things from scratch at home.

You may also be able to save money on your energy costs. Most power companies offer a free energy audit and will show you ways to cut costs. If you plan to live in your home during retirement, these savings can be a big help once you are on a fixed income.

Be creative in your attempts to save money. For instance, consider bartering. You may have a skill that others can use. Rather than paying for work you are not skilled at doing, see if you can trade with others who have different skills. Both people benefit by not having to use cash.

Social Graces

You may want to seek third-party assistance with your debt situation. One of the highly respected nonprofit groups is the National Foundation for Credit Counseling. You can find the organization online at www.nfcc.org. You can find an accredited local credit counseling service online at www.debtadvice.org/ContactUs/contactus.html.

There's no question that it's hard to change habits. Sometimes the best way to do it is to pick a friend with the same goal. You can support each other as you try to make these hard life choices and change your living style.

Starting to live frugally before you get to retirement will help you even more when you find yourself on a fixed income. You'll already have done the hardest work. Adjusting to retirement is much easier if you're not also struggling to control your budget.

Seeking Community Support

Chapter 14 discussed the government programs that are available to folks with limited income and low assets, such as Supplemental Security Income (SSI). Many older people are not that poor but still need help making it through each day. Most cannot afford to have 24-hour assistance in the home. Many communities today offer adult day services to help the elderly and give them a place to socialize and be active.

These adult day services are run by community-based organizations that help both active and impaired seniors by developing individual plans of care. How much the senior pays depends on the mix of health-care-related activities they take part in.

These programs provide health, social, and other related support services in a protective setting during the day, but they are not 24-hour care facilities. Most operate during normal business hours five days a week, but some have services available in the evenings and on weekends. Some of these programs cater primarily to the impaired, but others offer social, educational, and craft activities as well.

A survey conducted by the National Adult Day Services Association (NADSA) found that the average age of participants was 72. Two-thirds of all participants were women. Of these women, one quarter lived alone and three quarters lived with a spouse, adult child, or other family and friends. About half of the participants had some cognitive impairment, and one-third needed nursing services at least once a week. More than 59 percent needed help with two or more activities of daily living, including eating, bathing, dressing, and transferring. Forty-one percent required assistance with three or more of these activities.

Social Graces

There are more than 4,000 adult day centers in the United States. You can find the ones close to you at the National Adult Day Services Association online at www.nadsa.org.

If you don't have computer access, you can contact them by phone or by mail:

National Adult Day Services Association
2519 Connecticut Ave., NW
Washington, DC 20008
Phone: 1-800-558-5301

Services provided usually include transportation, social services, meals, nursing care, personal care, counseling, therapeutic activities, and rehabilitation therapies. Regulations for these centers differ by state and by funding source. Their costs vary greatly. They can be as low as several dollars a day or as high as $185, according to the NADSA.

You may be wondering how to pick a center. NADSA has set out these guidelines for a high-quality adult day center:

- Conducts an assessment of individuals before admission to determine their range of abilities and needs

- Provides an active day program that meets the social, recreational, and rehabilitative needs of the impaired adult

- Develops an individualized treatment plan for participants and regularly monitors their progress

- Provides referrals to other needed services in the community

- Has clear criteria for service and guidelines for termination of service based on the functional status of the person

- Provides a full range of in-house services, which may include personal care, transportation, meals, health screening and monitoring, educational programs, counseling, and rehabilitative services

- Provides a safe, secure environment

- Utilizes qualified and well-trained staff and volunteers

- Adheres to or exceeds existing state and national standards and guidelines

Other types of community services may be available to you locally. Many times, they are run by a church or other religious institution.

The social services office of your local or state government will probably be aware of alternatives if you don't know where to start locally. You can also ask at these offices about resources for finding someone to share your home.

> **Senior Moments**
>
> If you want to see what local governments are doing, stop by the Senior Link Age Line at www.tcaging.org for an example of an excellent program in the Twin Cities metropolitan area and greater Minnesota.

Sharing Your Living Space

Another way seniors can help make ends meet is by sharing their homes. This not only helps ease the economic difficulties of living on a fixed income, it also gives single seniors much-needed companionship.

As we've already discussed, more women than men are left living alone. Many religious organizations have matching programs to help people find housemates. Sometimes these housemates are also elderly people, but other times they are younger folks who are going to school or starting out in their career. They not only can help meet expenses, they can also help with some of the tasks of taking care of a home.

There are things you can start doing right away to make your retirement future much brighter. Getting control of your budget today will not only help you save more for retirement, but make it easier for you to live comfortably when you begin living on a fixed income.

The Least You Need to Know

- ◆ Living on a fixed income offers a new set of challenges for making ends meet.

- ◆ Medical expenses can really throw a budget out of whack when you are on a fixed income. Be sure you understand what those costs are.

- ◆ Adult day centers can help you continue to live independently or with family and friends. Services offered help seniors that need assistance with activities of daily living.

- ◆ Learning to live frugally before you retire will make the transition much easier when it comes time to live on a fixed income.

Chapter 16

Working Again

In This Chapter

◆ Rethinking work

◆ Looking at how working affects your benefits

◆ Calculating your income

◆ Going back to work again

We're living longer, sometimes 30 years into retirement. That's a long time to spend taking adult-learning classes, playing golf, or pursuing other interests. More and more people are going back to work after retirement, even while they are collecting Social Security benefits. They return to work for many reasons: some people need the money, some are bored, and some want to start a new business.

There appears to be a new way of looking at work after retirement—a more positive view of continuing to work. And with the passage of the Senior Citizens Freedom to Work Act, there are no longer penalties for working once you reach full retirement age. When he signed this act in 2000, President Bill Clinton said, "Today, one in four Americans between 65 and 69 has at least a part-time job. Eighty percent of the baby boomers say they intend to keep working past age 65."

In this chapter, we'll look at the rules for working after retirement and how they may affect your Social Security benefits. (This chapter only deals with the rules related to working again as a retiree. If you are a disabled worker on Social Security disability, the rules are in Chapter 13. If you are on Supplemental Security Income, read the rules about working in Chapter 14.)

I Don't Want to Quit

Because people are living a lot longer than they used to, there is more of a risk that they will outlive their savings if they aren't careful. At the same time, as the baby boomer population leaves the workforce, companies may be faced with a brain drain. Many older workers have skills and knowledge that cannot be easily replaced.

Insecurities

Seniors over the official retirement age (which will range from 65 to 67 depending on when you were born) sometimes are discouraged from working, because staying too long on the job could result in possible lost retirement benefits. Many companies encourage early retirement as a way to reduce their workforce. As we continue to hear of major corporations cutting their workforce (Ford and GM talk about cutting tens of thousands of workers over the next six years), this is just another reason for us all to be sure we are saving enough for retirement.

Companies are coming up with new "phased" retirement programs that let workers retire over a number years, usually working part-time during a designated period or working as a consultant. Both the worker and the company benefit from such programs. The workers don't face the drastic life change of going abruptly from being a full-time worker to a full-fledged retiree, and companies benefit from a smoother transition of work responsibilities to other staff members.

As part of this "phased" retirement, new benefit programs are being designed for workers who decide to stick around a bit longer. In the work environment, some companies are allowing workers to continue to build their retirement nest egg, even if they stay only part-time and begin drawing benefits.

Senior Moments

The AARP found that "Americans generally are enjoying longer and healthier lives than previously, which allows them to retire gradually, often using part-time work or stints of self-employment on their way out of the labor force. Surveys indicate that even more Americans would like to do so. If employers would be willing to structure compensation and job characteristics to meet the needs of these potential employees, society could tap a growing pool of older, experienced, and willing workers for years to come."

Social Security laws were originally written to penalize folks who went back to work. The *Retirement Earnings Test* (*RET*), a means of reducing benefits if a retiree started working, was part of the law when the Social Security Act was originally passed in 1935. In April 2000, Congress made a dramatic change to these rules. Although it kept the RET for workers who retired before their normal retirement age (NRA), it removed all penalties for working once people reached NRA.

Why was this so important? In the most recent data available before the passage of the bill, 960,000 beneficiaries were impacted by the RET. Approximately 806,000 of those impacted by the RET were 65 or older, and they lost a total of $4.1 billion in benefits because of the RET rules.

def•i•ni•tion

The **Retirement Earnings Test** was the method used administratively to manage the principle that "one must be retired in order to collect retirement benefits from Social Security's old-age insurance program." That statement was in the original law. The RET took many forms over the years, but its primary purpose was to reduce benefits if a retiree started working again.

As it became more popular for people to work after full retirement age, more and more people faced a loss of benefits. Today, Congress believes that these benefits are earned by years of work and should not be withheld from people who choose to go back to work—for whatever reason—once they reach their normal retirement age. (See Chapter 4 for a table showing when you will reach your normal retirement age.)

Now let's take a look at how the RET works for people who return to work and are collecting their Social Security retirement benefits before their normal retirement age.

Scouting the Rules

Under the new law, you don't have to worry about any earnings rules as long as you've reached your NRA. If you retire early, though, you could lose some benefits until you reach your NRA.

If you are subject to the RET, you are allowed to earn up to a certain amount each year that is exempt from the earnings rule. The exempt amount varies annually and is based on the national average wage index.

Two levels of exemptions for earnings are considered:

◆ **A lower earnings threshold for people between age 62 and their NRA.** The Social Security Administration withholds $1 of benefits for every $2 of earnings in excess of the lower threshold for younger retirees.

◆ **A higher earnings threshold for people in the year they will reach their NRA.** In the year of attaining their NRA, retirees are allowed a higher threshold of earnings and only $1 of every $3 will be withheld.

The higher threshold of exempt earnings for 2006 between the age of 62 and when they reach their NRA is $33,240. The lower threshold is $12,480, which is adjusted by a formula based on the national wage index each year.

Using the Formulas

So, what does this actually mean for the money that makes it into your pocket? Social Security has prepared a useful chart to give you a ballpark estimate of how different earnings levels can affect benefits:

For People Under Age 64

If Your Monthly Social Security Benefit Is	And You Earn	You Will Receive Yearly Benefits Of
$500	$12,480 or less	$6,000 (no adjustment)
$500	$15,000	$4,740
$700	$12,480 or less	$8,400 (no adjustment)
$700	$15,000	$7,140
$700	$20,000	$4,640

If Your Monthly Social Security Benefit Is	And You Earn	You Will Receive Yearly Benefits Of
$900	$12,480 or less	$10,800 (no adjustment)
$900	$15,000	$0,540
$900	$20,000	$7,040

Let's take one of these examples and show you how to apply the formula for an early retiree, age 63, who earns $20,000.

Social Security benefit   = $700/month ($8,400/year)

Earnings up to $12,480   = No adjustment

Remaining $7,520 ($20,000 – $12,480) reduces benefit by $1 for every $2 of earnings = $3,760 withheld

Amount paid to beneficiary   = $4,640 ($8,400 – $3,760)

Now we'll take a look at what happens to an early retiree in the year he reaches normal retirement age. This time, we'll look at a 64-year-old retiree who reaches his NRA (age 65 in this case) in August of the year. He earned $60,000 throughout the year (or $5,000 per month). The earnings from August to December are not subject to the RET. His Social Security benefit is $900/month. Here's how his earnings would be figured.

Earnings Subject to RET

January through July (7 months)   = $35,000

Earnings Exempt in 2006   = $33,240

Remaining $1,760 reduces benefit by $1 for every $3 earned   = $587

Benefits due January through July   = $6,300

Benefits withheld   = $587

Benefits paid January through July   = $5,713

August through December   = $4,500

Total benefits in NRA year   = $10,213

This early retiree would earn $60,000 plus get $10,213 in Social Security benefits for the year. His benefits would be reduced by $587 dollars.

Once you've reached your full retirement age, your benefits will no longer by subject to RET. You can earn as much as you want and there will be not reduction in your Social Security benefits.

Insecurities _____

Decisions you make at retirement can impact your life for 20 to 30 years or more, depending on how long you live in retirement. Don't make the decisions lightly or on the spur of the moment. Be sure to consider all the implications. Consider consulting with a professional financial planner if you are not sure of the consequences of the choices you are making.

What Counts as Income?

Not all the money that comes into a retiree's home counts as income. Nonwork income never counts. This includes government or military benefits, investment earnings, interest, pensions, annuities, and capital gains. Only wages earned by working for someone else or in self-employment count toward Social Security's earnings limits for retirees. If you are self-employed, the gross earnings are not considered. Only the net earnings are used in the RET calculations.

Special Rules for the Self-Employed

Self-employed people do face somewhat different rules in the year they retire. Money earned before retirement but paid after retirement will not count in the retirement year. For example, let's say you plan to retire in 2002. In 2001, you worked on a project during the months of October and November, but you won't get paid for that project until February of 2002. You will not have to count that income when calculating earnings for RET in 2001.

Another retirement earnings test for self-employed folks is whether they performed substantial services in their businesses. Business owners have found ways to hide their income when self-employed. One way Social Security tests self-employed retirees is to measure the amount of time a person spends on his or her business. The SSA considers working 45 hours in a month as substantially employed, which can reduce benefits. If you work fewer than 15 hours a month, you are considered fully retired. Between 15 hours and 45 hours per month your occupation and size of your business determine whether your work is substantial or not, according to Social Security standards.

If you plan to work for yourself at least part-time in retirement and want to collect Social Security before your normal retirement age, you could end up with a loss of benefits. To be sure you understand the impact your work could have on your benefits, set up an appointment with a Social Security claims representative.

If you are thinking about starting a business in retirement and are planning to retire early, you may want to sit down with a Social Security representative and figure out whether your business or the work you plan to do will be considered substantial. The loss of part of your monthly benefits because of RET may require you to alter your early-retirement plans.

> **Senior Moments**
>
> Earnings you get from an employer are considered income when they are earned. They are not based on when the money is actually paid to you. It is exactly opposite for earnings from self-employment; income counts when you actually receive it and not when you earn it.

Special Rules for the Year You Retire

In the first year of retirement, many people often exceed the earnings limit. Because of this, special rules apply to the year in which a person retires.

Instead of an annual earnings test, people in their first year of retirement are allowed to use a special monthly earnings test. In 2005, people were allowed to earn $1,000 a month under the special first-year rules. The special monthly earnings test figure for 2006 is $1,040. Let's look back at the situation of the retiree earning $60,000 a year. Instead of being in the middle of his early retirement, let's say he retired in 2005 at age 63 on July 31. Rather than earning an equal amount of $5,000 per month, we'll say he earned $55,000 through July and then worked part-time at $1,000 per month through the end of the year, earning another $5,000.

Even though his yearly earnings were well over the 2005 limit of $12,000 allowed at age 63, his monthly earnings of $1,000 meets the monthly test allowed in the first year. In this case, he would be entitled to his full retirement benefit of $900 for the months of August through December. After he gets through his first full year of retirement and until he reaches his normal retirement age, the yearly RET limits on earnings will affect him.

Reporting Earnings

You may be wondering how the SSA sets benefits based on earnings a year in advance. The benefit payments are based on earnings estimates that you give to the SSA when you apply or that you provide at the beginning of a year. If during the year you discover that your earnings will be different from your estimate, you should call the SSA and revise your estimate.

If your benefits are reduced because of the RET, any benefits received by family members will also be affected by your earnings. The offset for earnings will affect any family members collecting on your record. If you and your spouse are collecting benefits on your individual work records, one of you can go back to work without affecting the other one's benefits.

Social Graces

If you end up earning less than you estimated, your monthly benefit could be too low. You certainly want to be sure you are getting all that you deserve. If you end up getting too much because your earnings were higher than expected, you could end up having to repay some money.

Benefits of Going Back to Work

All is not lost if you do go back to work, especially if you had years of low or no earnings. Each year that you work—even while collecting benefits—the earnings are added to your work record.

Each year, after earnings reports are in, Social Security recomputes each person's earnings record. If a person is already collecting Social Security, that recomputation could result in a benefit increase.

In fact, according to an AARP 1999 Ageline Database study, 1.66 million primary beneficiaries aged 65 and older (about 7 percent of all retired workers) got an increase in their monthly benefit during 1995 (which was the year on which the study was based). The total increase in benefits in January 1996 because of these recomputations was $25 million, which averaged $15 per recomputation that month.

So, how does all this work? Let's take a look at one of the more common scenarios. A woman began working out of school and earned $10,000 per year. (Keep in mind that we're looking at someone who retired in 2005.) She started working at age 20 and retired at age 62, so we're assuming she started working in 1963. She got married and decided to have a family two years later, in 1965. At age 45 (1988), after raising her family, she decided to go back to work. She started collecting early Social Security retirement benefits at age 62, but she plans to continue to work for three more years. In this scenario, she has 22 years of paid work and 20 years in which she earned $0. Remember that the SSA averages the 35 highest years of earnings. So 13 of the years used in this calculation are $0. If she works even part-time after the age of 62, that part-time salary will raise her average.

At the end of each year that she works, the SSA will automatically recompute her life-time earnings and adjust her benefits accordingly. So even if she loses some of her monthly benefits because of the RET while she works during the three years before her NRA, she may end up increasing her benefit for many more years down the road once she reaches full retirement age.

Each year, more people are deciding to work during retirement. Some people go back to work because they need the income, others to pursue a passion they didn't have time for while working full time. No matter what you're reason for returning to work—especially if you retire early—be sure you understand how it may impact your Social Security benefits.

The Least You Need to Know

◆ You can go back to work without any loss of benefits as long as you have reached your normal retirement age.

◆ If you retire early and start collecting benefits, you will be subject to the Retire-ment Earnings Test. If you exceed the earnings allowed, your benefits will be reduced.

◆ There are special earnings rules for people in the first year of their retirement that allow them to earn more money.

◆ If you earn money once you start collecting Social Security benefits, those addi-tional earnings will be added to your work record and could result in an increase in your monthly benefit amount, depending on your work history.

Chapter 17

Using Your Assets

In This Chapter

- Taking account of what you have
- Organizing your finances
- Withdrawing your retirement savings
- Using your house as a source of income

When you retire, the SSA will tell you exactly how much you can expect to receive in monthly benefits for the rest of your life. I'm sure you've figured out by now that those payments probably will not be enough for you to live on. Hopefully, you have a lot more to draw upon so that you will be able to maintain the lifestyle you've become accustomed to living. The average wage earner can expect about 40 percent of his or her past earnings in monthly payments from Social Security, but will need at least 70 percent of past earnings to maintain his or her current lifestyle, according to financial planners. Where will you get that additional 30 percent? That's where saving for retirement becomes crucial.

In this chapter, we'll take a look at what you have and how you may be able to use those assets to improve your financial prospects for retirement.

Identifying Assets

The first thing you need to do is figure out how much you have right now. Once we've put that together, we'll take a look at how much of a gap you have to meet your retirement goals.

Let's start by filling out a worksheet of your current assets:

Asset	Value
Employer retirement plans (401[k], 403[b], SEP-IRA, SIMPLE-IRA, Keogh, profit sharing, pension lump sum, other)	_____
Other employer plans (stock options, stock purchase, other savings plans)	_____
Personal retirement plans (traditional IRA, Roth IRA, nondeductible IRA)	_____
Nonretirement market investments (mutual funds, stocks, bonds, treasury bills, other)	_____
Cash accounts (checking, savings, CDs, money market, other)	_____
Real estate (home, vacation property, rental property)	_____
Insurance (life insurance cash value, annuity surrender value, other)	_____
Other assets (value of business, precious metals, antiques and collectibles, other)	_____
Future assets (expected inheritance, trust fund, other)	_____
Total	_____

If you are one of the lucky few who do have a company pension, be sure to add your monthly benefit to the amount of cash you have to spend each month as you calculate your budget. Government retirees are more likely to have monthly pension benefits than retirees for private companies.

This should give you a good idea of what you may have to work with when you start your retirement. Do you think it will be enough? If you are like the majority of the population, the answer is no.

Now that you've taken the time to pull together your asset information, the next step is to look at how you can integrate it and make it work for you. One of the most important things to do is look more closely at your stock, bond, and cash investments. Be sure you have a good mix that matches your investment needs, including assets offering growth, safety, and income.

Senior Moments
Most people will be managing their own assets in retirement or seeking the help of a financial planner. Only about 10 percent of the population will have access to company pensions that will pay them a set amount through their retirement years.

Integrating Assets

As you get closer to retirement, you probably want to start shifting some of your investments, either to safer assets that have little chance of losing principal or to income-producing assets that can provide the cash you will need. You don't want to shift all your assets into these categories, though, because you probably will still need some growth; otherwise, you could outlive your assets. A good strategy is to categorize your holdings. If you haven't already done it, you'll need to pull out the statements from all your investments so you can list each asset by type. Here is a sample worksheet you can use to help you start the integration process:

Investment	Account	Amount	% of Portfolio	Purpose
XYZ mutual fund	IRA/wife	$5,000	25%	Growth
ABC stock	401(k)/husband	$5,000	25%	Growth
Government bonds	IRA/husband	$5,000	25%	Income
Cash savings	Bank (FDIC insured)/joint	$5,000	25%	Safety
Total		**$20,000**	**100%**	

Obviously, this is a very simple example, but it helps give you an idea of how to go about examining your assets. In this example, 50 percent of the portfolio is invested for growth, 25 percent for income, and 25 percent for safety. Most financial planners recommend that the growth portion of your portfolio should be no more than 20 to 25 percent once you reach retirement.

Social Graces

The American Savings Education Council offers you a way to figure out whether you have enough saved for retirement and, if not, how much more you will need: www.choosetosave.org/ballpark.

You can take some risks with your money, but you never want to be in a position in which you are forced to sell something at a loss because you need the money. By carefully balancing your assets among mutual funds, stocks, bonds, and cash, your goal should be to have some money that you can access in an emergency without being forced to sell something you are not ready to sell. How much you should keep in each type of asset depends on your monthly cash needs.

It's best to keep anything you know you will need in the next 12 to 24 months in an asset that you can quickly convert to cash or in a cash account without risking principal. It is best not to hold money you are sure you will need in five years or less in an asset as volatile as stocks.

If all this seems like gibberish to you, it's time to start working on your investment education or to make an appointment with a financial planner you can trust. You don't want to be forced to determine how to balance your assets when you don't understand what balance works best for you.

Insecurities

As we've seen in the early part of this decade, the stock market can take a downturn for a very long time, wreaking havoc on any long-term portfolio. You surely don't want funds you need on a short- or medium-term basis tied up in an asset that just lost 20 percent or more.

Some books that might help you understand the ins and outs of investing include *The Complete Idiot's Guide to Managing Your Money, Fourth Edition*, by Robert K. Heady and Christy Heady, and *Making the Most of Your Money*, by Jane Bryant Quinn. For retirement planning, my book, *Streetwise Retirement Planning (Adams Media Corporation, 2003)*, will help you get on the right retirement path.

You can mix a portfolio in many ways. This is called *asset allocation*. Mutual funds mix their assets among stocks, bonds, and cash, depending on the fund's stated goals. The way you mix your assets will provide different types of growth strategies. Here are five common asset mixes:

def•i•ni•tion

Asset allocation is the method you use to proportionally allocate your assets among cash, bonds, or stocks within an investment portfolio. Cash deposited in an insured bank account is the safest place to put your money, but there is little growth potential. Stocks offer the greatest growth potential, but also have the highest risks of losing money. Bonds fall in between cash and stocks for both safety and risk.

♦ **Conservative portfolio.** 25 percent stocks, 40 percent bonds, 35 percent cash

♦ **Conservative growth portfolio.** 40 percent stocks, 40 percent bonds, 20 percent cash

♦ **Balanced portfolio.** 50 percent stocks, 35 percent bonds, 15 percent cash

♦ **Moderate aggressive growth portfolio.** 60 percent stocks, 35 percent bonds, 5 percent cash

♦ **Aggressive growth portfolio.** 75 percent stocks, 25 percent bonds, 0 percent cash

The conservative portfolio offers the greatest degree of safety but the least chance for growth. The aggressive growth portfolio offers the greatest opportunity for growth but the least amount of safety.

Just to give you an idea of what to expect, historically over a 20-year period, stocks have averaged returns of 10 to 12 percent, bonds have averaged returns of 5 to 6 percent, and cash accounts have averaged returns of 2 to 3 percent. As the old saying goes, the greater the return you want, the greater the risk you must take.

Using Your Investments

Now for the scary part. Once you've got everything neatly stocked away in its little compartment, you've got to figure out how you want to start using the assets. There are a lot of things to consider.

A big factor in deciding how to spend your assets once you reach retirement is the tax implications of your decisions. Any money you move around outside of a sheltered retirement fund can immediately cost you tax-wise. When you sell an asset such as a stock, any profit you make will result in a capital gains hit. If you sell stock inside the walls of a sheltered retirement plan, such as an IRA, there will be no immediate tax hit.

You can't avoid the taxman forever, though. Unless you are holding your funds in a tax-free investment such as the Roth IRA, you will take a hit when you start withdrawing funds from an IRA. In the next chapter, we discuss tax issues in greater detail.

The next decision you'll need to make is how much you can take out each year during retirement and what type of funds you should use first. According to financial planners, a good rule of thumb is to plan to withdraw 4 percent of your funds per year if you don't want to outlive your money. You can withdraw funds more quickly if you expect a short retirement, but you might want to draw them down more slowly if your family has a history of living longer than average.

Social Graces

MSN Money has three useful calculators to help you plan how to use your retirement savings—the life expectancy calculator, the retirement expense calculator, and the retirement income calculator. You can find them at moneycentral.msn.com/investor/calcs/n_retireq/main.asp.

Another factor in determining how much money to withdraw each year is how much risk you take with your portfolio. A riskier portfolio that grows more quickly may allow you to take a bit more money out each year. By taking that risk, however, if the market tumbles, you could end up with less than you need to make it through retirement.

In addition to how much you might want to take out, you also have to be concerned with how much the IRS will let you take out if your funds are in an IRA or other tax-sheltered retirement plan. For most of these types of retirement plans, you can start taking money out at the age of 59½ without having to worry about tax penalties, and you must start taking them out by age 70½.

Believe it or not, you also risk tax penalties by taking your money out too slowly. The IRS has minimum withdrawal rules for retirement accounts such as IRAs and 401(k)s. Here's a chart from the IRS that gives you the information you need to figure out how much you must take out each year after you reach age 70. I show you how to figure it out below.

Age	Life Expectancy Divisor	Age	Life Expectancy Divisor
70	27.4	85	14.8
71	26.5	86	14.1
72	25.6	87	13.4

Age	Life Expectancy Divisor	Age	Life Expectancy Divisor
73	24.7	88	12.7
74	23.8	89	12.0
75	22.9	90	11.4
76	22.0	91	10.8
77	21.2	92	10.2
78	20.3	93	9.6
79	19.5	94	9.1
80	18.7	95	8.6
81	17.9	96	8.1
82	17.1	97	7.6
83	16.3	98	7.1
84	15.5	99	6.7

Senior Moments

The primary exception to the withdrawal rules is the Roth IRA. There are no withdrawal requirements for the Roth IRA once you reach retirement. The law under which the Roth IRA was established allows you to determine when you want to withdraw the money in retirement. The only restriction is that the money must be in the Roth account for at least five years.

This chart might look a bit overwhelming, but calculating the minimum amount you must withdraw isn't difficult. The formula is as follows:

$$\frac{\text{Total assets in retirement account}}{\text{Life expectancy divisor}} = \text{Required minimum distribution}$$

Let's practice with some make-believe numbers. Gary and Mary have $100,000 in their IRA retirement plans. They just turned 71 and want to know how much they must take out of their retirement plans this year to avoid an IRS penalty. You can figure it out as follows:

$$\frac{\$100,000}{26.5} \quad = \quad \$3,773.58$$

Interestingly, in this example, it comes close to matching the dollar that financial planners recommend. Four percent of $100,000 is $4,000. If they had just turned 80, they would need to withdraw more. We'll again look at a $100,000 portfolio.

$$\frac{\$100,000}{18.7} \quad = \quad \$5,681.82$$

The penalty for not taking the right amount is stiff. You will have to pay a 50 percent excise tax on the amount that was not properly distributed in a year. If it was an error in calculation, you might be able to get this penalty waived by explaining the error and showing the IRS how you plan to fix it.

I'm not trying to make recommendations as to how you should use your retirement assets. That is definitely beyond the scope of this book. I'm just trying to give you an idea of the types of decisions you'll need to make when you retire. I want to be sure you understand how complicated these decisions can be and encourage you to learn more about managing your assets in retirement *before* you get there.

Tapping Your Home Equity

If you are like the majority of people, your home is probably one of your largest assets, and by the time you reach retirement age, the mortgage will be paid off or be very close to being paid off. You may want to tap into your home equity without having to move.

At retirement, you can do one of three things to turn your home into a source of retirement income:

1. Sell your home and move into something smaller, using the cash from the sale of your house to buy a smaller home and banking the leftover money for future use. You may also decide that you don't want the hassles of owning and rent instead, banking all the profits for future use.

2. Take an equity line or a new mortgage to free up the cash so you can use it to live on.

3. Use a reverse mortgage that will pay you a set amount per month.

I'll discuss each of these options briefly, but it's important to remember when taking out any type of loan that you need to be sure you understand the implications of the decision and how it might affect you—and your heirs—if you are not able to make payments on the loan.

Selling Your House and Moving

Some people decide to move to a warmer climate or a smaller home during retirement for reasons other than money. For these folks, it's an easy decision to sell the home and invest whatever money is left over after purchasing their new retirement home.

You may find that although you weren't intending to move, cutting down on your living costs might be a good idea. If you live in a large home with high utility bills, it might make sense to move to something smaller so you can live on less. A nice bonus would be the extra cash you'll free up by selling the home and buying something less expensive.

Home Equity Line of Credit or a New Mortgage

Taking an equity line or a new mortgage may be an option, but remember that either choice will leave you with monthly payments that will have to be made on a fixed income. It might help you through a short-term crunch, but it could result in greater financial difficulties later. If you can't pay your monthly payment, you could face losing your home.

The Reverse Mortgage Option

The reverse mortgage is a newfangled option being promoted heavily to seniors. In these deals, rather than making a monthly payment to the bank, the bank makes a monthly payment to you. Sound too good to be true? It can be.

Reverse mortgages are complicated. You could end up owing more to the bank than the house is worth, even though your liability is limited to the house's value. You won't have to pay the money back, but your heirs will lose all rights to the property. If this happens, when you die,

 Social Graces

The AARP has an excellent collection of articles about reverse mortgages at www.aarp.org/money/revmort.

the bank will foreclose on the house and sell it. You probably should not plan on a reverse mortgage as your first choice, but it may be a good option if you suffer severe financial difficulties in retirement.

The Least You Need to Know

◆ Be sure you know where your assets are and how they are invested.

◆ Integrate your assets wisely, carefully balancing your money to make sure you will have access to it when you need it without incurring a large loss of principal.

◆ Withdrawing your money in retirement can be tricky. Be sure you understand the withdrawal rules for each of your investments. Don't withdraw assets too quickly; otherwise, you could end up outliving your assets and being forced to live solely on Social Security.

◆ Your house could be one of your largest assets, but be careful how you decide to tap those funds. Don't put yourself in a position that could result in the loss of your home.

18

Minimizing the Tax Bite

In This Chapter

◆ Going by the tax rules

◆ Figuring out what's taxable

◆ Figuring out what's not taxable

◆ Earning too much

You won't have to answer to your boss after you retire, but you certainly don't get a break from the taxman. In fact, you could find that your tax returns become even more complicated after you retire!

Many people will have amassed an incredible mixture of income sources in addition to their Social Security benefits. You could have pensions, life insurance policies, annuities, tax-deferred savings, and taxable savings, just to name a few.

Most of that income will need to be reported, and if you have enough of it, your Social Security benefits may even become taxable. You can even earn *too* much and end up with higher taxes than before you retired.

You may find it very beneficial to work with a tax advisor as you get ready for retirement. An advisor can help you develop tax-wise strategies for drawing down your retirement assets to minimize the tax bite and be sure you don't outlive your savings. I'm not trying to be a tax advisor here, I just want to give you an overview of the tax rules and how they might affect your Social Security and other income in retirement.

Tax Rules in Retirement

Every year in retirement, you will have to determine whether your Social Security benefits are taxable. You can do this by comparing your base amount for your filing status to one-half of your Social Security benefits plus all your other income, including tax-exempt interest.

What is your base amount? It depends on how you are filing. By Internal Revenue Service (IRS) standards, your base amount is as follows:

- ◆ $25,000 if you are single, head of household, or qualifying widow(er)
- ◆ $25,000 if you are married filing separately and lived apart from your spouse for the current tax year
- ◆ $32,000 if you are married filing jointly
- ◆ $0 if you are married filing separately and lived with your spouse at any time during the current tax year

When you complete this comparison, if your total income is more than your base amount, your benefits could be taxable. If you file a joint return, you and your spouse must combine your incomes and your benefits when doing this comparison. Even if your spouse is not collecting benefits, you must add in your spouse's income when trying to determine whether your benefits are taxable.

If the only income you receive is from Social Security, your benefits are most likely not taxable. You may not even have to file a tax return. If you do have income in addition to your benefits, you may be stuck filing a return even if none of your benefits are taxable.

Putting Worksheets to Work

I'm sure you are familiar with IRS worksheets. Most of us have filled out hundreds of them for various reasons by the time we get to retirement. Let me assure you that you will still have plenty more to fill out in your retirement years.

Here's a sample of the IRS worksheet you will be filling out yearly to determine if your benefits are taxable:

Worksheet. You can use the following worksheet to figure the amount of income to compare with your base amount. This is a quick way to check whether some of your benefits may be taxable.

A. Write in the amount from box 5 of all your SSA-1099 and RRB-1099 forms. Include the full amount of any lump-sum benefit payments received in 2005, for 2005 and earlier years. (If you received more than one form, combine the amounts from box 5 and write in the total.)   A.

Note. If the amount on line A is zero or less, stop here; none of your benefits are taxable this year.

B. Enter one half of the amount on line A.   B.

C. Add your taxable pensions, wages, interest, dividends, and other taxable income and write in the total.   C.

D. Write in any tax-exempt interest (such as interest on municipal bonds) plus any exclusions from income (shown in the list under Exclusions, earlier).   D.

E. Add lines B, C, and D and write in the total.   E.

---

*Note. Compare the amount on line E to your **base amount** for your filing status. If the amount on line E equals or is less than the **base amount** for your filing status, none of your benefits is taxable this year. If the amount on line E is more than your **base amount**, some of your benefits may be taxable.*

def•i•ni•tion

SSA-1099 is the form every Social Security beneficiary receives each year. If you are getting benefits on more than one Social Security record, you may get more than one form. The form will include all the benefits you received from the Social Security Administration and adjustments to those benefits. Railroad retirees get an **RRB-1099** instead.

Overearning

You can earn too much in retirement and end up with higher taxation on your Social Security benefits. Remember that the amount of your benefits that is taxable depends on the amount of your benefits plus other income. In most cases, the higher that total is, the greater your tax bill will be.

For most people, the taxable part of their benefits will be no greater than 50 percent, but it can be as high as 85 percent. If the total of one half of your benefits plus all your other income is more than $34,000 if you are single (or $44,000 if you are married and filing jointly), more than 50 percent of your benefits will be taxable. The amount of your benefits that is taxable depends on how much you exceed those maximums but will not be higher than 85 percent.

Adding Children's Benefits to the Mix

This entire process can get even more complicated if you and your child are getting benefits. If your child's check is made out in your name, you only use 50 percent of the benefits to determine whether any benefits are taxable to you. One half of the benefits that belong to your child will need to be added to any other income your child receives. You'll have to do a worksheet for your child to see if any of his or her benefits are taxable.

Social Graces

You can find full details about taxation of Social Security benefits in IRS Publication 915, "Social Security and Equivalent Railroad Retirement Benefits," available online at www.irs.gov/pub/irs-pdf/p915.pdf. You can also order copies by calling 1-800-829-3676.

If for some reason you have to repay benefits, you will be able to deduct your repayment amount from the benefits received, even if the repayment is for a prior year's benefits. Any repayments you make will be reported on your SSA-1099.

Withholding Taxes from Your Benefits

You may prefer not to be stuck with an unexpected tax bill at tax time. If you think you will owe taxes on your benefits, you can request that federal income taxes be withheld from your Social Security benefits by filing Form W-4V with the SSA. You can elect to withhold 7 percent, 10 percent, 15 percent, or 25 percent, depending on your expected tax obligations.

If your benefits are taxable, you will have to file either Form 1040 or Form 1040A. You will not be able to use the simpler Form 1040EZ. If none of your benefits is taxable, you do not report any of them on your tax return. In fact, you may not even have to file a return.

What Is Taxed?

Income that is taxed in retirement is not that different from the income you receive prior to reaching the retirement milestone. Taxable income can include compensation for services, interest, dividends, rents, royalties, income from partnerships, estate and trust income, gains from sales or exchanges of property, and business income of all kinds.

Any wages or other compensation you receive for services is treated as income in the same way as before you retired. You do not need to report any income amounts for supportive services or out-of-pocket expense reimbursements if you are involved in certain volunteer programs, including the Retired Senior Volunteer Program (RSVP), Foster Grandparent Program, Senior Companion Program, and Service Corps of Retired Executives (SCORE).

We'll take a brief look at the various types of income that are common primarily when people reach retirement. These include retirement plan distributions, purchased annuities, railroad benefits, and military benefits. I won't go into an extensive discussion of these benefits, but I will give an idea of what the typical tax impact might be.

Retirement Plan Distributions

For most people, some type of distribution from retirement savings will be part of their reported income. Few will have pensions because only about 10 percent of the population currently working for public or private companies is covered by traditional pensions today. People working for government entities are more likely to have traditional pension benefits. A majority of folks will have individual retirement arrangements (IRAs). A smaller percentage will have annuity income. We'll take a quick look at the tax implications of each.

Taxation of IRAs varies by the type of IRA, which for retirement can include a traditional tax-deductible IRA, a nondeductible IRA, a Roth IRA, a *SIMPLE IRA*, or a *SEP-IRA*. These IRA types have different tax implications when you start withdrawing the money.

Social Graces

For detailed information about the taxation of IRAs, read IRS Publication 590, "Individual Retirement Arrangements (IRAs) (Including Roth IRAs and Education IRAs)." You can find it online at www.irs.gov/pub/irs-pdf/p590.pdf. Publication 575, "Pension and Annuity Income," can be found at www.irs.gov/pub/irs-pdf/p575.pdf. You also can order copies by calling 1-800-829-1040.

You do not pay taxes on the money going into tax-deductible IRAs, SIMPLE IRAs, or SEP-IRAs, so everything coming out will be taxable in retirement. The money contributed to a nondeductible IRA is taxed when you put it in, so that money isn't taxed again at retirement, but any gains on that money are taxable.

def•i•ni•tion

SIMPLE IRAs and SEP-IRAs are retirement plans used by small businesses that do not want to create a more complicated 401(k) plan. IRAs are cheaper to set up and easier to administer. The IRAs are taken out in the employee's name and are portable if you change jobs. Self-employed folks will use one of these plans or another plan called the Keogh. For more information on small business plans, go to www.irs.gov/pub/irs-pdf/p560.pdf.

Roth IRA contributions are taxed before being put into the IRA, so there are no taxes when you take out that money. The Roth IRA has an even greater advantage, however, because even your gains are not taxed as long as the money was in the Roth for five years and you are at least 59½ years old.

Insecurities

If you do not take out the required minimum distribution from your qualified retirement plans, you will have to pay a 50-percent excise tax for that year on the amount that was not distributed. Sometimes you can avoid this penalty by explaining the error and showing the IRS how you plan to fix it.

In most cases before the age 59½, you will have to pay a 10-percent penalty if you withdraw the money from your retirement plan, unless the distribution qualifies as an exception. If you are thinking about taking out the money early, be sure to check with your tax advisor to find out the tax implications of your decision.

If you have a type of IRA that is taxable, the withdrawals will be taxed at your current tax rate in retirement. As I mentioned in Chapter 17, you will have to take a required minimum distribution each year for all but the Roth IRA once you reach age 70½.

If you are one of the lucky few who has a pension or an annuity from your employer, most likely you did not pay any of the cost of that benefit. So like most IRAs, you will have to pay taxes as you receive the money. If you did contribute to any part of your employer plan, you will be able to exclude part of the distribution based on the portion you contributed.

You may also receive your qualified retirement plan in a lump-sum distribution when you retire. In most cases, the wisest thing to do with a lump-sum distribution is to roll it over into another qualified retirement vehicle, such as an IRA, to avoid being hit with a huge tax bill all at once. There is also a 10-year tax option you can use on the ordinary income part of the distribution. You will pay a portion of the tax over a 10-year period. Check with a tax advisor to figure out what works best for your individual situation.

Tax on Early Distributions

As I previously mentioned, there is a 10-percent penalty if you withdraw money from a qualified retirement plan or a deferred annuity before you reach age 59½. And, as expected for the government, there are exceptions to this rule. The most costly is a 25-percent penalty for certain early distributions from a SIMPLE IRA made within the first two years of participation in the plan.

Some exceptions allow you to make withdrawals from a qualified retirement plan early without having to pay a penalty at all. These exceptions include …

♦ Leaving a job involuntarily after you reach age 55 (does not include IRA).

♦ To pay deductible medical expenses (expenses in excess of 7.5 percent of your adjusted gross income) even if you don't itemize your deductions.

♦ To pay medical insurance premiums if you are unemployed.

♦ To pay qualified higher education expenses.

♦ To buy your first home.

If you plan to withdraw funds early, be sure you understand what is permitted and what the tax bite will be before you take the funds out of your qualified retirement plan.

Purchased Annuities

You can also purchase an annuity directly from an issuer, such as an insurance company, bank, or mutual fund group. These are treated as *nonqualified retirement plans* and taxation is much more complex.

Most people purchase annuities to get a guaranteed income over a set number of years or for the rest of their life. There are different distribution options for annuities based on your lifespan or the lifespan of you and your spouse. After you have one, if you decide that you are not happy with the product, it can cost you to switch in both fees and taxes. Be certain if you choose to purchase an annuity that you understand all its provisions, its fees, and its tax implications.

def•i•ni•tion

A Qualified Retirement Plan meets the requirements of the Internal Revenue Code (IRC) and the Employee Retirement Income Security Act of 1974 (ERISA). By passing the qualification test, a plan qualifies for four important tax benefits:

1. Employers may deduct allowable contributions that were made on behalf of plan participants.
2. Plan participants may exclude contributions and all earnings from their taxable income until the year they are withdrawn.
3. Earnings on the funds held by the plan's trust are not taxed to that trust.
4. Participants and/or beneficiaries may further delay taxation on a plan's benefits by transferring those amounts into another tax-deferred vehicle, such as an Individual Retirement Arrangement (IRA).

If a plan does not meet the requirements of IRC and ERISA it is a **Nonqualified Retirement Plan** and does not have these tax benefits.

Railroad Retirement Benefits

A few times I mentioned that railroad retirees have a separate retirement program all to themselves. The program is similar to Social Security, but it falls under the Railroad Retirement Act.

Railroad retirees have two types of benefits. Tier 1 benefits equal the Social Security benefit that a railroad employee or beneficiary would have been paid under the Social Security system. Tier 2 is treated as the amount received from a qualified employer plan. Tier 2 benefits are taxable.

Military Retirement Pay

In addition to your qualified retirement plan, you may also be collecting military retirement pay if you served for a long enough time. The pay is based on age and length of service and is fully taxable. Some military and government pensions that are based on disability from active service in the armed forces are not taxable. Be sure to verify whether your benefits are taxable or not.

What Isn't Taxed

Believe it or not, some things aren't taxed. Most of them are things you likely would hope to avoid. I'll list them briefly here:

- Compensation for sickness or injury (such as workers' compensation) is not taxable.

- Benefits you collect from an accident or health-insurance policy are not taxable as long as you paid the premiums or the premiums paid by your employer were included in your gross income.

- Payments from long-term care insurance contracts generally are not taxable.

- Compensation for permanent loss or loss of the use of a part or function of your body is not taxable.

- Life insurance proceeds paid after the death of an insured person are not taxable unless the policy was turned over to you for a price.

- Veterans' benefits from the Department of Veterans Affairs are not included in gross income.

- Payments you receive from a state fund as a victim of a crime should not be included in your income, but you cannot deduct as medical expenses any expenses reimbursed by the fund.

Some government programs are designed to help the elderly cope on a fixed income. These programs include mortgage assistance, help with energy bills, and food benefits from the Nutrition Program for the Elderly. None of the benefits received under these programs is taxable.

I've just given you a brief overview of the tax issues you'll face once you start collecting Social Security and other distributions from your retirement plans. Filling out tax forms doesn't get easier in retirement. You may want to seek professional help at least the first few years of retirement to be sure you are doing things right and to find out about any state tax breaks available for seniors.

The Least You Need to Know

◆ Social Security benefits are taxable, but for most people, only 50 percent of the benefits are taxed.

◆ If you exceed maximum earning limits, you may face a higher tax bite on your Social Security benefits.

◆ Most distributions from your qualified retirement plans will be at least partially taxable in retirement. The key exception is the Roth IRA.

◆ It's important to know what types of income are taxed and what types are not taxed.

Part 5

Staying Healthy

Keeping healthy and active in retirement is a major goal for everyone. We all hope to be healthy enough to do many things once we finally retire. Seniors face more medical problems than most of the population, and it's important for you to know what kind of health coverage will be available once you reach that age and retire. Medicare is a big part of almost everyone's life once he or she reaches age 65. As the largest public health-care system in the United States, it's an incredible maze of bureaucracy.

In the following chapters, we sort through all its rules and then talk about other supplemental health plans you may want to consider. I also explore the complex rules of the new Medicare Prescription Drug Plan and help you to decide whether or not to sign up for the coverage.

Chapter **19**

Getting Medicare Coverage

In This Chapter

♦ Qualifying for Medicare

♦ Deciding whether to go on Medicare while still working

♦ Knowing your rights

♦ Recognizing fraud

Today, Medicare seems almost like a rite of passage when you turn 65, so you might be surprised to learn that medical care wasn't added to the federal retirement package until 1966. It's grown quickly, though. Medicare is run by the Centers for Medicare and Medicaid Services (CMS) under the Department of Health and Human Services and is the largest public health program in the United States. In 2004, more than 41 million people received their health care through Medicare. In 2004, Medicare expenses totaled more than $280 billion. Eighty-five percent of beneficiaries were retired folks over the age of 65. Other beneficiaries were people on disability.

Let's now take a look at how you start your Medicare benefits and what rights you have once you get them.

Medicare: Starting Coverage

Anyone who pays into Social Security also pays into Medicare. In fact, some folks who are not part of the Social Security system, such as state and local workers, may pay Medicare taxes. If you haven't paid into the system, you can buy into Medicare at age 65 (more on that later in this chapter).

Medicare is divided into four parts: Parts A, B, C, and D. Part A is hospital insurance, Part B is medical insurance, Part C is health maintenance organizations (HMOs) and other forms of managed care, and Part D is prescription drug coverage. In this chapter, we concentrate on Parts A, B, and C. Part D is discussed in Chapter 20.

There is no charge for Part A if you qualify for it. Medicare Part B is optional for people who qualify for Part A, but most people elect to take it. The monthly premium for Part B is $88.50 in 2006, and it is deducted directly from your Social Security benefits. We look more closely at what each part covers later in this chapter.

If You're 65 and Already Collecting Social Security ...

If you are collecting Social Security at the age of 65, Medicare Part A coverage is automatic, and you will get a Medicare card in the mail without having to do anything. If you are not yet collecting Social Security, there is an enrollment period during which you must apply for benefits. If you don't apply for benefits during your enrollment period, you risk a delay in your benefits and even an increase in their cost.

Your Medicare card will become a part of your daily wardrobe. You'll need to carry it every day because it is your passport to health care in retirement.

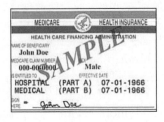

(Source: Medicare website www.medicare.gov)

If You're 65 and Not Collecting Social Security ...

If you're nearing 65 and aren't collecting Social Security yet, you should sign up for Medicare about three months before your sixty-fifth birthday. You can do the paperwork for Social Security and Medicare at the same time at your local Social Security office. Unlike Social Security, you have a limited time to apply for Medicare, or you could miss out on coverage.

Delaying an application for Medicare Part B can also cost you. If you are already getting Social Security, your Part B enrollment will be automatic. If you don't want Part B, you will have to cancel it.

For those of you not yet receiving Social Security, you can apply for Part B coverage at the same time you apply for Part A. If you don't, you will face a penalty of 10 percent of the Part B premium for each 12-month period you delay. The 10 percent penalty will be a permanent addition to the $88.50 premium. So, if you delay for two years at 10 percent per year, it could cost you an additional $17.70 a month for Part B, or a $106.20 monthly premium rather $88.50.

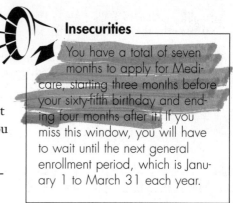

Insecurities

You have a total of seven months to apply for Medicare, starting three months before your sixty-fifth birthday and ending four months after it. If you miss this window, you will have to wait until the next general enrollment period, which is January 1 to March 31 each year.

You can avoid the Part B premium penalty if you delayed signing up because you had health coverage at work. We talk more about working and Medicare later in this chapter.

First, let's look at how you can get Medicare even if you don't qualify for Social Security.

Buying Into Medicare

As you know, some people are exempt from paying into Social Security. In some cases, they may still pay into Medicare. Medicare taxes are 1.45 percent of a person's salary, and this is matched dollar-for-dollar by a person's employer. For anyone who hasn't paid into Medicare or who hasn't paid in long enough, Medicare is still available but at a cost.

Medicare eligibility is based on the number of quarters you paid into the system. Anyone with fewer than 40 quarters of participation in Medicare must pay for coverage. Each year you pay for Medicare, you earn four quarters. You must have worked and paid into Medicare for 10 years (or be married to someone who worked and paid into Medicare for 10 years) to qualify for Part A benefits without a premium.

If you have fewer than 40 quarters of participation, all is not lost. You can still get Medicare at age 65. If you have fewer than 30 quarters of Medicare covered employment, your Part A premium will be $393 per month. Part B will be $88.50 per month, for a total of $481.50.

Folks who have between 30 and 39 quarters of Medicare-covered employment can get Part A for $216 per month. Part B is still $88.50 per month.

What should you do about Medicare if you've reached age 65 but still want to work and have medical coverage at work? It depends on the size of the company that employs you. Let's take a look at the rules.

Should You Apply If You Are Still Working?

Folks who want to keep working at age 65 face different rules when it comes to Medicare enrollment. If you work for a company with 20 or more employees (100 or more if you are disabled), you can decide to remain on the company's health plan.

Insecurities

If you delay starting your Medicare benefits because you have health benefits at work, you must apply for Medicare within eight months of leaving your job; otherwise, you will face penalties when you try to get coverage.

Carefully compare the benefits when deciding whether to stay on the company plan or switch to Medicare. In most cases, you'll find that your company's plan offers more coverage for less out-of-pocket expense.

If you work for a small company of fewer than 20 employees, you don't have a choice. You must sign up for Medicare within the seven-month window previously mentioned, starting three months before your sixty-fifth birthday. Private insurers for small companies will only pay what is not normally covered by Medicare. By not signing up for Medicare, you risk not having full coverage, plus you will end up with Part B penalties because you didn't sign up in time.

What's in Part A

As noted earlier, everyone who is eligible for Medicare is covered by Part A at no cost. This is essentially the in-patient portion of Medicare. Coverage includes hospital stays, care in skilled nursing facilities, home health care after being released from a hospital, and hospice care.

In the hospital or a skilled nursing facility, your Medicare coverage includes a semi-private room, meals, general nursing, and other hospital services and supplies. Part A does not cover private duty nursing or a television or telephone in the room. You also can't get coverage for a private room unless it is medically necessary.

To get coverage for the skilled nursing facility, it must be after a three-day hospital stay. That is when things can get interesting. Sometimes a physician will order in-patient hospital testing, rather than testing as an outpatient, to make it possible for the patient to qualify for a skilled nursing facility.

After a hospital stay, you can also get coverage for home health care if the doctor recommends it. This can include part-time skilled nursing care, physical therapy, occupational therapy, speech-language therapy, home health aide services, medical social services, durable medical equipment (including wheelchairs, hospital beds, oxygen, and walkers), medical supplies, and other services.

People who have been diagnosed with a terminal illness can get *hospice care* from a Medicare-approved hospice, including drugs for symptom control and pain relief and other services not otherwise covered by Medicare. Hospice care frequently can be given in your home. However, short-term hospital and inpatient *respite care* may also be possible when needed.

def•i•ni•tion

Hospice care is a specialized type of health care for terminally ill people. This holistic approach frequently includes legal, financial, and emotional assistance for the patient and his or her family in addition to medical care. Care can be provided in the home, a hospital, or specialized hospice facilities.

Respite care is short-term care given to a hospice patient or other homebound person who needs around-the-clock medical or daily living assistance by another caregiver, such as a hospital or respite care home, so that the usual caregiver can take a break. For Medicare purposes, respite care is only covered if the patient is terminally ill.

It's Not Free!

You've probably already guessed that Part A does not cover 100 percent of your costs. You will have to pay both a deductible and coinsurance for each stay in a hospital. Before we get into your costs, I first must explain something unique to Medicare, called benefit periods.

Benefit Periods

Benefit periods are the way Medicare tracks your use of hospitals and skilled nursing facilities. A benefit period begins when you enter a hospital or skilled nursing facility. It ends when you haven't received hospital or skilled nursing care for 60 days. As long as you are out of hospital or skilled nursing care for 60 days, a new benefit period begins. There is no limit to the number of new benefit periods you can have.

Your Costs

Why are benefit periods so important? Because each benefit period requires that you pay a new inpatient deductible of $952 in 2006. Coinsurance also is impacted by the benefit periods. In 2006, coinsurance for an inpatient hospital stay is $238 a day for the 61st to 90th day of each benefit period. Coinsurance then jumps to $476 a day for the 91st to 150th day, which would be covered under the provision for *lifetime reserve days*. You are responsible for all costs after the 150th day. Coinsurance amounts are set each year by Medicare. Deductibles and coinsurance rates are adjusted yearly by CMS.

Insecurities _____

Lifetime reserve days are another unique feature of Medicare. Each person gets 60 lifetime reserve days that can be used after the standard 90-day inpatient allowance. Coinsurance amounts for the lifetime reserve days are set each year by Medicare. These days can be used at any time once a person needs hospitalization for more than 90 days within a benefit period. For example, if you are in the hospital for 100 days in a row, you would use up 10 of the 60 lifetime days. You only have 50 days left for the rest of your life. Once you use them up, they are not renewable. Once the 60 days are used up, you're stuck with the full bill.

Let's take a look at how much a 100-day hospital stay could cost you out-of-pocket on Medicare:

Day 1 to day 60	$952	deductible
Day 61 to day 90	$7,140	coinsurance
Day 91 to day 100	$4,760	coinsurance
Out-of-pocket cost	$12,852	

Coinsurance in a skilled nursing care facility is less costly. Medicare covers the costs completely for the first 20 days. After that your cost per day most likely will be $119 a day for the twenty-first to one-hundredth day. Sometimes you can find a nursing home facility that will charge you less than $119 per day. You are responsible for all costs beyond the 100 days in a benefit period. One way to avoid the higher costs of extended stays in skilled nursing facilities is for the patient to go home after the one-hundredth day and spend at least 60 days at home, if possible. Then, if the patient needs to go back into the hospital for at least three days, the clock is restarted, and a new benefit period is available for another 100 days. Remember, however, that at the start of a new benefit period you'll have to pay a new hospital deductible!

So you can see how quickly a major illness can eat up someone's resources on a fixed income. Chapter 22 looks at supplemental coverage called Medigap, which you can use to minimize your out-of-pocket expenses, as well as long-term care policies.

If you go home after an inpatient stay but still need some home health care services approved by Medicare, you pay nothing for those services. There is a 20-percent copayment for Medicare-approved durable medical equipment. Medicare may also approve respite care up to a certain amount. If respite care is approved, your copayment would be 5 percent of the amount.

Now that you know the coverage for Part A, let's move on to Part B.

What's in Part B

Part B is optional, but because it's just $88.50 a month, few people reject it. Part B is essentially your medical insurance. The 2006 deductible for Part B is $124. A copayment of 20 percent is required for most Medicare-approved services and equipment under Part B, but there is a 50-percent copayment for outpatient mental health care.

In addition to covering doctor expenses, Part B also covers outpatient medical and surgical services and supplies, diagnostic tests, ambulatory surgery center facility fees for approved procedures, and durable medical equipment (such as wheelchairs, hospital beds, oxygen, and walkers). There is also coverage for second surgical opinions, outpatient mental health care, and outpatient physical and occupational therapy (including speech-language therapy).

As with any other medical policy, there are hundreds of items specific to various diseases. I'm not going to list them all here. When you start getting Medicare, however, you will get a booklet similar to those you've probably received from your employer-sponsored health insurance that details everything that is covered.

Senior Moments

If you haven't had a recent hospital stay to qualify for Part A coverage, Part B will cover home health care needs. These can include part-time skilled nursing care, physical therapy, occupational therapy, speech-language therapy, home health aide services, medical social services, durable medical equipment (such as wheelchairs, hospital beds, oxygen, and walkers), and medical supplies. There is also coverage for ambulance services (when other transportation would endanger your health); artificial eyes and limbs; braces for arms, legs, back, or neck; limited chiropractic services; and emergency care.

Preventive Care Coverage

In addition to these medical services, Medicare pays for preventive services. Some of the key covered preventive tests are …

- **Bone mass measurements.** The frequency of this testing varies with your health status.

- **Cardiovascular screenings.** Screening tests for cholesterol, lipid, and triglyceride levels are covered every five years.

- **Colorectal cancer screening.** You and your doctor determine your level of risk for colorectal cancer and the frequency of which preventive screening tests should be used. These tests can include Fecal Occult Blood Test, Flexible Sigmoidoscopy, Colonoscopy, and Barium Enema.

- **Diabetes screenings plus services and supplies.** Screenings to check for diabetes are covered every year if you have any the following risk factors: high blood pressure, abnormal cholesterol or triglyceride levels, obesity, or a history of high blood sugar. Medicare will also pay for screenings if you have two or more of these characteristics: age 65 or older, overweight, family history of diabetes, or a history of diabetes during pregnancy. In addition to screenings, Medicare pays for glucose monitors, test strips, and lancets as well as diabetes self-management training.

- **Glaucoma screening.** You can have a screening once every 12 months. It must be done or supervised by an eye doctor who is legally allowed to do this service in your state.

- **Mammogram screening.** You can get a mammogram once every 12 months. Medicare also covers new digital technologies for mammogram screening.

- ◆ **Pap test and pelvic examination.** If you have no evidence of cancer risk, you can get a Pap test and pelvic exam once every 24 months. You can have test once every 12 months if you are at high risk for cervical or vaginal cancer or if you are of childbearing age and have had an abnormal Pap test in the past 36 months. This does include a clinical breast exam.

- ◆ **Prostate cancer screening.** A digital rectal examination and a prostate-specific antigen (PSA) test can be done once every 12 months.

- ◆ **Shots (vaccinations).** You can get a flu shot once a year in the fall or winter. You can also get a Pneumococcal pneumonia shot (one shot may be all you ever need; ask your doctor). Hepatitis B shots are covered by Medicare for people at high or medium risk for Hepatitis B.

- ◆ **"Welcome to Medicare" Physical Exam.** You get a one-time review of your health, as well as education and counseling about preventive services, within the first six months of coverage under Part B. This exam is required and will include screenings, shots, and referrals for other care if needed.

When you go to a doctor, you must be aware of something called *assignment*. If the doctor or supplier does not accept assignment, you will have to pay the entire charge at the time of service because the doctor will not take the responsibility of billing and collecting from Medicare. You will then have to file a claim with Medicare to be reimbursed for what you paid minus your 20-percent co-payment. There is a risk that you could end up paying more than 20 percent of the bill if the doctor's charges for the service are above what Medicare normally pays for that service in your area.

def•i•ni•tion

Assignment, in Medicare terminology, means that a doctor agrees to accept Medicare's fee as full payment even if his or her normal fee for the same service is higher. It can save you money if your doctor accepts assignment.

Don't Forget Those Ugly Exclusions

Most private health insurances have exclusions from coverage, and Medicare is no exception. Exclusions are services, drugs, or other medical supplies that the insurance company will not pay.

Some of Medicare's exclusions from coverage include routine or yearly physical exams (the first one is included—see "Welcome to Medicare" Physical exam above), outpatient prescription drugs (not covered under Part B, but you can get coverage under

Part D, see Chapter 20), custodial care, acupuncture, dental care, cosmetic surgery, hearing aids and exams, orthopedic shoes, routine foot care, routine eye care, and most shots.

Privatizing Medicare: Medicare Advantage Plans

So far, I have described the traditional fee-for-service Medicare plan. You may still have a fee-for-service plan in the workplace, but you probably also have a choice between a health maintenance organization (HMO) or other health insurance options.

Social Graces

In a fee-for-service plan you usually have both an annual deductible (for Medicare Part A, it's $952, Part B, it's $124) to pay plus a co-insurance percentage (for Medicare Part B it's 20 percent) for every medical appointment and other medical services. You can select any doctor or specialist you want to use. In a health maintenance organization (HMO), your appointments are usually a pre-set amount ($5 to $25) per appointment and there aren't any deductibles to meet. Your choice of doctors is limited to those who are part of the HMO.

In 2003, when Congress passed the Medicare Prescription Drug, Improvement and Modernization Act of 2003, it did more than add a provision for prescription drug coverage (covered in Chapter 20). This bill also offers monetary incentives to get private insurers to jump on board the Medicare bandwagon. Congress has tried this before, most recently with the failed Part C program called Medicare+Choice. This time around they've added more financial incentives and renamed it Medicare Advantage.

The new Medicare Advantage health plans give seniors the option to choose from among several different types of plans, including Medicare HMOs, Medicare Preferred Provider Organizations (PPOs), Provider-Sponsored Organizations (PSOs), Private Fee-for-Service Plans (PFFS), and Medical Savings Accounts (MSAs) coupled with high-deductible insurance plans.

Sorting out the Plans

Here's how the different plans work:

◆ **Medicare Health Maintenance Organizations (HMOs).** If you enroll in an HMO, you can only use doctors, hospitals, or other providers in the HMO network. You choose a primary care doctor, who decides when you should see a specialist and which specialist you can see. Neither Medicare nor the HMO will pay for unauthorized visits to specialists. They also will not pay for visits to medical providers outside the plan. If you pay additional premiums, some HMOs do offer partial coverage for point-of-service (POS) benefits outside the plan, which means you can choose your own doctors but you'll pay more. HMOs usually provide more benefits than traditional Medicare, which includes coverage for some of the out-of-pocket deductibles and co-payments mentioned above.

> **Social Graces**
>
> You can search online to find out which Medicare Advantage Plan options are available in your area. Use Medicare's Personal Medical Plan Finder at www.Medicare.gov/MPPF/home.asp.
>
> You also can get the information about specific plans by calling 1-800-MEDICARE (1-800-633-4227) and asking for health plan quality information.

◆ **Medicare Preferred Provider Organizations (PPOs).** PPOs, while similar to HMOs, offer you more flexibility than an HMO. Your reimbursement for medical care will be higher if you see in-network doctors, but you can get reimbursed for care from doctors or hospitals outside the network. You don't have to see a primary care physician before being permitted to contact a specialist. Expect to pay higher premiums for the increased flexibility.

◆ **Provider-Sponsored Organizations (PSOs).** PSOs are medical-provider owned and sponsored ventures that operate much like an HMO. The big difference is that rather than being owned and managed by an insurer, they are owned and managed by a medical-provider group (which can include doctors, laboratories, and hospitals). These are a totally new entity being established for Medicare with different rules in different states.

◆ **Private Fee-for-Service Plans (PFFS).** These plans work much like traditional Medicare. You pay an initial premium for the plan plus pay deductibles and co-payments.

◆ **Medical Savings Accounts (MSAs).** You can choose to save for your own medical costs in tax-advantaged medical savings accounts. With this option, you buy a high-deductible insurance plan (usually with a deductible of $1,000 to $3,000) and pay all medical costs up to that deductible. As of November 2005, there were no MSAs available for Medicare recipients, but you can learn more about how they work if they do become available at hiicap.state.ny.us/medicare/msa.htm.

Whether or not you have these plans available in your state depends upon which companies bid to operate in your state. You can see a state-by-state breakdown of the types of plans available at www.medicare.gov/medicarereform/map.asp. In order to participate in these plans you must be eligible for Medicare Part A and pay the premium for Medicare Part B plus pay any additional premiums for the Medicare Advantage plan you choose.

Determining What's Best for You

While you will likely need to pay an additional premium to participate in the private plans, you will also likely get additional benefits by choosing a private provider. Be sure you understand the provisions of any of these new plans and how they will impact your health care before switching from traditional Medicare.

You will only be able to switch plans once a year, so you could get stuck in the wrong plan for 12 months. In 2006, if you want to make a change you must make that change in the first six months. After that you will only be able to change plans once during the enrollment year in the first three months. Here are some key things to consider:

- ◆ **Keeping your doctors**. If you want to use specific doctors, specialists, or hospitals, be sure they are part of the network of doctors within the plan you are considering. If they are not, you are better off staying in traditional Medicare and taking what is called a Medigap policy, explained in more detail in Chapter 22.

- ◆ **Getting more benefits to reduce medical costs.** If reducing your out-of-pocket costs is more important than your choice of doctors, you may want to consider one of the Medicare Advantage plans offered in your state. Be sure you understand the benefits being offered and how much you will have to pay out-of-pocket for the specific drugs and other therapies you need before signing up for these plans. Many of these plans prefer to insure only the healthiest seniors and don't provide all the benefits you may need for a chronic health condition. Before switching to a health plan, ask specific question about the coverage for any medical conditions you have.

◆ **Keeping your supplemental coverage from a former employer or union.** If you are currently getting additional medical coverage from your former employer or union, talk to the provider of your current coverage before considering a Medicare Advantage Plan. You could lose your valuable retiree health benefits.

◆ **Coordinating Medicaid benefits.** If you are currently receiving Medicaid benefits, be sure to contact your state Medicaid office for assistance before considering any Medicare Advantage plan. Your state may even pay the costs of your enrolling in some of the Medicare Advantage options, but if you choose the wrong ones you could lose Medicaid benefits.

Why All the Medicare Changes?

Congress hopes to move seniors away from the traditional government-run Medicare fee-for-service plan into privately run medical insurance plans. So far Medicare has failed to convince seniors to make the move, and only 5 million of the 41 million on Medicare chose private insurers in 2005.

To sweeten the pot for private insurers, Congress gave insurers added incentives to get them to participate more aggressively. In fact, reimbursements to insurers for these private plans will be higher than those for seniors who stay in the traditional plan. Private plans will be paid 107 percent of what it would cost to treat the same people in the traditional Medicare plan. These incentives allow insurers to lower their premiums and offer more benefits than the traditional plan to entice seniors to choose the private plans. Some estimate these incentives could result in overpayments by as much as $80 billion dollars in the first 10 years of the program. The stated goal is to give seniors more choice of doctors, benefits, convenience, and quality, as well as cost options. Ultimately, we are left asking two very important questions about this strategy:

◆ How long will government sustain these overpayments before Congress figures out it can no longer afford to pay them?

◆ What will happen when the insurers no longer get the incentives? Will they raise prices and/or reduce benefits? It's a possibility.

◆ Will they eat the extra costs? I seriously doubt that. Based on what insurance companies have done historically (Medicare+Choice's failure is a prime example), when they no longer get these incentives they will likely start dropping out of Medicare Advantage. Medicare+Choice could not succeed because so many insurers dropped out once the reimbursements for patient care were lowered.

Social Graces

There are other options for supplementing Medicare to minimize your cost risks. Some are specific to groups such as railroad workers and veterans. The most common group of options is Medigap insurance policies. If you are lucky enough to have worked for a company that offers retiree health benefits, you have a plan that coordinates its benefits with Medicare. There are also insurance policies for long-term care. We look at the various options more closely in Chapter 22.

Medicare Rights

Once your Medicare starts, you will have certain guaranteed rights to protect your medical care. If for any reason your coverage is denied, you will be able to appeal that decision. You can appeal if …

♦ You don't agree with the amount that is paid.

♦ You believe you were denied a service that you should have gotten.

♦ You believe a service was stopped before it should have been stopped.

Each time you get a statement of what Medicare pays, you will get instructions about how to file an appeal. If you decide to appeal, be sure to work with your doctor or provider to get any information that may help your case.

In addition to the right to appeal, you also have the right to get emergency services, to get treatment by doctors and at hospitals, to participate in treatment decisions and know your treatment choices, and to maintain privacy of personal and health information.

Senior Moments

Appeals rights are very important because it can take Medicare up to five years or more before it approves new medical technologies for coverage. If you are denied coverage for a new medical technology, you must use the appeals process to question that ruling. Newly approved advanced diagnostic tests are sometimes delayed in being added to the agency's coding and payment procedures. If the test is not coded, it cannot be paid through regular channels and must be appealed.

You may also have additional rights if you are in a hospital or skilled nursing facility or if your home health care ends. If you have any questions about rights and protections, you can call Medicare at 1-800-633-4227.

Detecting and Preventing Fraud and Abuse

You may have seen horror stories on television about Medicare patients being abused in substandard care situations. You may have seen stories of doctors overcharging patients for care they never received.

Medicare is combating these abuses by giving recipients a list of tips on how to detect fraud. Medicare believes you should be suspicious of a provider who tells you …

◆ The test is free; he only needs your Medicare number for his records.

◆ Medicare wants you to have the item or service.

◆ He knows how to get Medicare to pay for it.

◆ The more tests he provides, the cheaper they are.

◆ The equipment or service is free; it won't cost you anything.

Other signs of fraud may be detected with providers who …

◆ Routinely waive copayments without checking on your ability to pay.

◆ Advertise "free" consultations to Medicare beneficiaries.

◆ Claim they represent Medicare.

◆ Use pressure or scare tactics to sell you high-priced medical services or diagnostic tests.

◆ Bill Medicare for services you do not recall receiving.

◆ Use telemarketing and door-to-door selling as marketing tools.

If you suspect a provider of fraud or abuse, you should call Medicare. One of the best ways to recognize problems is to carefully review your statements from Medicare when payments are made. These payment notices show how much Medicare was billed, how much Medicare paid, and what you owe. If you see services or equipment on the bill that you did not receive, you may want to question them.

Medicare recommends that you do a number of things to prevent fraud:

◆ Don't give out your Medicare health insurance claim number (on your Medicare card) except to your doctor or other Medicare provider.

◆ Don't allow anyone, except appropriate medical professionals, to review your medical records or recommend services.

◆ Be careful in accepting Medicare services that are represented as being free. Also be cautious when you are offered free testing or screening in exchange for your Medicare card number.

◆ Be cautious of any provider who maintains that he has been endorsed by the federal government or by Medicare.

◆ Avoid a provider of health-care items or services who tells you that the item or service is not usually covered but that he knows how to bill Medicare to get it paid.

When you receive your statement, if you see something that you did not get or do not understand, your first call should be to your doctor, hospital, or other provider. The bill may be correct, and a staff member can help explain any services, supplies, or equipment charges you don't understand. There could also be a billing error that can be corrected.

Social Graces

If you suspect fraud, there is a hotline for tips. You can call 1-800-447-8477. If you report fraud and it turns out to be true, you might receive a reward of 10 percent of the amount recovered up to a maximum of $1,000, provided at least $100 in Medicare money was recovered and the fraud and abuse you report is not already being investigated.

If you think fraud may be involved, call the Medicare claims-processing company that paid the claim. When you get your statement that shows what Medicare paid, the name, address, and telephone number of the claims company will be on that statement.

You'll need to give the Medicare claims-processing company the provider's name and any identifying number, as well as the item or service you are questioning. You'll also need the date when the item or service was supposedly furnished and the amount approved and paid by Medicare. In addition, you'll need any information you might have that explains why the service or item should not be paid.

Fraud costs everyone that uses Medicare. As a few people get rich, others are stuck with increases in health-care costs. Recognizing and preventing fraud is one way to help keep costs down.

The Future of Medicare

You hear a lot about Social Security running out of money, but Medicare is actually more at risk. As with Social Security, Medicare taxes not used for current benefits are put into trust funds. Tax inflows for Medicare will start running short of outlays by 2014, when they will begin spending down the trusts. Insolvency is expected by 2020, according to the 2005 annual report by the trustees of the Social Security and Medicare trust funds. We look more closely at Medicare's future in Part 6, "What Next for the Nest Egg."

The Least You Need to Know

- ◆ Medicare is automatic for anyone who qualifies for Social Security at age 65. If you start collecting Social Security before age 65, your Medicare card will be mailed to you.

- ◆ Medicare is divided into three kinds of coverage. Part A coverage is for hospitalization; Part B coverage is for medical expenses and Part D is for prescription drugs.

- ◆ If you haven't paid into Social Security and Medicare, you can buy into Medicare at age 65.

- ◆ In some areas, you can choose between the traditional fee-for-service Medicare and private plans offered through Medicare Advantage.

- ◆ Beware of Medicare fraud—it can take many forms.

Chapter 20

Paying for Your Drugs

In This Chapter

◆ Making sense of Plan D

◆ Costing out the plan

◆ Applying for coverage

◆ Making changes in your plan

Confusing! That's the word you'll hear most often when you ask a senior what he or she thinks of the new Medicare prescription drug plan, called Part D, which made its debut on January 1, 2006. And I agree with them 100 percent. I don't think the government could have designed a more confusing benefit if they deliberately set out to do so.

Unfortunately, whether you like it or not, you need to understand how the plan works, how to sort out the myriad options, how to compare the costs, and how to pick the right plan for you. If you don't do so on time, you'll end up paying a penalty of 1 percent per month for every month you delay—and you'll have to pay that penalty for the rest of your life.

In this chapter, I help you to get past the drug plan's daunting options so you can make the best decision for your needs.

What the Medicare Prescription Drug Plan Covers

What does the Medicare prescription drug plan cover? Here's a summary of the basic provisions of Medicare Plan D:

♦ Each senior can voluntarily decide to enroll in the Medicare prescription drug plan. If a senior does enroll, he or she will pay a monthly premium for the plan.

♦ A senior will have to pay a deductible of $250, which means seniors will have to spend $250 on drugs before drug costs will be covered under the plan.

♦ Once the deductible is met, the senior will pay 25 percent of prescription costs and the insurer will pay 75 percent of the costs. The 25 percent is the senior's co-pay. The payment scheme continues until the senior spends $500 out of pocket on drugs and receives drugs worth $2,000.

♦ Seniors then lose all coverage until they spend another $2,850 on drugs. This is what people call the *donut hole* because seniors must pay for 100 percent of the cost of their drugs at this point.

def•i•ni•tion

For seniors the **donut hole** is a big hole in the coverage of Medicare's prescription drug plan. Once you're received $2,000 worth of drugs under the plan, you'll then get nothing to help pay for your drugs until you've spent $3,600 out-of-pocket.

♦ Once a senior spends $3,600 out-of-pocket (that includes the $250 deductible plus $500 co-pay plus $2,850 in the donut hole) and the total value of drugs received is $5,100 ($250 deductible plus $2,000 paid by insurer plus $2,850 paid by senior once the donut hole was reached), then the senior will only pay 5 percent of all future drug costs and the insurer will pay 95 percent. The amount to be paid out-of-pocket will be adjusted yearly.

If this isn't confusing enough, there are a lot more options from which you can choose. That's because the Congress decided to make this plan available through private insurers rather than directly from Medicare. Insurers were given great flexibility in how they could design their plans, provided they meet the minimum requirements I just outlined. Insurers came up with many alternatives to this design, which I discuss in greater detail later in this chapter.

Although this flexibility, which includes at least 40 choices in all but two states (Alaska only has 27 choices and Hawaii has 29 choices), makes choosing a plan more difficult, it also means there's a better chance of finding a plan to suit your needs.

There are two ways to get Medicare's Plan D prescription coverage: through the stand-alone Prescription Drug Plan (PDP) or through the Medicare Advantage Prescription Drug Plan (MA-PD).

The average PDP costs $32 per month nationwide, but there are options in some states for less than $2 per month or more than $100 per month. I tell you how to sort out the options below.

You can find out more about Medicare Advantage Plans in Chapter 19. If you enroll in this type of plan, your prescription drug coverage would be included in that enrollment. Some plans charge no additional premium for drug coverage; others do charge an additional monthly premium.

Who Is Eligible?

Anyone who is enrolled or entitled to enroll in Medicare Part A or Part B is also eligible to enroll in a new Medicare Prescription Drug plan, which the government now calls Part D. (Catchy isn't it? Part D for drugs.)

Eligible folks include …

♦ Anyone 65 years old or older.

♦ Anyone receiving disability payments from Social Security for at least 24 months.

♦ Anyone who has end-stage renal disease.

You're Eligible, but Take Action Carefully!

You may fit in the category of being eligible, but don't apply too fast. Many people who are eligible already get their prescription drugs from other sources, such as state plans, Medicaid, retirement benefits from a company or union, Medigap, or an alphabet soup of other plans including COBRA, TRICARE, VA, FEHB, PACE, ESRD, ADAP and SPAP. If you do get prescription drug coverage from somewhere else, check with your current provider before signing up for the new Medicare plan.

You should get a letter from your current provider stating whether or not your plan is creditable. If your plan is creditable, that means that its coverage is at least as good as Medicare and may even be better. If you are currently in a creditable plan you don't need to do anything and most likely will be better off keeping your current coverage. If you are in a creditable plan and you sign up for the new Medicare plan, you likely will lose your existing drug coverage and you may even lose your coverage for other medical needs, so proceed with caution.

Insecurities

If you already have prescription drug coverage from a source other than Medicare, don't sign up for Medicare Part D before checking with your current provider of prescription drug coverage. If you do sign up for Medicare Part D you will likely lose your current prescription drug coverage automatically.

Here's a brief overview of what you should do if you are eligible for Medicare Part D but receive prescription drug coverage from another source:

◆ **Medicaid.** Beginning January 1, 2006, all Medicaid recipients who qualified for Medicare Part D got assigned to a prescription drug plan. The only exceptions to this were seniors in a Medicare Advantage Plan or PACE (Program for All Inclusive Coverage for the Elderly). In these two cases prescriptions are paid through one of those plans instead of a separate Medicare Part D plan. While the transition to the new Part D was supposed to be automatic for Medicaid recipients, hundreds of thousands of these recipients, called "dual eligibles," left pharmacies without their medications in the first 30 days after the implementation of Part D. More than 20 states declared a health emergency by February 2006 and started paying for the drugs. At the time of this writing, solutions to this health emergency were still being worked out. When the problems are finally worked out, dual eligibles will have their premiums paid for them, will have no deductible, and will not have a coverage gap. They will pay $1 or $2 for generic and preferred drugs and $3 to $5 for non-preferred drugs. Some dual eligibles in a nursing home or other institution will not have to pay anything for their drugs, depending on their income.

◆ **Employer or Union Plan.** Most employers and unions plan to continue offering prescription coverage in 2006. In fact, 93 percent of employers who provided prescription drug coverage to their retirees in 2005 planned to continue to do so in 2006, according to a survey by Kaiser/Hewitt in 2005. The future doesn't look as rosy though for this coverage, which is usually better than what is offered under Medicare Part D. By 2010, 50 percent of employers said they

Alternative II is what the trustees believe is the best estimate of likely future economic and demographic conditions.

The trustees believe that Alternative III is the worst-case scenario. This set of assumptions expects the highest costs, the slowest economic growth, rapid inflation, and the worst combination of demographic conditions financially.

Now that we have an overview of the projections, let's take a closer look at how the funds will be drained.

Insecurities

Reading these figures can be frightening for folks who are counting on Social Security benefits in their retirement. It's important to keep in mind that when the trust funds are exhausted, it does not mean Social Security and Medicare will end. What it does mean is that any shortfall in the taxes collected for Social Security and Medicare will have to be paid by other federal receipts or benefits will have to be cut.

Draining the Trust Funds

Each year the trustees of Social Security and Medicare prepare an annual report to the public that details the current status of the trust funds and a projection of what their condition is expected to be over the next 75 years. Let's review how the trustees believe the trust funds will be drained unless some significant reforms are put in place very soon.

Medicare's Troubles

Medicare is expected to be the first program hit with a shortfall, and its long-term problems are considered more severe than Social Security's. The trustees conclude that …

Medicare still faces financial difficulties that come sooner—and in many ways are more severe—than those confronting Social Security. While both programs face essentially the same demographic challenge, underlying health-care costs per enrollee are projected to rise faster than the wages per worker on which the payroll tax is paid and on which Social Security benefits are based.

The reason for Medicare's dire situation is that, in addition to an influx of baby boomers into the program, it also faces health-care costs that are increasing faster than income. Most of us probably understand this problem because we have watched our health insurance premiums increase dramatically since the mid-1990s.

def•i•ni•tion

The **gross domestic product (GDP)** is the total market value of all final goods and services produced in this country in any given year. GDP equals total consumer, investment, and government spending, plus the value of exports minus the value of imports.

Today, Part A and Part B of Medicare combined make up 2.6 percent of the *gross domestic product (GDP)*. Part D will increase that, but no one knows by how much because it depends upon how many people choose to participate, since it is a voluntary program. In 2079, it is expected to rise to 14 percent of the GDP. By comparison, the revenues collected for the programs will only grow from 2.4 percent of the GDP today to 5.3 percent in 2079. In other words, projected income doesn't meet projected need. Premiums for Parts B and D pay for only 25 percent of the program costs.

Medicare Expenditures and Noninterest Income by Source as a Percent of GDP

This chart from the 2005 trustees' report shows you the expected shortfall for Medicare expenditures. Medicare expenses are paid through payroll taxes, taxes on benefits, Part B premiums, and general revenue. You can see that the shortfall rises dramatically beginning in 2019, after the HI trust fund is exhausted.

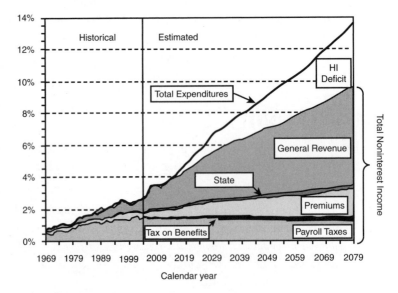

Medicare spending is expected to exceed the costs of Social Security. The financing gap for the hospital program alone, which is about one half of total Medicare costs, is larger than the Social Security gap. Medicare's annual expenditures are expected to surpass Social Security's by 2024.

The Hospital Insurance trust fund is projected to remain solvent until 2019, but projected tax income is expected to fall short of outlays in 2014. After 2014, benefits will be paid using tax income plus spending down of the trust fund.

The Supplemental Medical Insurance trust fund, which pays the benefits for Part B, will remain adequately financed into the indefinite future, according to the 2005 trustees' report. This is not because it is in better shape but because current law sets financing each year to meet the next year's expected costs. Funding for the SMI trust fund comes primarily from general tax revenues plus the Part B premiums paid by recipients. This will require a growing share of general federal revenues each year and most likely substantial beneficiary premium increases.

Social Security Shortfall

Social Security's trust funds are in somewhat better shape than the Hospital Insurance trust fund. The Old-Age and Survivors Insurance (OASDI) trust fund is projected to be able to pay full benefits until 2041. The Disability Insurance trust fund is in a bit more trouble and will only be able to pay full benefits until 2027 without a fix.

The situation for the trust funds will rapidly deteriorate when the baby boomers start to retire in about 2010. Tax income will fall short of outlays beginning in 2017, according to the 2005 trustees' report.

Long-Range Outlook for the Funds

The long-range outlook is not good for the OASI, DI, and HI trust funds. In making their predictions, the trustees use a percentage of taxable payroll, which is the portion of total wages and self-employment earnings. The trustees expect income rates to remain relatively constant but project cost rates to rise substantially.

Why will costs rise faster than income? Baby boomers. Cost will rise steeply between 2010 and 2030 as the number of people receiving benefits rather than paying payroll taxes increases rapidly as the baby boomers retire.

In the year 2000, there were 3.4 workers for every retiree. Historically, there have been 3.7 workers paying into Social Security for every retiree. That number will fall dramatically. The trustees expect it to be as low as 1.9 workers per retiree in 2075.

Income and Cost Rates (as a percentage of taxable payroll)

This chart from the 2005 trustees' report shows the expected imbalance. As you can see, beginning in 2017, the cost rate for OASI will exceed the income rate by increasing amounts.

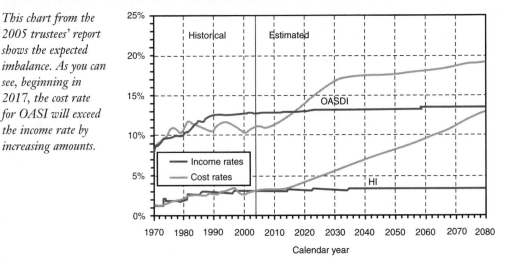

After the Trusts

So what happens when the trusts are fully drained? OASDI and DI are projected to be exhausted in 2041. Payroll taxes will still be coming into the program, but they are estimated to cover only 73 percent of the program costs. By 2075, payroll taxes will cover even less of the costs—67 percent—if there isn't a fix.

The HI trust fund will be in even worse shape. The fund is expected to be exhausted in 2019. Payroll taxes in that year will only pay 68 percent of the costs. By 2075, the trustees expect payroll taxes to cover only 32 percent of the costs.

When the trust funds are exhausted, the battle over how to fix the programs will truly begin if a solution hasn't already been found. Social Security and Medicare will compete with other federal programs for money from general revenues. The only choices the government will have are to increase taxes, decrease benefits, or cut other federal spending. It won't be a pretty picture.

Luckily, the baby boomer storm will rise gradually. Not everyone will retire in one year. The government still has time to figure out a plan, but the longer Congress and the president wait to implement a fix, the more difficult the fix will be.

In the 2005 report, the trustees said that Social Security can be brought into actuarial balance over the next 75 years by an immediate 15 percent increase in the amount of payroll taxes collected or an immediate reduction of 13 percent in benefits paid or some combination of the two. If Congress were to adopt the increase in payroll taxes, your contribution and the contribution of your employer would go up by .93 percentage points each to 7.13 percent.

The trustees also stated that the Hospital Insurance program will need an immediate increase in income of 107 percent. If Congress adopts that recommendation, your payroll taxes for Medicare would increase from 1.45 percent to 3 percent, with an equal match by your employer. The only other alternative would be to cut program outlays by 48 percent. If I were to take my best guess about what will happen, it will probably be a compromise that mixes the two alternatives.

Many different alternatives have been discussed for fixing Social Security and Medicare. In Chapter 24, we focus on the specific ideas proposed for Medicare. In Chapter 25, we zoom in on Social Security reforms.

The Least You Need to Know

- Trust funds for Social Security and Medicare are running out of money, and the shortfall will be in the trillions.

- Although Social Security's troubles are primarily caused by the baby boomer wave soon to hit retirement, Medicare faces a double whammy of baby boomers plus rapidly rising medical costs.

- When the trust funds are exhausted, Social Security and Medicare will compete with other federal programs for money to meet their financial obligations. The federal government will be faced with cutting spending, raising taxes, or increasing debt.

Chapter 24

Modernizing Medicare

In This Chapter

- ◆ Finding drug money
- ◆ Sharing the costs
- ◆ Combining Parts A and B
- ◆ Privatizing Medicare
- ◆ Controlling costs

Fixing Medicare will be a lot harder than fixing Social Security. Social Security involves payments to retirees and disabled folks with no other stakeholders, but any change in Medicare has to take into account the impact of the change on beneficiaries, hospitals, doctors, insurance companies, and other medical service and equipment providers. You can imagine the number of lobbyists who take over the halls of Congress anytime someone even mentions the possibility of a change in Medicare.

The 2003 Medicare Prescription Drug Improvement and Modernization Act was supposed to help fix Medicare by offering managed care options (Plan C) and prescription drug coverage (Plan D), but neither of these new programs helped to solve Medicare's financial woes—in fact they made the situation much worse.

This chapter takes a look at more proposals on the table and how the Medicare was impacted by 2003 law. I won't make any guesses as to what you can expect in a modernized Medicare program or when you can expect that modernization to take place.

Dealing With the Shortfall

As you know by now, Medicare's number one problem is money. Medicare's hospital insurance trust fund began paying more in benefits than it collected in 2004. In their 2005 report, the trustees overseeing Social Security and Medicare projected the Medicare trust fund would be exhausted by 2019.

Insecurities

Medicare's total unfunded liability projected infinitely is $65.4 trillion, almost six times that of Social Security's, according to independent Social Security Trustee Republican Thomas R. Saving.

In addition to rising medical costs, a big factor in Medicare's shortfall is the new prescription drug coverage, which began in January 2006 as part of the 2003 Medicare Prescription Drug Improvement and Modernization Act. The unfunded liability for the prescription drug benefit is expected to be $18.2 trillion dollars projected out infinitely. When projected to just 2014, the Trustees 2005 report said the new drug benefit would cost $1.1 trillion, and it represents an unfunded government obligation of $8.7 trillion through 2079. The benefits offered in Part D are not covered by the trust fund.

The Battle to Add Prescription Drug Coverage

The monumental battle to pass the Medicare prescription drug coverage culminated in an arm-twisting middle-of-the-night vote of the House of Representatives. Controversy surrounding the vote—one member even indicated he was promised a payoff—and the information given to Congress prior to that vote continues to haunt the legislation today.

Richard Foster, chief actuary at the Centers for Medicare and Medicaid Services (CMS) reported that he was threatened with being fired if he gave Congress his analysis of the cost of the bill, which showed that costs would exceed by more than $100 billion the promised $400 billion maximum promised to members of Congress. Although an investigation into the withholding of information was halted, former

CMS administrator Thomas Scully, who became a health-care lobbyist shortly after the bill was passed, admits that he did stop Foster from providing the information to Congress.

Pharmaceutical and managed care industries spent $141 million in 2003 to push for passage of the bill, according to the watchdog group Public Citizen, which regularly analyzes lobbying efforts in Washington. Its director, Frank Clemente, said, "The Medicare Modernization Act, a top priority of President Bush, promises to safeguard industry profits at the expense of America's taxpayers. Considering the legion of lobbyists unleashed by pharmaceutical companies, HMOs, and allied industry front groups, no wonder taxpayers ended up with a bill tailor-made to serve these special interests instead of senior citizens." You can find out more about the drug program in Chapter 20.

Aside from the massive government costs, the bill drew opposition because …

◆ It restricts the government from seeking volume drug discounts to reduce prices for seniors, which it can do for veterans who get their drugs from the Veterans Administration. In fact, in early reports about the prescription plans offered to seniors in November 2005, pharmacy benefit managers raised red flags because some drugs would be cheaper for seniors to buy directly from retail pharmacies than through the prescription drug plans being sold. I explain that in greater detail in Chapter 20.

◆ Insurance and drug companies will fill their pockets with additional revenues. The government is expected to spend $720 billon on the program over the next 10 years. The fact that the government can't negotiate lower prices for the drugs means the pharmaceutical companies will make more profits on seniors than they do on veterans. Insurance companies were given a lot of latitude in how they could structure the drug programs offered, so they can expect healthy profits if they negotiate well with the pharmaceutical companies. The insurance companies also will receive millions of dollars in incentives to offer Medicare Advantage plans..

◆ Many fear drug companies will stop offering assistance to low-income seniors. November 2005 reports indicated that at least some drug companies would stop offering assistance to low income seniors when the new drug benefit was put in place.

◆ Some fear that employers who offer drug coverage as part of their retirement benefits will cut out that benefit. Congress tried to fix that problem paying companies to keep their drug plans in place. Companies do receive payments from the government for each retiree who gets company retirement benefits. According to a study done by the Kaiser Family Foundation and Hewitt Associates at the end of 2005, 89 percent of the companies that offered drug coverage in 2005 expect to continue offering drug coverage for their retirees in 2006. Companies that offer drug coverage with their retiree medical coverage will get an average payment from the government of $826 per retiree. If they do not offer drug coverage, the payment drops to an average of $626 per individual retiree. In 2007, only 50 percent of the companies said they were very likely to continue drug coverage and, by 2010, only 20 percent said they were very likely to continue drug coverage.

New Bill Causes Increases in Medicare Premiums

Monthly Medicare part B premiums increased 17 percent to $78.20 per month in 2005. In 2006, the monthly part B premium increased another $10.30 to $88.50 for a total two-year increase of $21.90, which is almost a 33 percent increase. Compare this to the cost of living increases from Social Security, which were only 2.7 percent in 2005 and 4.1 percent in 2006.

What caused these dramatic increases in Medicare premiums? Provisions of the new 2003 Medicare law.

The Minority staff of the House Committee on Government Relations analyzed the increase based on data from the Office of the Medicare Actuary and provided this breakdown of the 2005 increase of $11.60:

◆ $4.60 for increased payments to HMOs, insurance companies, and other fee-for-service providers mandated by the 2003 law.

◆ $.70 for increased administrative costs of the new programs mandated by the 2003 law

◆ $1.50 to increase payments to the Medicare reserve fund mandated by the 2003 law

◆ $.10 for new preventive benefits added in the 2003 law

◆ $3.20 to cover Medical inflation costs

◆ $1.50 for the Medicare reserve fund mandated by law prior to the 2003 law

If the 2003 law had not been implemented, the premium increase for seniors would have been only $4.70 in 2005. Of the $6.90 in Medicare premium monthly increase required because of the 2003 law, only 10 cents represents increased services for seniors. The largest share of the increase, $4.60, goes to profits for the insurance companies, HMOs, and other fee-for-service providers. Add to that the 70 cents for additional administrative costs tied to these payments as well as $1.50 in additional Medicare reserve costs, and you find that 59 percent or $6.80 of the increase can be directly tied to required provisions of the 2003 act that will not directly benefit seniors. Analysis of the increase for 2006 was not available at the time this was written.

In 2005 government projections indicated the 2003 provisions would cost $720 billion. That includes costs for prescription drugs plus incentive payments to get private medical insurers, HMOs, and fee-for-service providers to offer private alternatives to traditional Medicare. Medicare is reimbursing these private plans at a higher rate then they will reimburse providers offering services through the traditional plan.

Improving Information Management

Getting costs under control is Medicare's biggest problem. Many believe that with better information management Medicare could improve its ability to control costs.

Why is information sharing so critical? One major obstacle is that there are different contractors for Part A, which involves hospital costs, and B, which involves all other medical costs, so beneficiary payments must be compared through a system at the Centers for Medicare and Medicaid (CMS). So information is not easily shared between a Medicare recipient's inpatient and outpatient medical billing.

This brings us to the second major obstacle—the outdated information systems CMS must contend with to monitor billing patterns and beneficiary service use.

Working with an Outdated System

Claims are processed through two common files: the *Common Working File* and the *National Claims History File*. The data is compiled much too slowly, and the information about services delivered and claims paid isn't available until long after they've been completed. Whereas private insurance companies have almost instant data to work with to find problems developing with claims and services, HFCA is hampered by its outdated systems, according to the U.S. General Accounting Office (GAO).

def•i•ni•tion

The **Common Working File** is a prepayment validation and authorization system for Medicare run by the HCFA. The **National Claims History File** is a system HFCA uses to analyze Medicare payment trends.

Not only does this outdated system limit HFCA's ability to respond quickly to problems, it can also raise program costs. The Office of the Inspector General for Medicare has found that some claims are paid twice, once under Part A and once under Part B, because of information system difficulties. Improvements are being implemented in the information system and a steady drop is being reported in improper payments. The error rate dropped from $23.2 billion in 1996 to $11.9 billion in 2000.

Many private insurers have gotten a handle on costs by setting up preferred provider networks, which are lists of approved doctors and hospitals. Insurance beneficiaries face lower out-of-pocket costs by staying within the network. Not only do people benefit by paying less, the private insurers can negotiate lower payment rates and save money. Unfortunately, Medicare cannot go out and negotiate individual contracts for providers without a major change in the way the law is written. As a national program, it must establish a set of rules that everyone can play by to ensure a level playing field.

Insecurities

Disease management programs have been very successful in the private sector, but there is a big question regarding how they could be implemented for Medicare recipients. For example, let's take notification of an annual preventive test such as a mammogram. Medicare could collect information about testing using payment information and send out a notice to recipients when their annual test is needed. The fear is that this could cause major complaints by recipients because they may protest the government telling them how they should monitor their own health care.

Disease Management Programs

Improved sharing of information between Medicare Parts A and B would also make it possible for Medicare to implement a disease management program. Private insurers use these programs to provide patient education, patient monitoring, and specialized services. Their goal is to improve the quality of care and reduce costs by identifying patients with high-risk conditions. When a patient with a high-risk condition is identified, contact is made with his or her health provider to coordinate treatment and be sure the patient is taking the medication as prescribed, showing up for physician appointments, and completing tests ordered by the physician. These programs are designed to encourage patients to follow health-promoting behaviors and to support a strong patient-doctor relationship.

Demonstrations for Modernization

A less publicized portion of the 2003 bill requires CMS to conduct a series of demonstration projects to look for ways to modernize Medicare and cut costs. The most controversial of these is sure to be the Comparative Cost Adjustment project to test whether direct competition between private plans and the original Medicare fee-for-service program will enhance competition and improve health care delivery for all Medicare beneficiaries.

Some members of Congress wanted this competition to start immediately, but others opposed it completely. The demonstration project was a compromise for those pushing for privatization of Medicare. The six-year project is slated to begin on January 1, 2010. The demonstration project will be conducted in six metropolitan areas, including one that crosses state lines. No specific plans for this demonstration project were announced at the time this book was written.

Other demonstration projects include …

- **Competitive Bidding Demonstration for Clinical Laboratory Services.** This project will look at cost savings by encouraging competitive bidding for laboratory services.

- **Demonstration Project for Use of Recovery Audit Contractors.** This project will pay audit contractors on a contingency fee basis to identify Medicare underpayments and overpayments and recoup overpayments.

- **Rural Hospice Demonstration Project.** This project will provide hospice care at three facilities of 20 or fewer beds in rural areas where services are currently not available for up to five years. CMS must report back to Congress at the end of the project and Congress will decide whether or not to extend it.

- **Rural Community Hospital Program.** This project will test the advisability and feasibility of establishing rural community hospitals to provide Medicare-covered inpatient hospital services in rural areas.

- **Frontier Extended Stay Clinic Demonstration.** This project will designate frontier extended stay clinics located in isolated rural areas as Medicare providers. Clinics must be located at least 75 miles from the nearest acute care hospital.

◆ **Medicare Replacement Drug Demonstration.** This project will test whether drugs for certain life-threatening diseases, such as cancer, that are traditionally given in the doctor's office can be replaced by drugs that can be taken in the home. CMS must report to Congress by July 1, 2006. The project will evaluate the cost savings (if any) to the Medicare program by reducing physician services and hospital outpatient services for the administration of study drugs.

This is just a sampling of the many demonstration projects mandated in the 2003 act. Other projects will look at patient care quality, quality of care for patients with chronic conditions, health information technology, expansion of coverage for chiropractic services, home health care, and day care services.

The only thing I can say for certain about Medicare is that there will continue to be changes in the program. No doubt as the bill comes due for Medicare, Congress will look for ways to cut expenditures. The big question is who will be most impacted by those cuts: seniors or drug companies, insurers, HMOS, and medical providers.

The Least You Need to Know

◆ Medicare's shortfall represents an unfunded liability for the government of $8.7 trillion through 2079.

◆ Prescription drug coverage provided by Medicare Plan D began in January 2006.

◆ Medicare Part B premiums increased because of certain provisions in the 2003 prescription drug bill that gave incentives to private insurers, HMOs, and fee-for-service providers.

◆ Medicare must look for ways to cut costs. Information sharing between Parts A and B is crucial to this goal.

◆ Demonstration projects mandated by the 2003 act will be conducted to look at ways to improve Medicare and cut costs.

Chapter 25

Rescuing Social Security

In This Chapter

- ◆ The plot
- ◆ The players
- ◆ The changes
- ◆ What other countries are doing
- ◆ What's next

Although the public debate about how to fix Social Security has not come up with any ideas that have received broad public support, it has certainly taken its toll on public confidence in the system.

The American Council of Life Insurance found in a recent survey that more than half the public lacks confidence in Social Security. Nearly two thirds of folks younger than age 55 have little confidence that they can depend on Social Security being there when they retire.

Is this lack of confidence warranted? I don't think so. There is no doubt that a fix is needed, but Social Security is so popular that any politician who even suggests that it isn't possible to save Social Security would soon be voted out of office. Remember, seniors are some of the most active voters.

We'll take a look at the fixes being considered, review the key players, discuss privatizing the system, explore the success of other countries that have privatized their retirement systems, and lay out the process for reforming Social Security.

Setting the Stage

As discussed in previous chapters, Social Security is primarily a pay-as-you-go system. Today, 85 percent of the money collected in Social Security taxes is paid to current beneficiaries; most of the rest is set aside in the Social Security trust funds. These funds will be exhausted by 2041, according to the 2005 annual report of the Social Security trustees.

The Crisis Isn't Immediate

When the trust funds are depleted in 2041, Social Security payments will not stop. If there is no fix between now and 2041, the trustees predict that Social Security taxes would still be able to pay about 70 percent of the promised benefits. At least some portion of the difference would likely be paid through general revenues even if no fix were put in place. The amount covered by Social Security taxes would gradually decrease to about 40 percent in 2075. So you can see that we're not in an immediate crisis.

It's not that we shouldn't work toward finding a fix quickly, but there's no reason to panic. The last fix in 1983 occurred when the trust funds' balances were expected to be zero within months of its passage. The sooner the fix is put in place, the less pain we all will feel in either tax increases or benefit cuts or, more likely, a mix of the two.

Senior Moments

Dean Baker, co-director of the Center for Economic Policy Research and co-author of the book *Social Security: The Phoney Crisis*, points out that the 1983 Social Security Commission headed by Alan Greenspan deliberately decided to build up the trust funds to accommodate the baby boomers. He says, "The fact that at some point we will actually start drawing on that leaves one pretty hard pressed to view it as a crisis."

The Trust Funds *Are* Real

Another myth being circulated to cause panic is that the trust funds are not real and are not an asset to the government. As I pointed out earlier, the trust funds are held in what most pension planners consider to be the safest investment: U.S. Treasury bonds. Alan Blinder, former Federal Reserve governor and currently a professor of economics at Princeton, has been quoted as saying, "Blood would run in the streets if Wall Street believed that Treasury bonds were worthless."

So why would anyone suggest that the trust funds aren't real? Because Congress essentially created I.O.U.s for the trust funds and used the money for current government expenditures. As recently as 1999, President Bill Clinton and both Democratic and Republican Congressional leaders mandated that the Social Security surplus be placed in a lockbox and be used to pay down the federal debt. Unfortunately, the events of September 11, 2001, plus the massive tax cuts pushed by President George W. Bush and Republicans in Congress, dissolved most of the surplus and put us back into deficit spending. Add to that the wars in Afghanistan and Iraq and the rebuilding of the Gulf Coast after the 2005 hurricanes and there will be deficit funding into the foreseeable future.

So now we are facing a greater need for a fix to get ready for the influx of baby boomer retirees, but it still hasn't gotten to crisis level. There are basically five different approaches being considered:

- **Benefit reductions.** While most plans don't suggest major changes for current retirees, some plans floating around suggest reductions in benefits ranging from 10 to 40 percent for future retirees. The ones on the higher end of the spectrum expect that the reduction in guaranteed benefits will be offset by personal accounts through privatization of Social Security (discussed later in this list).

- **Tax increases.** The most common measures being considered include raising the Social Security tax by 1 percent or raising the salary level on which taxes are collected. In 2006, the Social Security tax ends once a person makes $94,200. The maximum salary level to be taxed is indexed to inflation.

- **COLA change.** Some people have suggested reducing the Cost of Living Adjustments. Right now, they are based on the consumer price index. Some proposals suggest that the change factor be a standard that would guarantee lower annual increases.

♦ **Change in investment strategies.** Some proposals suggest that a good part of the shortfall could be made up by investing in equities as well as bonds. People concerned about this strategy worry about the impact that major government investment in stocks could have on the market. Others are concerned about the politics that could drive investment choices.

♦ **Privatization.** Basically, the idea is to put some portion of your Social Security tax payment into a personal account. Some plans suggest that it should be "carved out" of current tax payments; others suggest that it should be in addition to current tax payments. It has polarized the debate about Social Security's future into two camps: proprivatization and antiprivatization. The proposals for establishing personal accounts as an add-on to current payments do have some support in the antiprivatization camp.

Let's now take a look at the key players.

Key Players

As previously mentioned, the privatization of Social Security has polarized the debate. President Bush tried to push for a privatization plan, but the public is actually more opposed to privatization after hearing his arguments for it. In a March 2005 CNN/Gallup poll only 38 percent of the population supported President Bush's call for major changes in the Social Security program in the next two years.

Although increasing taxes, decreasing benefits, decreasing COLA adjustments, and shifting trust fund investment options are being discussed by all players, where a group stands on privatization pretty much defines its side. There are lots of players. I've decided to introduce you to three key leaders on the proprivatization side, three key leaders on the antiprivatization side, and one large and influential player that is straddling the fence. On the proprivatization side, there is the President's Commission to Strengthen Social Security, the Alliance for Worker Retirement Security, and the Heritage Foundation. The AARP is sitting on the fence and hasn't taken a strong stance yet. On the antiprivatization side, there is the National Committee to Preserve Social Security and Medicare, Women and Social Security, and the Campaign for America's Future.

The Proprivatization Side of the Fence

Setting the stage for President Bush on the proprivatization side of the fence was the President's Commission to Strengthen Social Security.

Unlike most presidential commissions, which seek a membership that is more inclusive to get a well-rounded report, President George W. Bush only appointed members who support some form of privatization. He set up the commission on these guiding principles for modernizing Social Security:

- Modernization must not change Social Security benefits for retirees or near-retirees.

- The entire Social Security surplus must be dedicated only to Social Security.

- Social Security payroll taxes must not be increased.

Social Graces

You can read the findings of the commission and how it got to those results at www.csss. gov. The commission disbanded in 2001 and its recommendations were never formalized into a bill in Congress.

- The government must not invest Social Security funds in the stock market.

- Modernization must preserve Social Security's disability and survivors' insurance programs.

The commission members decided that they would be unable to reach an agreement on a single plan. The members sent President Bush several alternatives for privatizing Social Security. None of the options resulted in fixing its long-term financial problems.

Each alternative included some form of private retirement accounts, but several substantially different approaches to establishing this goal were proposed. The key reason they could not reach a conclusion was the financial strains baby boomers will put on the system. Big surprise? Nope.

Social Graces

All three proprivatization groups are closely tied to the conservative think tank the Cato Institute, which has been a proponent of Social Security privatization for 20 years. You can read more about their research at www. socialsecurity.org.

The Alliance for Worker Retirement Security is a coalition formed in 1988 by the National Association of Manufacturers. Members include the American Bankers Association, Securities Industry Association, U.S. Chamber of Commerce, and many other business trade associations. So although the name might make you think it's a workers' group, it actually represents business owners rather than employees. You can find the group online at www.retiresecure.org. You can also contact the group at the following address:

Alliance for Worker Retirement Security
1331 Pennsylvania Ave., N.W., Suite 600
Washington, D.C. 20004-1290
Phone: 202-637-3453

The Heritage Foundation is the third key player in the proprivatization fight. The Foundation sounds the alarms for Social Security at www.heritage.org.

You can contact The Heritage Foundation at:

The Heritage Foundation
214 Massachusetts Ave NE
Washington D.C. 20002-4999
Phone: 202-546-4400

The Fence Straddler

The middle-of-the-roader on privatization is the AARP, which is the largest membership organization for seniors. Membership is open to anyone over the age of 50. The AARP not only is involved in legislative matters affecting seniors, it also provides members with information on health and wellness issues, computers and technology, retirement and other life-transition issues, and places for fun and leisure.

The AARP has been straddling the fence on the privatization issue because its membership is so diverse politically. Its former executive director expressed great disappointment in President Bush's Social Security Commission when it was first appointed. In a statement in May 2001, Horace Deets said, "Unfortunately, this commission may represent a missed opportunity because it lacks the balance of opinion that is essential for public credibility."

After the interim commission report was released in 2001, the AARP's current executive director, Bill Novelli, was quoted in AARP's bulletin as saying, "By portraying Social Security finances 'in the worst possible light,' the Social Security report 'demonstrates how far outside the mainstream the commission appears to be headed.'" He also let it be known that the AARP would support some form of privatization as long as it involved *add-on accounts* that would create savings accounts on top of Social Security, but the group would oppose *carve-out accounts* that would divert some existing payroll tax dollars because they would worsen the problem.

In a June 2005 bulletin, AARP said, "Now is the time to put aside polarizing ideas that won't work and get serious about strengthening Social Security so it's fair for everybody …. Private accounts that take money out of Social Security are not part of the solution. These accounts drain money out of Social Security, cut benefits, and pass the bill to future generations …. We will not waiver in our commitment to Social Security and will remain firm in our stance against any plan that takes money out of Social Security." You can read more about the AARP position at www.aarp.org/issues/policies/econ_sec.

def•i•ni•tion

Carve-out accounts would be accounts set up in each individual's name using money from existing Social Security taxes. **Add-on accounts** also would be set up for each individual, but instead of using current taxes these accounts would be funded with additional money collected over and above current Social Security taxes.

The Antiprivatization Side of the Fence

The antiprivatization forces also continue to lead a major public relations effort to kill any move toward privatizing Social Security. The National Committee to Preserve Social Security and Medicare was formed in 1982 to serve as an advocate for Social Security and Medicare. The committee is led by Martha McSteen, who was the former acting commissioner of the Social Security Administration during the Reagan administration after working for 39 years at Social Security.

The committee's position is clearly stated by McSteen, "We are committed to preserving America's Social Security system and protecting it from those who would privatize it and leave today's and tomorrow's retirees with risky individual investment accounts that rise and fall at the whims of Wall Street and with the burden of huge transition costs for the switch to a privatized system."

You can find out more information about the committee at www.ncpssm.org. You can also write to the committee at the following address:

National Committee to Preserve Social Security and Medicare
10 G Street, NE, Suite 600
Washington, D.C. 20002
Phone: 1-800-966-1935

Social Graces

The primary research arm for the National Council of Women's Organizations is the Institute for Women's Policy Research, which is an independent, nonprofit, research organization that works in affiliation with the graduate programs in public policy and women's studies at The George Washington University. Their website address is www.iwpr.org.

The Women and Social Security Project was formed in the fall of 1998 and is run by the National Council of Women's Organizations. The council is a bipartisan network of more than 100 women's organizations representing more than 6 million women. The council has formed a Women and Social Security Task Force to develop a unified position on Social Security reform. You can find out more about the project at the council's website: www.womensorganizations.org/pages.cfm?ID=182.

The Campaign for America's Future was founded in 1996 to offset then Speaker of the House Newt Gingrich's move toward a conservative agenda. The group strongly believes that there is an attempt underway to undermine Social Security and Medicare.

Roger Hickey, a co-director of the campaign's sister organization, the Institute for America's Future, said, "The basic reason we oppose the commission's mandate to create private accounts from Social Security taxes is that it will inevitably lead to draining money out of Social Security in order to finance these private accounts. That, in turn, will require severe cuts in Social Security's guaranteed benefits and increases in the retirement age as well." You can contact the campaign online at www.ourfuture.org. You can also write to the campaign at the following address:

Campaign for America's Future
1025 Connecticut Avenue, NW, Suite 205
Washington, D.C. 20036
Phone: 202-955-5665

Private Parts

Why has privatization overtaken the Social Security debate? What the heck is privatization, anyway? Basically, privatization of Social Security would establish individual accounts for every person paying into Social Security.

These accounts could be financed by using a portion of the current Social Security taxes that you pay; this is known as carved-out accounts. Another method of financing these accounts would be additional payments over and above your current Social Security taxes; these are known as add-on accounts.

The carved-out accounts are the most controversial type of account because they will draw money from funds either being paid out to current beneficiaries or being deposited into the Social Security trust funds. Since our current system is primarily a pay-as-you-go system, to "carve-out" these funds, current benefits and savings could be at risk or taxes would have to be raised.

Proponents of privatization believe that private accounts would give individuals more control over their Social Security funds and would permit more investment choices, which would potentially allow participants to maximize their investment in the Social Security program. In other words, proponents of privatizing Social Security view the program basically as a retirement account and feel that people should get their money's worth for having paid into the system all of their working life. As fixes were put in place over the years to make the system more viable, Social Security became less of a good deal for future recipients.

Opponents of privatization don't think that Social Security should be viewed exclusively as a retirement account in which maximum return on investment is the primary goal. They remind us that Social Security was designed as a social insurance program to ensure that the elderly have the adequate resources they need in retirement (even if they had low earnings while they were young) and to pay benefits for disability and survivors of deceased workers.

Senior Moments

The Congressional Research Service reports that workers who earned average wages and retired in 1980 at age 65 took 2.8 years to recover what was put into Social Security on their behalf by themselves and their employers plus interest. After the 1983 fix with the increase of Social Security taxes, a 65-year-old who retired in 2000 will need 16.7 years of benefits to recover money paid in, and a retiree in 2025 will need 27.4 years.

The Cost of Privatization

The cost of privatizing Social Security would be huge because Social Security taxes would have to cover current beneficiaries as well as pay for the establishment of individual accounts for future retirees. The only alternative to the dual-pay structure would be a drastic cut in benefits for current retirees and near retirees, and given the political clout of seniors in this country, it's unlikely that any politician would do this.

The Kolbe-Stenholm Bill

President Bush decided not to draft his own bill after the commission finished its work. Instead he wants Congress to take the lead. In 2004, for the tenth year in a row, a bipartisan bill was introduced in Congress by Representatives Jim Kolbe (R-Ariz.) and Charles Stenholm (D-Tex.). This bill gives us a glimpse of the difficult choices that will need to be made.

The Kolbe-Stenholm bill calls for a reduction of the guaranteed benefit, an increase in the level of earnings subject to the Social Security tax, and a reduction of Cost of Living Adjustments to get the Social Security system on sound footing. There is also a call for speeding the change in retirement age to 67 and diverting tax revenues away from Medicare.

Social Graces

An interactive calculator is available online to help you find out how you would fare with privatization. You can find it at www.cepr.net/calculators/ss/calculator.html.

The core of the Kolbe-Stenholm bill is mandatory personal investment accounts for all workers covered by Social Security. It calls for 3 percent of the first $10,000 in earnings to be directed to these personal accounts and 2 percent of additional earnings up to the maximum amount taxed ($94,200 in 2006) to go into personal accounts. Using these numbers, a worker making $10,000 per year would add $300 to his or her account, while someone making the maximum taxable amount of $94,200 would add $12,526.

You can quickly see that rather than a progressive system in which low-income workers get a greater part of the benefits, the high-income workers would benefit more from this program. The bill does allow voluntary contributions up to $5,000, but how many low- or even middle-income workers would have the extra money to put in? To help low-income workers, the bill does call for a government match, but only if the worker adds voluntary contributions.

This is just one example of a privatization proposal. I selected it because it comes closest to President Bush's proposals during the campaign. Literally dozens of bills about reforming Social Security have been proposed in the past few Congresses.

Administering the Accounts

No matter what scheme is chosen, the biggest challenge will be administering the personal accounts. Dallas Salisbury, president of the nonpartisan Employee Benefits Research Institute, which oversees employee benefits policies, said, "Large and uncertain amounts of revenue and time would be involved in establishing computer systems, offices, and personnel to handle 15 times as many participants as the largest defined-contribution record keeper." He believes that "conservatively, any type of universal individual account program could take 10 years to put in place and require a staff of more than 100,000."

Salisbury's comments are not surprising when you look outside the United States at countries who have already experimented with privatization. Let's take a quick look at two programs touted by proprivatization forces.

International Players

The country most often mentioned when discussing privatizing Social Security is Chile, which had the oldest social insurance program in the Americas until its military dictatorship privatized the system in 1981. Employees were required to contribute 10 percent of their salary (up to $22,000) plus an additional 2.5 percent to 3.7 percent for death and disability insurance and administrative fees. They also had the option of voluntarily contributing up to an additional $2,000.

Employers in Chile were not required to contribute, but they were ordered to give raises of 18 percent to make the mandatory system more acceptable to workers. Can you imagine the uproar from employers if the U.S. government mandated a sizeable salary increase?

At first, the system worked great. Returns over 15 years averaged 16.6 percent. But when Chile's economy cooled, retirement funds started to see losses. By 1995, average returns fell to 2.5 percent, and since 1995 they have averaged 1.8 percent. A United Nations Development Program report estimates that 40 percent of contributors in this government plan will need additional assistance.

Insecurities

In Chile, 80 percent of the money in these private plans is controlled by five companies who average more than 22 percent in profits. Now you know why the investment companies are quickly jumping on the bandwagon in favor of privatization plans. There's big money to be made.

In addition to the volatility of the investments, program expenses for participants have averaged 15 to 20 percent. About one third of these expenses were for marketing costs, which more than doubled as a portion of total expenses from 1988 to 1995. World Bank economist Hemant Shah found that commissions reduced individuals' average rates of return between 1982 and 1995 from 12.7 percent to 7.4 percent and even more drastically between 1991 and 1995 from 12.9 percent to only 2.1 percent.

Looking at the UK

The United Kingdom faces similar problems with its move to privatization. The United Kingdom has a two-tier pension system. Starting in 1945, the UK offered a Basic State Pension funded by employer and employee payroll deduction, which replaced only 15 percent of a worker's earnings. In 1975, a second tier was added based on earnings, called the State Earnings Related Pension Scheme (SERPS). To participate, additional employer/employee contributions were required. This tier originally guaranteed 25 percent of average annual wages.

In 1986, as the ratio of retirees to workers increased, SERPS benefits were reduced to 20 percent. Workers were given the choice to forego a public benefit and instead opt for a private personal pension. Workers who chose the personal pension were given tax breaks. Today, one in four British workers have a personal pension, but in 1997, the UK's Office of Fair Trading reported that 570,000 of these pensions were under investigation for being misrepresented to buyers.

Insecurities

In the UK, 10 private firms have 80 percent of the personal pension market. According to the Office of Fair Trading, "firms compete not on the basis of the cheapest product, that is, the one with the lowest expenses, but on the basis of specious claims about investment returns." Since 1995, firms have enjoyed a profit margin of 22 percent, the same profit level Chile's companies have enjoyed.

Three economists who conducted research for the World Bank estimate that fees and costs will consume an average of 43 percent of the value of an individual account during the course of a typical 40-year working career. These fees are not all for administering and managing the account; they also include costs incurred when plans are switched from one provider to another or when a worker drops out of the workforce.

As the United States considers privatization, serious attention must be paid to how the accounts will be managed, how much profit the managing firms will be permitted to make, and how much the holders of these accounts will have to pay in fees. Right now, it costs less than 2 percent to administer Social Security in the United States, but that is because the money is managed in a lump sum. Costs will rise dramatically if individual accounts need to be established for every worker.

Next Steps

President Bush's push for privatization has so far gone nowhere. The Republicans briefly toyed with a face-saving bill to carve personal Social Security accounts out of the trust fund surplus, but those plans were quietly shelved.

Hopefully, there will be numerous opportunities for you to hear about and question the options for Social Security in public forums before any extensive changes are made to the system.

The Least You Need to Know

- Most people agree that Social Security needs to be reformed, but there is a lot of disagreement about the kind of reforms to make.

- The battle lines are drawn between proprivatization and antiprivatization forces. The key privatization question is whether there should be personal accounts for each Social Security participant.

- Privatization of Social Security could increase costs of administering the program.

- Privatized national retirement programs in Chile and the United Kingdom have expenses ranging from 20 to 40 percent versus less than 2 percent for our current Social Security system.

Chapter 26

Following the Changes

In This Chapter

- ◆ Tracking government moves
- ◆ Bringing in more private players
- ◆ Digging deeper
- ◆ Getting involved in the reform movement

I hope I have convinced you of the importance of maintaining a strong and active interest in the future of Social Security and Medicare. It's up to all of us to take the initiative to learn how these critical parts of our nest egg could be changed. Although it may seem daunting to keep track of everything that is happening, I'll give you some good resources to help make this task a bit more manageable.

The fastest way to track the changing forces is to join one or two organizations that share your viewpoint. They will definitely alert you when key moves are being made legislatively or administratively and will give you an idea of actions you need to take.

If you are like most folks and just don't know enough yet, take the time to research the issues more deeply. Your retirement future is at stake. You are better off putting in the effort now. Waiting until it is time for you to retire will probably be too late. The changes most likely will already have occurred, and you will just have to live with them.

This chapter takes a look at some of the ways for you to get more actively involved in the future of Social Security and Medicare.

Monitoring the Government

Obviously, your first step is to find out what is being considered both by the president and Congress. If there is going to be a major change, these are the folks who will do it.

The Administration

The president will set the tone for members of his own political party. Although he may not control them, most congressional members will follow his lead.

> **Social Graces**
>
> Two links on President Bush's website will help you track what he is doing.
>   Social Security: www.whitehouse.gov/infocus/social-security
>   Medicare: www.whitehouse.gov/infocus/medicare
> On the websites, you will find details of the president's positions.

Congress

When it comes to monitoring Congress, it gets much more tricky. First, let's take a quick lesson in legislation 101.

Congress has about 250 committees and subcommittees to handle the high volume and complexity of its work. Standing committees have legislative responsibilities and are broken into subcommittees for handling work in specific areas. There are also select and joint committees, which are primarily involved in oversight and housekeeping tasks. Each committee is made up of members from the majority and minority parties. The distribution on committees reflects proportionately the distribution of the parties in Congress.

Each Congress, which serves for two years, refers thousands of pieces of legislation to its committees. Only a small percentage of these bills actually reach full consideration by committee members. The committees are very powerful because they pick the issues they want to consider for further action, and this drives the agenda of the full Congress.

When a committee decides to act on a piece of legislation, it usually goes through the following legislative process: first, it asks relevant executive agencies for written comments on the bill. Next, it holds hearings to collect information from experts and the public, usually at the subcommittee level. The subcommittee then revises the original legislation using amendments and votes on whether to approve it. If the subcommittee approves the bill, it is then sent to the full committee. Sometimes the full committee will hold additional hearings, but not always. The full committee may act on the bill without hearings, but it could still amend the bill further before voting on whether to send it to the floor of its respective congressional chamber, either the House or Senate.

Senior Moments

In the 2006 Congress, the Senate has 55 Republicans, 44 Democrats, and 1 Independent who votes with the Democrats. This gives the Republicans strong control over what legislation will actually make it to the floor of the Senate. They serve as the majority party on committees and subcommittees and pick the chairmen. The party distribution on the House side also gives the Republicans control. There are 229 Republicans, 204 Democrats, and 1 Independent. This all could change after the 2006 elections if the majority in the Senate or the House shifts parties.

Once a bill is passed out of committee it goes to the leadership, which will then decide when the bill will come to a full vote on the floor and under what rules that vote will be taken. I won't go into the complicated rules here—that could be a book in itself, but the rules can have a major impact on the bill. Sometimes no amendments will be allowed; sometimes unlimited amendments will be permitted. It's all about political gamesmanship, and these folks are the masters at playing politics.

Here's a quick list of the key committees and their related subcommittees where action may be considered in Congress related to Social Security or Medicare:

♦ **House Committee on Energy and Commerce (http://energycommerce. house.gov).** When you get to this website, you'll want to look at full committee actions as well as the actions of the Subcommittee on Health and the Subcommittee on Oversight and Investigations for activities related to Medicare.

- **House Committee on Ways and Means (http://waysandmeans.house.gov).** At this website, you'll want to look at full committee actions as well as the actions of the Subcommittee on Social Security and the Subcommittee on Health.

- **House Appropriations Committee (http://house.gov/appropriations).** The Appropriations Committee does not have separate websites for its subcommittees, but the one whose actions you need to watch regarding Social Security and Medicare is the Subcommittee on the Departments of Labor, Health and Human Services, Education, and Related Agencies.

- **Senate Committee on Health, Education, Labor, and Pensions (http://help.senate.gov).** There are no separate websites for its subcommittees, but you'll want to follow the Subcommittee on Retirement Security and Aging.

- **Senate Finance Committee (http://finance.senate.gov).** Subcommittees of interest are the Subcommittee on Health Care and the Subcommittee on Social Security and Family Policy.

- **Senate Committee on Appropriations (http://appropriations.senate.gov).** The Subcommittee on Labor, Health and Human Services, Education, and Related Agencies controls money appropriated for Social Security and Medicare.

- **Senate Special Committee on Aging (http://aging.senate.gov/public/).** This Committee focuses on policies and laws that deal with the needs of the aging population. It studies issues, conducts oversight of programs and investigates reports of fraud and waste.

In addition to the committee websites, there are also two additional places to find out about congressional activities related to pending legislation and oversight of existing programs: the Congressional Research Service and the U.S. Government Accountability Office.

The Congressional Research Service (CRS), which is part of the Library of Congress, develops reports for Congress. Its reports are balanced and well-respected throughout Congress. CRS reports are not provided to the general public, but you can access some of them online. Links for finding reports online can be found at the Open CRS Network (www.opencrs.com), an organization that advocates making these reports public. If you hear about a report that interests you, you can contact your Congressman and ask that he send you a copy.

The U.S. Government Accountability Office (GAO) is the investigative arm of Congress. GAO studies the use of public funds, evaluates federal programs and activities, and provides analysis, options, recommendations, and other assistance to help Congress make effective decisions relating to oversight, funding, and policy issues. Any member of Congress can request a GAO study. You can search for GAO studies at www.gao.gov.

The Congressional Budget Office (CBO) is the budget and economic policy arm of the Congress. It provides reports on budget and economic issues, as well as appropriations legislation. The agency is composed primarily of economists and public policy analysts. About 70 percent of its professional staff hold advanced degrees in economics or public policy. You can find CBO publications at www.cbo.gov.

Tracking Private Advocacy Groups

Private advocacy groups are the ones down in the trenches fighting for causes they believe in. These groups try to find friendly partners in Congress who will champion a needed change.

Chapter 25 focused on seven of the key advocacy groups. In addition to those groups, this section introduces some others. While some of these groups do get involved in reform and modernization issues, I'm also including many here because of their activities related to improving existing services and regulations for elderly care issues, financial issues, Social Security, and Medicare.

First, let's start with a government site that pulls together all these service groups extremely well—the U.S. Department of Health and Human Service's Administration on Aging (www.aoa.gov). The resources on this site, as well as the links to other resources, will give you an incredible place to begin your search for information when looking for any issue related to retirement and medical services for the elderly.

Social Graces

The Administration on Aging also runs the National Aging Information Center. One of its best sites for families with aging parents or other relations is the Intergenerational Programs site (www.aoa.gov/prof/notes/notes_intergenerational.asp).

The Alliance for Aging Research (www.agingresearch.org) seeks to improve the health and independence of elderly Americans through public and private funding of medical research and geriatric education.

The Medicare Rights Center (www.medicarerights.org) is based in New York and primarily is involved in advocacy for that state, but it also gets involved nationally on some issues. The center has an excellent collection of Medicare consumer publications.

The Medicare HMO Web Link Directory (www.medicarehmo.com/mcweb.htm) is a great starting point if you are looking for organizations involved in services or legislation regarding Medicare HMOs.

The National Women's Law Center (www.nwlc.org) is a leader on Social Security issues affecting women. The center works to promote Social Security reforms to ensure adequate benefits for future generations and to improve the economic security of women.

The Women's Institute for a Secure Retirement (www.wiser.heinz.org) was created by the Heinz Family Foundation to educate women about retirement issues. In addition to information about Social Security, you will also find sections on pension, divorce, and widowhood.

SaveOurSecurity.org (www.saveoursecurity.org/a/national/secure_retirement) is run by the Democratic National Committee. If you stop by, you will see that the group clearly believes that privatization is a dangerous plan.

Team NCPA: Save Social Security (www.teamncpa.org) is run by the National Center for Policy Analysis, which is a nonprofit, nonpartisan, policy-research organization that develops and promotes private alternatives to government programs. The group is a big proponent of Social Security privatization.

The National Organization of Social Security Claimants Representatives (www.nosscr.org) helps claimants find representation for cases involving Social Security or Supplemental Security Income. The organization provides an excellent resource for basic disability questions at www.nosscr.org/faqind.html.

Key Research Studies and Websites You Shouldn't Miss

A number of websites offer comprehensive research on Medicare and Social Security. Here are some of the best:

The Employee Benefits Research Institute (www.ebri.org) is a highly respected, nonpartisan organization that researches information about all types of employee benefits. You will find numerous studies on the site about Social Security and its role in retirement benefits planning.

The Urban Institute (www.urban.org) is a nonpartisan economic and social policy research organization. The institute's site has special sections related to Social Security and Medicare.

The Michigan Retirement Research Center (www.mrrc.isr.umich.edu) is a national research and education resource focusing on Social Security, pensions, and retirement-related policies.

The Center for Retirement Research at Boston College (www.bc.edu/bc_org/avp/csom/executive/crr/index.shtml) promotes research on retirement issues, especially when it can promote initiatives that encourage cooperation among academic and policy communities.

The Century Foundation (www.tcf.org) supports a number of projects intended to add depth and balance to issues relating to the future of Social Security, Medicare, Medicaid, and other government activities that affect the elderly. The foundation also runs an excellent site for consumers called the Social Security Network (www.socsec.org).

The Heritage Foundation (www.heritage.org) is a conservative think tank. You will find a lot of comprehensive research in favor of privatization on this website.

The Disability Research Institute (www.dri.uiuc.edu), with the support of the Social Security Administration, established a small grant program to support research projects related to Social Security and disability.

The National Center on Women and Aging (www.heller.brandeis.edu/national/research.htm) promotes security, health, and dignity of women in their later years. Activities focus on income security, health, and care giving.

The Kaiser Family Foundation (www.kff.org) provides useful information about health issues and Medicare.

Your Role in Social Security and Medicare's Future

You may wonder how you can have a significant impact with so many organizations out there working on the issues. In reality, you can make a difference by staying on top of the issues, understanding how any changes will impact you, and taking the initiative to contact key players and let them know what you think.

You can also help by encouraging others to learn more and become more involved. For you, Social Security and Medicare may seem like a distant phase of life that you are not ready to face. If you don't take the initiative now, however, it may be too late to impact the benefits you will receive from Social Security and Medicare when it is your turn to use them.

The Least You Need to Know

◆ You can follow legislation as it passes through Congress by keeping a close watch on a few key congressional committees.

◆ Advocacy organizations for just about any viewpoint are available once you take the first step to find them.

◆ Take the time to research the key issues related to Social Security and Medicare reform so that you can be more informed when attempts are made to change the benefits of these programs critical to your retirement future.

Glossary

actuaries   People who analyze the financial consequences of risk. They use mathematics, statistics, and financial theory to study uncertain future events, such as how long people will live and collect payments from Social Security.

assignment   In Medicare terminology, this means that a doctor agrees to accept Medicare's fee as full payment even if his or her normal fee for the same service is higher. It can save you money if your doctor accepts assignment.

case review   A reconsideration of your application for Supplemental Security Income that doesn't involve an in-person meeting. You do have the right to review your file before the reconsideration. If you feel that additional information may help your appeal, you can provide the information before the case review.

Common Working File   A prepayment validation and authorization system for Medicare run by the Centers for Medicare and Medicaid (CMS). The National Claims History File is a system the HFCA uses to analyze Medicare payment trends.

consumer price index (CPI)   One of the tools used to measure inflation. It measures changes in the cost of a cluster of products and services, including housing, electricity, food, and transportation. This index is published monthly by the federal government. You may also have seen it called the cost-of-living index.

Cost of Living Adjustments (COLAs)   Annual adjustments to Social Security payments indexed by inflation. These were added as a provision of Social Security in 1972. Prior to that, Congress had to pass legislation each time a COLA was made.

Disability Determination Service (DDS)   A state-based team of specialists that includes a disability evaluation specialist and a doctor. Each applicant's case is reviewed by this team to determine whether he or she meets the Social Security Administration's definition of disability.

durable power of attorney   A document that allows you to make legal and financial decisions for another person. How much control you have depends on how the document is written. Sometimes broad power of attorney arrangements allow you to set up trusts and other similar financial arrangements.

Federal Insurance Contributions Act (FICA)   Established as a payroll deduction in 1939, both employers and employees are taxed. Today, the amount of this tax is established each calendar year. The employee's portion of the tax is deducted from his or her paycheck. The employer matches this deduction 100 percent. All the money is paid to the federal government.

gross domestic product (GDP)   The total market value of all final goods and services produced in this country in any given year. The GDP equals total consumer, investment, and government spending, plus the value of exports minus the value of imports.

hospice care   A specialized type of health care for terminally ill people. This holistic approach frequently includes legal, financial, and emotional assistance for the patient and his or her family in addition to medical care. Care can be provided in the home, a hospital, or specialized hospice facilities.

identity theft   This occurs when a criminal uses another individual's personal information to take on that person's identity. It can be much more than misuse of a Social Security number. The theft can also include credit card and mail fraud.

informal conference   This allows you to meet with the person who will be reviewing your Supplemental Security Income case and tell him or her why you disagree with the decision. You can bring witnesses to this informal conference to talk about your case. You can also bring a representative if you have chosen to have one. Before the conference, you will be able to review your file, and if you think it would be helpful, you can bring new information to the conference.

medical underwriting   A process used by insurance companies to review your medical history and health status. Insurance companies use this process to decide whether or not to accept your application for insurance.

Medicaid   A federal program that provides medical assistance to families with low income and resources.

Medigap   Private insurance that retirees can buy to supplement the cost of medical coverage not paid by Medicare. The insurance is closely regulated by the federal government and is even more closely monitored in some states. To get Medigap insurance, you must have Medicare Part A and Part B.

Old-Age Survivor and Disability Insurance (OASDI)   The largest social insurance program run by the Social Security Administration. It provides monthly benefits that replace lost income because of retirement, disability, or death. Over 90 percent of the jobs in the United States are covered by OASDI through mandatory payroll tax contributions.

President's Committee on Economic Security   Formed in June 1934, it was asked to devise "recommendations concerning proposals which in its judgment will promote greater economic security." Five top cabinet members made up the committee, led by the Secretary of Labor Francis Perkins. It took them only six months to design the first comprehensive federal social insurance program in the nation's history.

Primary Insurance Amount (PIA)   The amount you will receive at your full retirement age. As long as you were born before 1938, that age is 65. Beginning with people who were born in 1938, that age gradually increases to 67 for people born after 1959. See the chart in Chapter 5 to find out your full retirement age.

respite care   Short-term care given to a hospice patient or other homebound person who needs around-the-clock medical or daily living assistance by another caregiver, such as a hospital or respite care home, so that the usual caregiver can take a break. For Medicare purposes, respite care is only covered if the patient is terminally ill.

Retirement Earnings Test (RET)   People who retiree before their full retirement age will lose some benefits once they reach the earnings maximum or RET. In 2006, any early retiree that earned than $12,480 faced a benefit reduction until they reach full retirement age.

SIMPLE IRAs and **SEP-IRAs**   Qualified retirement plans used by small businesses that do not want to create a more complicated 401(k) plan. IRAs are cheaper to set up and easier to administer. The IRAs are taken out in the employee's name and are portable if you change jobs. Self-employed folks can use one of these plans or another qualified plan called the Keogh.

Social Security Board (SSB)   Appointed by President Franklin D. Roosevelt to implement Social Security. The three-member bipartisan board was chaired by John G. Winant. The SSB's biggest challenges were informing the public, setting up field operations, and staffing those operations with trained people. It then had to design a system for collecting information and managing that information so that people could get the appropriate benefits at retirement.

Social Security Disability Insurance   This is paid only if you cannot do the work you did before becoming disabled and cannot adjust to other work because of your disability. Your disability must be expected to last for at least a year or be expected to result in your death. There are no benefits for short-term disability.

Social Security Trust Fund   This includes the Old-Age and Survivors Insurance (OASI) trust fund, which pays retirement and survivors' benefits, and the Disability Insurance (DI) trust fund. The funds can only be used to pay benefits and program administrative costs. The trust fund holds money not needed in the current year to pay benefits and administrative costs. It must, by law, be invested in interest-bearing securities that are guaranteed by the U.S. government.

SSA-1099   The form that every Social Security beneficiary receives each year. If you are getting benefits on more than one Social Security record, you may get more than one form. The form will include all benefits you received from the Social Security Administration and adjustments to those benefits. Railroad retirees get an RRB-1099 instead.

Supplemental Security Income (SSI)   Provides benefits to people who become disabled but who have not worked long enough to qualify for Social Security Disability Insurance. These people must also meet a financial-needs test. SSI also provides benefits to disabled people over age 65 who qualify based on financial need. It provides cash to meet basic needs for food, clothing, and shelter. SSI is run by Social Security, but the money for the program does not come from Social Security taxes or the Social Security trust fund. SSI payments are financed by the general revenue funds of the U.S. Treasury. Most SSI recipients also qualify for Medicaid and food stamps.

W-2 form (Wage and Tax Statement)   Provided by your employer at the end of each year, usually by January 31 of the following year, to report your earnings and the taxes paid on those earnings. This is the form you send in with your tax return each year.

W-4 form (Employee Withholding Allowance Certificate)   This form gives your employer the information needed to withhold the correct federal income tax from your pay. If your financial situation changes, it is good to revisit what you told your employer on this form because the amount of tax being taken out of your check may need to be adjusted. Major changes that could warrant a difference in tax deductions include marriage, the birth of a child, or the purchase of a new home, just to name a few.

Windfall Elimination Provision   This affects the way your retirement or disability benefits are calculated if you receive a pension from work not covered by Social Security. The formula is modified, which results in you receiving a lower Social Security benefit. This formula is used to figure your Social Security benefit beginning with the first month you get both Social Security and the other pension.

Resources

In this appendix, I summarize the key resources you can use to find additional information about Social Security and Medicare.

Social Security Officials

Your official contact for Social Security information is the Social Security Administration. Its mail and phone contact information is as follows:

Social Security Administration
Office of Public Inquiries
Windsor Park Building
6401 Security Blvd.
Baltimore, MD 21235
UNITED STATES OF AMERICA
Phone: 1-800-772-1213
TTY: 1-800-325-0778

The administration also has an incredible amount of information available on its website. Here are some of my favorite spots:

You can find out your estimated benefits online at www.ssa.gov/planners/calculators.htm.

You can order your benefits statement online at https://s044a90.ssa.gov/apps6z/isss/main.html.

You can get the location of the Social Security office nearest you by using the online locator at https://s044a90.ssa.gov/apps6z/FOLO/fo001.jsp.

You can find out what benefits you are eligible for by using the benefits eligibility screening tool at http://best.ssa.gov.

You can apply for benefits online at https://s044a90.ssa.gov/apps6a/ISBA/main.html.

When you apply for benefits, you will need your birth certificate. If you don't have a birth certificate, you can order it online at www.doh.wa.gov/EHSPHL/CHS/cert.html.

Social Security has partnered with the American Savings Education Council to offer you a way to figure out whether you have enough saved for retirement and, if not, how much more you will need. You can find this information at www.choosetosave.org/ballpark.

If you own a small business and want more information about your obligations as an employer, an excellent place to start is www.ssa.gov/employer.

If you'd like to learn more about SSA rules and how the money is invested, an excellent overview of the Social Security trust fund can be found at www.socialsecurity.gov/OACT/ProgData/fundFAQ.html.

For history buffs, the best place to start is at www.socialsecurity.gov/history/history.html.

You may not be aware that you can tell where someone was born (or where the person first applied for a Social Security number) by the first three numbers of his or her card. People who work regularly with SSN cards have come to recognize the states. If you're curious and want to check it out yourself, here is a list of the geographical number assignments: www.ssa.gov/foia/stateweb.html.

Are you living or traveling outside the United States? You are not cut off from services. If you will be outside the United States and think you might need services, you can find information about where to get help when you are outside the country at www.ssa.gov/foreign/index.html.

Are you disabled, or do you know someone who is? You can review a list of impairments for adults online at www.ssa.gov/disability/professionals/bluebook/AdultListings.htm.

Online information about assistance for working if you are disabled can be found at www.ssa.gov/work/index.html.

You can find a listing of impairments for children online at www.ssa.gov/disability/professionals/bluebook/ChildhoodListings.htm.

Some noncitizens can qualify for SSI. For more information on noncitizen qualifications, go to www.ssa.gov/pubs/11051.html.

You can read more detailed information about the financial state of Social Security in the trustees report at www.ssa.gov/OACT/TR/index.html.

Social Security and Taxes

Taxes on Social Security and other assets during retirement can make a big difference in your income. Some good resources are available at the IRS site. You can order any of these publications by calling the IRS at 1-800-829-1040.

You can find full detail about taxation of Social Security benefits in IRS Publication 915, *Social Security and Equivalent Railroad Retirement Benefits*, available online at www.irs.gov/pub/irs-pdf/p915.pdf.

For detailed information about the taxation of IRAs, read IRS Publication 590, *Individual Retirement Arrangements (IRAs) (Including Roth IRAs and Education IRAs)*. You can find it online at www.irs.gov/pub/irs-pdf/p590.pdf.

You can find out more about the taxation of pension and annuities in Publication 575, *Pension and Annuity Income*, available online at www.irs.gov/pub/irs-pdf/p575.pdf.

If you run a small business or are self-employed, you can find an excellent resource about retirement plans at www.irs.gov/retirement/page/0,,id=136836,00.html.

You can find out more about taxes for the self-employed at www.irs.gov/businesses/small/content/0,,id=98942,00.html

Retirement Planners

Social Security has excellent calculators for planning your retirement benefits package at www.ssa.gov/planners/calculators.htm.

MSN Money has three useful calculators to help you plan how to use your retirement savings—the life expectancy calculator, the retirement expense calculator, and the retirement income calculator. You can find them at http://moneycentral.msn.com/investor/calcs/n_expect/main.asp.

If you have a home, AARP has an excellent collection of articles about home loans at www.aarp.org/money/wise_consumer/financinghomes.

The Motley Fool's Insurance Center is a great place to start investigating insurance needs. You can find it at www.fool.com/Insurancecenter/Insurancecenter.htm.

Senior Services

To help you sort out some of the issues, the Administration on Aging (AOA) offers a comprehensive website at www.aoa.gov/retirement/default.htm. If you don't have Internet access, you can contact the administration at the following address:

Administration on Aging
330 Independence Ave., SW
Washington, D.C. 20201
Phone: 202-619-0724

One of the best first stops if you have Internet access is the Elders and Families web-page of the AOA at www.aoa.gov/eldfam/eldfam.asp.

The center also offers its services toll free for persons with hearing impairments using TTY devices at 1-800-877-8339, which is a federal relay service. The call should be placed to AOA.

Some particularly helpful services can be found on the Internet if you are caring for your parents. The Eldercare Locater from the Administration on Aging is at www.eldercare.gov/Eldercare/Public/Home.asp, and the Guide for Caregivers is at www.aoa.gov/eldfam/For_Caregivers/For_Caregivers.asp.

There are more than 4,000 adult day centers. You can find the ones closest to you at the National Adult Day Services Association online at www.nadsa.org.

If you don't have computer access, you can contact the association at the following address:

National Adult Day Services Association
2519 Connecticut Ave., NW
Washington, D.C. 20008
Toll Free Phone: 1-800-558-5301
Phone: 202-508-1205

If you would like to find out more about the Family and Medical Leave Act, go to www.nationalpartnership.org/Default.aspx?tabid=31&folderid=9.

You can also contact the National Partnership for Women & Families at the following address:

National Partnership for Women & Families
1875 Connecticut Avenue, NW, Suite 650
Washington, D.C. 20009
Phone: 202-986-2600
Fax: 202-986-2539

If you want to see what local governments are doing, stop by the Senior Link Age Line for an example of an excellent program in the Twin Cities metropolitan area and greater Minnesota. This information can be found at www.tcaging.org.

The National Organization of Social Security Claimants Representatives (www.nosscr.org) helps claimants find representation for cases involving Social Security or Supplemental Security Income. The organization provides an excellent resource for basic disability questions at www.nosscr.org/faqind.html.

Financial Services

You may decide you need some help organizing your finances. The Board of Standards for Certified Financial Planners is a good place to start if you don't know how to find a planner. Simply go to www.cfp-board.org/search.

If you don't have an Internet connection, you can contact the board by phone or by mail:

CFP Board
1670 Broadway, Suite 600
Denver, CO 80202-4809
Phone: 1-888-237-6275

Another good source for financial services is a Certified Public Accountant with a Personal Financial Specialist designation. You can find a good resource online at pfp.aicpa.org/Resources/Consumer+Content.

You can also find one by phone or by mail:

American Institute of Certified Public Accountants
201 Plaza 3
Harborside Financial Center
Jersey City, NJ 07311-3881
Phone: 1-888-777-7077

You may want to seek third-party assistance with your debt situation. One of the highly respected nonprofit groups is the National Foundation for Credit Counseling. You can find the group online at www.nfcc.org. You can also contact it by phone at 1-888-850-6322.

Social Security Fraud

If you think your Social Security number is being used fraudulently, the Federal Trade Commission has developed an excellent website about identity theft and what you should do. It can be found at www.consumer.gov/idtheft.

If you don't have Internet access, you can reach the commission by phone or by mail:

Federal Trade Commission
CRC-240
Washington, D.C. 20580
Phone: 1-877-FTC-HELP (382-4357)

Social Security also has a fraud hotline. You can contact the Social Security Fraud Hotline at 1-800-269-0271. If appropriate, an investigation will be started by the Office of the Inspector General. You can also contact Social Security by mail or by fax:

Social Security Fraud Hotline
P.O. Box 17768
Baltimore, MD 21235
Fax: 410-597-0118

It's also important to contact the credit bureaus if you suspect Social Security fraud. Here's the contact information:

◆ Equifax
www.equifax.com
To report fraud: 1-800-525-6285
To order a credit report: 1-800-685-1111
P.O. Box 740241
Atlanta, GA 30374-0241

◆ Experian
www.experian.com
To report fraud: 1-888-397-3742
To order a credit report: 1-888-EXPERIAN (397-3742)
P.O. Box 9532
Allen, TX 75013

◆ Trans Union
www.transunion.com
To report fraud: 1-800-680-7289
To order a credit report: 1-800-916-8800
Fraud Victim Assistance Department
P.O. Box 6790
Fullerton, CA 92834

Medicare

You can call Medicare 24 hours a day at 1-800-MEDICARE (1-800-633-4227), or you can find information online at www.medicare.gov.

You can use Medicare's Personal Medical Plan Finder to research medical options for seniors at www.medicare.gov/MPPF/home.asp.

You can use the Medicare Prescription Drug Plan tool to find options for prescription coverage at www.medicare.gov/MPDPF/Public/Home.asp.

You can find out more about medication-related problems for seniors at the Alliance for Aging Research. The website is at www.agingresearch.org, or you can contact the alliance at the following address:

Alliance for Aging Research
2021 K St. New, Suite 305
Washington, D.C. 20006
Phone: 202-293-2856

Not only must you be familiar with the care, you also have to check out medical insurance companies. You don't want to pay premiums for years and then find out the company is no longer around when you need it. You can check on a company's financial health through two key ratings services online:

◆ A.M. Best (www3.ambest.com/ratings/Advanced.asp)

◆ Standard and Poors (www.standardandpoors.com)

If you don't have online access, you can find this information at a local public library.

The Medicare Rights Center (www.medicarerights.org/Index.html) is based in New York and primarily is involved in advocacy for that state, but it also gets involved nationally on some issues. The center has an excellent collection of Medicare consumer publications.

The Medicare HMO Web Link Directory (www.medicarehmo.com/mcweb.htm) is a great starting point if you are looking for organizations involved in services or legislation regarding Medicare HMOs.

Social Security and Medicare Advocacy

The following websites will allow you to track the progress of Social Security and Medicare reform and to see what advocacy groups are doing.

President George W. Bush's White House Sites

Social Security:

www.whitehouse.gov/infocus/social-security

Medicare:

www.whitehouse.gov/infocus/medicare

House Committees

House Committee on Energy and Commerce:

http://energycommerce.house.gov

In particular, the Subcommittees on Health and Oversight and Investigations are involved with issues related to Social Security and Medicare reform.

House Committee on Ways and Means:

http://waysandmeans.house.gov

In particular, the Subcommittees on Social Security and Health are involved with issues related to Social Security and Medicare reform.

House Appropriations Committee:

http://appropriations.house.gov

In particular, the Subcommittee on the Departments of Labor, Health and Human Services, Education, and Related Agencies is responsible for Social Security and Medicare appropriations.

Senate Committees

Senate Committee on Health, Education, Labor, and Pensions:

http://help.senate.gov

The Subcommittee on Aging and the Subcommittee on Public Health both cover issues related to Social Security and Medicare.

Senate Finance Committee:

http://finance.senate.gov

The Subcommittee on Health Care and the Subcommittee on Social Security and Family Policy cover issues related to Social Security and Medicare.

Senate Committee on Appropriations:

http://appropriations.senate.gov

In particular, the Subcommittees on Labor, Health and Human Services, and Education have information on Social Security and Medicare.

In addition to the committee websites, there are also two additional places to find out about congressional activities related to pending legislation and oversight of existing programs: the Congressional Research Service and the U.S. General Accounting Office.

The Congressional Research Service (CRS), which is part of the Library of Congress, develops reports for Congress. The reports are balanced and are well-respected throughout the Congress. CRS reports are not provided to the general public, but you can access some of them online. These reports are not protected by law or copyright. Links for finding reports online can be found at the Open CRS Network (www.opencrs.com), an organization that advocates making these reports public. If you hear about a report that interests you, you can contact your Congressman and ask that he send you a copy.

The U.S. Government Accountability Office (GAO) is the investigative arm of Congress. GAO studies examine the use of public funds, evaluate federal programs and activities, and provide analysis, options, recommendations, and other assistance to help Congress make effective decisions relating to oversight, funding, and policy issues. Any member of Congress can request a GAO study. You can search for GAO studies at www.gao.gov.

The President's Commission to Strengthen Social Security was appointed to develop a privatization alternative for Social Security. You can find information about the commission online at www.csss.gov.

Private Groups

The Alliance for Worker Retirement Security is a coalition formed in 1988 by the National Association of Manufacturers. It supports Social Security privatization. Members include the American Bankers Association, Securities Industry Association, U.S. Chamber of Commerce, and many other business trade associations. You can find the alliance online at www.retiresecure.org.

The Campaign for America's Future was founded in 1996 to offset Newt Gingrich's move toward a conservative agenda. One of the campaign's strong beliefs is that there is an attempt to undermine Social Security and Medicare. You can contact the campaign online at http://socialsecurity.ourfuture.org.

Team NCPA: Save Social Security (www.teamncpa.org/main/index.php) is run by the National Center for Policy Analysis, which is a nonprofit, nonpartisan, policy-research organization that develops and promotes private alternatives to government programs. The group is a big proponent of Social Security privatization.

The National Women's Law Center (www.nwlc.org) is a leader on Social Security issues affecting women. The center works to promote Social Security reforms to ensure adequate benefits for future generations and to improve the economic security of women.

SaveOurSecurity.org (www.saveoursecurity.org/a/national/secure_retirement) is run by the Democratic National Committee. If you stop by, you will see that the group clearly believes that privatization is a dangerous plan.

The Women's Institute for a Secure Retirement (www.wiser.heinz.org) was created by the Heinz Family Foundation to educate women about retirement issues. In addition to information about Social Security, you will also find sections on pension, divorce, and widowhood.

The National Committee to Preserve Social Security and Medicare was formed in 1982 to serve as an advocate for Social Security and Medicare. You can find out more information about the committee at www.ncpssm.org.

The Women and Social Security Project was formed in the fall of 1998 and is run by the National Council of Women's Organizations. The council is a bipartisan network of over 100 women's organizations representing more than 6 million women. You can find out more about the project at www.womensorganizations.org.

Research Sites

A number of sites offer comprehensive research on Medicare and Social Security. Here are some of the best:

The Cato Institute is a conservative think tank that has been a leading proponent of Social Security privatization. You can read more about the institute's research at www. socialsecurity.org.

The Employee Benefits Research Institute (www.ebri.org) is a highly respected, non-partisan organization that researches information about all types of employee benefits. You will find numerous studies on the site that impact Social Security.

The Urban Institute (www.urban.org) is a nonpartisan, economic and social policy research organization. It's website has special sections related to Social Security and Medicare.

The Michigan Retirement Research Center (www.mrrc.isr.umich.edu) is a national research and education resource focusing on Social Security, pensions, and retirement-related policies.

The Center for Retirement Research at Boston College (www.bc.edu/bc_org/avp/csom/executive/crr/index.shtml) promotes research on retirement issues, especially when it can promote initiatives that encourage cooperation among academic and policy communities.

The Century Foundation (www.tcf.org/list.asp?type=TP&topic=2) supports a number of projects intended to add depth and balance to issues relating to the future of Social Security, Medicare, Medicaid, and other government activities that affect the elderly. The foundation also runs an excellent site for consumers called the Social Security Network (www.socsec.org/facts/index.htm).

The Heritage Foundation (www.heritage.org/Research/SocialSecurity/index.cfm) is a conservative think tank. You will find a lot of comprehensive research in favor of privatization on this website.

The Disability Research Institute (www.dri.uiuc.edu), with the support of the Social Security Administration, established a small grant program to support research projects related to Social Security and disability.

The National Center on Women and Aging (www.heller.brandeis.edu/national/research.htm) promotes security, health, and dignity of women in their later years. Activities focus on income security, health, and care giving.

The National Council of Women's Organizations' research arm is the Institute for Women's Policy Research (www.iwpr.org), which is an independent, nonprofit, research organization that works in affiliation with the graduate programs in public policy and women's studies at The George Washington University.

Special Rules for State and Local Government Workers

Over 23 million state and local government workers face unique rules when it comes to Social Security. In some states they can qualify for full Social Security and Medicare coverage, in others they can get only Medicare coverage, and in still others it depends on an employee's position whether he or she gets Social Security coverage.

When Social Security was started, only private sector workers were covered, because lawmakers at the time weren't sure if it was constitutional for the Federal government to tax state and local governments (remember, an employer is responsible for one half of the FICA and Medicare tax). As a consequence, many state and local employees had no retirement coverage at all.

Legislation for State and Local Government Workers

That all changed in 1951 when Section 218 was added to Social Security, allowing states to voluntarily elect Social Security coverage for public employees not already covered under a public retirement system. Each state that wanted to participate entered into a Federal-State Agreement, which is more commonly referred to as a Section 218 Agreement, with the Social Security Administration. These agreements gave public employees the same benefit rights and responsibilities as any other employee who had Social Security coverage. The Social Security and Medicare taxes are the same for state and local government employers and their employees as they are for the private sector.

Section 218 Agreements are only possible for employers and employees in the 50 States, Puerto Rico, the Virgin Islands, and interstate entities. The District of Columbia, Guam, and American Samoa cannot be part of these agreements. In 1955, the law was amended to allow coverage for individuals who did have a public employee's retirement system.

Mandatory Medicare coverage became law in 1986. Any public employee hired after March 31, 1986, must pay the Medicare-only portion of the Federal Insurance Contributions Act (FICA) tax, unless they are covered for full FICA. The government entity is required to match their portion of the tax as well.

Until 1991, participation in Social Security was entirely voluntary, but on July 2, 1991, all state and local government employees who were not covered by a public retirement system or covered under a Section 218 Agreement became subject to mandatory Social Security and Medicare coverage. States and local governments that do offer a public retirement system are not yet required to participate in Social Security. Today, as part of the discussions to fix Social Security, many Congressmen are pushing to make Social Security mandatory for all government workers. State and local workers who pay into their government retirement plan plus Social Security are entitled to collect benefits from both plans.

All states have a Section 218 Agreement in place, but each state's agreement is unique.

Who Gets Coverage?

The Section 218 Agreements cover positions, not individuals. If the position is covered for Social Security and Medicare under a Section 218 Agreement, then any employee filling that position must pay Social Security and Medicare taxes. The employees under a Section 218 Agreement are placed in coverage groups. There are two basic coverage groups: absolute coverage groups and retirement system coverage groups. An absolute coverage group includes employees not covered under a public retirement system. A retirement system coverage group includes employees who do have coverage under a public retirement system.

For new coverage to start, if it isn't mandated by law, a majority of eligible members in a group must vote in favor of coverage. If the majority of the eligible members vote in favor of coverage, all current and future employees in positions under the retirement system will be covered. Once it is instituted the coverage cannot be cancelled.

Some states did provide in their initial Section 218 Agreements for people to opt out of Social Security coverage after the initial vote. In these states employees who voted "no" are not covered as long as they work continuously in the same public retirement system. All employees who vote "yes" are covered, and all future employees will be covered.

How the referendum is conducted is a state matter, but there are certain conditions that must be met under Section 218. As part of the legislation, certain employee services are mandatorily excluded from Social Security coverage, and some services and positions may, if requested by the State, be excluded from Social Security coverage under the State's Section 218 Agreement (optionally excluded).

Positions mandatorily excluded include:

◆ Services performed by individuals hired to be relieved from unemployment.

◆ Services performed in a hospital, home, or other institution by a patient or inmate who is an employee of a state or local government employer.

◆ Services performed for a state or local government by workers hired on a temporary basis in emergencies such as a fire, storm, snow, earthquake, flood, or similar emergencies.

◆ Other services not defined as employment under section 210 (a) of the *Social Security Act*. (The services most commonly excluded here are those performed by a nonresident alien temporarily residing in the United States. These services are performed to carry out the purpose for which the alien was admitted to the United States.)

Services that can be optionally excluded are:

◆ Services in elective positions.

◆ Services in part-time positions.

◆ Services in positions paid on a fee basis (usually independent contractors).

◆ Agricultural labor.

- Student services.

- Services of election workers and officials if the remuneration paid is less than the threshold amount established by the state's agreement, which is commonly $1,000.

A public employee who is not covered by a Section 218 Agreement cannot voluntarily participate in Social Security. It is not possible to pay Social Security taxes voluntarily on work that is not covered for Social Security under the terms of the Social Security Act and the Internal Revenue Code.

In each state there is a Social Security Administrator who coordinates the coverage for all the various state and local government entities in the state under the Section 218 Agreement. The Administrator also serves as a liaison with Social Security and is responsible for educating public employers about the Social Security benefits available in the state.

If you are a state or local government employee and want to research the provisions of Section 218 further, there are several good places on the Internet where you can start.

The Social Security Administration has a website for local and state government employers:

www.ssa.gov/slge

You can find a list of regional offices with state and local coverage specialists here:

www.ssa.gov/slge/specialists.htm

The National Conference of State Social Security Administrators has excellent information on its site:

www.ncsssa.org

The State of Colorado Department of Labor and Employment has developed a website for its public employers and employees that provides information useful to employers and employees in other states:

pess.cdle.state.co.us

Index

Q-R

S

Check Out These
Best-Sellers

More than *450 titles* available at booksellers and online retailers everywhere

www.idiotsguides.com

ALPHA